autumn into winter

Gary
Rhodes
cookery year

autumn into winter

In loving memory of John Miller
A man whose art we love
A man we loved

This book is published to accompany the television series entitled *Gary Rhodes Cookery Year* first broadcast on BBC2 in 2002.

Executive producer: Nick Vaughan-Barratt
Series Producer: Siobhan Mulholland

Published by BBC Worldwide Ltd,
Woodlands, 80 Wood Lane,
London W12 0TT

First published 2002

ISBN 0 563 53421 4

Commissioning Editor: Nicky Copeland
Project Editor: Sarah Miles
Copy Editor: Lewis Esson
Art Director: Linda Blakemore
Designer: Andrew Barron @ Thextension
Production Controller: Christopher Tinker
Food prepared for photography
by Gary Rhodes
Food Economists: Jo Pratt and
Wayne Tapsfield
Stylist: Bo Chapman

Typeset in Century ITC and Gothic 720
Printed and bound in Great Britain by
Butler & Tanner Ltd, Frome and London
Colour separations by
Radstock Reproductions Ltd,
Midsomer Norton
Jacket printed by Lawrence-Allen Ltd,
Weston-super-Mare

Photographs page 1: *Green garden soup* (page 28);
page 2 left: *Steamed chicken leg jardinière* (page 152); right: *Bramley and Russet apple pie* (page 90);
page 3: *Beenleigh Blue and courgette egg cake* (page 24)

Acknowledgements

As you will find within the pages that follow, autumn and winter dishes so often require extra ingredients and time to achieve the very best results. Finding and enjoying all of these flavours would not have been possible without the following list of 'ingredients', who all added a touch of seasoning, to produce the best of finishes to the overall dish. A personal thank you then to Wayne Tapsfield, Lissanne Kenyon, all Rhodes' restaurant teams, Sîan Irvine, Jo Pratt, Sharon Hearne, Nicky Copeland, Sarah Miles, Andrew Barron, Nick Vaughan-Barratt, Siobhan Mulholland, Claire Popplewell, Borra Garson and Lynda Seaton (*Fresh Produce Journal*).

contents

autumn fruit and puddings **78**

winter

winter vegetables **100**

One of the delights of being in tune with the seasons is the effortless way we rediscover simple classic fare, turning the daily job of cooking into pure pleasure. It was with this in mind that I wrote the first part of my cookery year, *Spring into Summer*. The next and very natural step was to turn to the more hearty and warming dishes that fit so well with our produce during the latter half of the year. It is during this time that our culinary instincts lean towards the heavy, with stews, casseroles and pies coming to the fore. The purpose of *Autumn into Winter*, therefore, is to add warmth to our lives and show us the wealth of good food we can create.

Autumn into Winter has a chapter devoted to each season and, as you'll see, many ingredients cross over both. Just because a recipe appears in one chapter doesn't mean you can't adapt its concepts at any other time of year. Within each chapter I've divided the recipes into vegetables, fish, meat, and fruit and puddings. Often you'll find the lead ingredient is the seasonal one, although sometimes it's the accompaniment; either way, whatever's at its prime has been colour coded to highlight it. I've kept as close to our own British produce as possible, but have chosen not to deprive us of a selection of many delicious imports, particularly exotic fruits, like pineapples, lychees and kumquats.

There are a few recipes within these pages that demand a little more attention and planning than usual, but many of the others, approached during the right season, will make life easier in the kitchen for everyone. And wherever possible, I have given alternatives that will save time, if you need it. Basically these recipes are not here to dictate; they are more to direct you towards tastes that are at their best, offering more respect to the ingredients, rather than to the method itself. I want you to approach all of these pages in the same spirit; it's not always intense dishes that provide pleasure – quite often the simplest of components on the plate will truly excite the palate and will be rewarded with great accolades.

I find that dinner parties come into season during the autumn and winter months. For me, these don't need to be formal events; it's more about a gathering of friends who are together to enjoy each other's company, with the star of the show – the food – opening, maintaining, entertaining and ending the whole event. The table is a place for sharing both food and conversation. The food is likely to become the main focus of discussion, particularly when there are dishes that need a helping hand to reach your plate. An autumn apple pie, for example, with its accompanying sauceboat of pouring cream or custard, makes for a really convivial event.

This is where seasonal flavours and thoughts will help you. It doesn't take much to prove what flavour can offer. If treated carefully and with respect, it will lead the table conversation, rather then be lost amongst it, and make life easier for the cook as well.

These two seasons of recipes within our cookery year should be given room to breathe and speak for themselves. Whether it be the unusual flavours of Swiss chard, Jerusalem artichokes, kohlrabi and quince, or old favourites, such as parsnips, leeks, cabbage and apples, why not, once you've seen what I would do, follow some of your own instincts and not completely those of mine?

Here are a few tips and guidelines that will help you achieve the best possible results with the recipes that follow.

Ingredients

Butter Unsalted butter is mostly used because it gives greater control over the seasoning of a dish.

Cooking oil Vegetable or groundnut oil can be used. Groundnut oil is a product sourced from peanuts.

Egg sizes All eggs used are large, unless otherwise stated.

Herbs All herbs are fresh, unless otherwise stated. All soft herbs, such as tarragon, flatleaf parsley and basil, are best torn by hand to prevent them bruising and to avoid breaking the texture. If you substitute fresh herbs with dried, remember to use only half the amount specified.

Instant sources and stocks There are a number of sauce and stock recipes included in the book (with a quick *Instant stock* recipe on page 194), but there are also many good bought alternatives (tinned consommé, carton, fresh, dried or cubed) available in supermarkets.

Seasoning Or 'season' simply means seasoning with salt and pepper – preferably freshly ground white pepper, unless otherwise stated.

Vinegars I use a selection of vinegars in this book. Red wine vinegar is a favourite. Because many of those available are shallow in flavour, I urge you to spend a little more and buy a vinegar that bears the hallmark of a good wine – a Bordeaux, say, or a Cabernet Sauvignon. If balsamic vinegar is a personal favourite, the older it is, the thicker and better the flavour.

Techniques and guidelines

Cooking green vegetables All green vegetables can be cooked at the last minute. However, with many other things happening on the stove, it can become overcrowded. Pre-cooking vegetables gives you time to ensure that they are perfectly tender and full of flavour.

To reheat them, most green vegetables can simply be dropped into simmering water for 30 seconds to a minute, then drained and seasoned. Cabbages, greens, spinach and other leafy vegetables are best rewarmed with a knob of butter and just a few tablespoons of water – the water creates steam. Dropping leafed vegetables in a large saucepan of water to reheat them will only spoil their texture. A modern choice is to microwave. This is a very successful route to take, particularly for all leafed vegetables and broccoli. If microwaving them, once they have been cooked and refreshed in iced water, the vegetables can be drained, seasoned and buttered, before microwaving and serving.

There are a few golden rules that should never be broken when cooking green vegetables. Always use a large saucepan up to three-quarters full of boiling salted water and never use a lid at any time during the cooking, even when the water has boiled and the vegetables are cooking. This guarantees that the rich colour is kept. One more important point – try not to cook too many green vegetables at once. If you do, the water temperature decreases and then takes too long to return to boiling point, which often results in the loss of colour.

Once cooked, drain immediately, seasoning and buttering before serving. If cooking in advance, drain the vegetables and plunge into iced water. This stops the cooking process and preserves the flavour and colour of the vegetables. It is also important not to leave the vegetables sitting too long in the iced water; after a period of time they will absorb it, becoming watery. So once cold, drain immediately and refrigerate until needed.

Measurements Follow one of the measurements only; do not mix metric and imperial. All spoon measurements are level unless otherwise stated.

- a tablespoon is 15g (½oz) for solids and 15ml (¼fl oz) for liquids
- a dessertspoon is 10g for solids and 10ml for liquids
- a teaspoon is 5g for solids and 5ml for liquids

Oven temperatures Be aware that if you are using a fan-assisted oven the temperatures may need to be adjusted and lowered to your oven manufacturer's recommendations.

Removing pin bones from fish Fine pin bones are found in round fish fillets, that is, red mullet, trout, salmon, cod and so on. The bones run down the centre of most of these fillets and are easily removed with fine pliers or tweezers. It's worth spending the time needed to remove them, as the fish then becomes more comfortable to eat.

Sterilizing jars It is important to ensure that any jars to be used for jams, etc., are sterilized. First wash the jars in soapy water and rinse well. Place in a large saucepan, cover with water and bring to the boil. Cover with a lid and continue to boil for 15 minutes. Remove from the heat, leaving the lid on the pan, and allow to cool slightly. Remove the jars and stand upside down on a clean tea towel to drain.

The jars must still be hot when you fill them with the jam. (Alternatively, heat the sterilized jars in a moderate oven for 5–10 minutes before use.)

Once the jars are filled, cover the preserve or chutney with waxed paper before closing and placing in a cool dark place, making sure the jars are not touching. Most jams and marmalades will have a 12-month shelf life if left unopened, providing the right quantity of sugar has been used. Once opened, any jar should be kept refrigerated and used within 3–4 weeks.

Using a gas gun Powerful blow torches fuelled by butane gas canisters can be used in the kitchen to give a crispy glaze to many dishes. They are available from almost any hardware store and can also be found in the kitchen sections of department stores. Follow the instructions and use carefully and, of course, keep them away from children.

autumn

After the weeks of summer, September arrives with its bright, sharp mornings. In fact, the most distinctive contrast between these two seasons is the sudden change in morning temperatures. This may appear to some a rather negative turn but, in fact, September is a beautiful month, filled with golden colour, giving us four very positive weeks, with fresh aromas and piquant flavours presented on our tables for us to savour.

It's the time of the year to introduce the English apple, the fruit of so many faces, each carrying a quite distinctive personality that can enhance so many desserts and savoury dishes. Pears are also beginning to reach their peak, particularly the Conference. The almost-forgotten and too-often-ignored damson is now reaching its prime, usually between late September and October, but is still with us in late autumn too.

Other culinary characters to look out for include Swiss chard, an all-year-round vegetable that is at its prime right now, and sweetcorn, with its bright yellow kernels, which adapts so easily to poultry, game and many a fish or vegetarian dish. Game, which has been with us since the start of the grouse season in mid-August, now begins to introduce partridge, wild duck, woodcock and plump wood pigeons. Another cast of characters to join us are the wild mushrooms, each with their own individual structure, flavour and texture, and with different colours to please and tempt the eye.

What also must not be forgotten, of course, are the fruits, leaves and other morsels still with us from previous warmer days. Tomatoes are still much in evidence, while summer cabbages, peas, courgettes and spinach are all as green as ever. Summer cauliflowers offer a contrasting shade, their brilliant-white still showing proud. And a great favourite of mine, runner beans, are still peaking right now.

And what about the fruit world? Raspberries, in particular the finest of the Scottish, are plentiful, strawberries are still with us, and plums are waiting to be bottled or simmered into jam. Probably the most fruitful of the summer berries during this season are the blackberries, always happy to be simmering with the apple in a crispy pie or beneath a crunchy soft crumble topping.

Shorter days and early dark evenings confirm that autumn is now truly with us. Pumpkins, butternut squash and more of the orange-fleshed vegetables begin to make an appearance, with their rich-flavoured structure adapting well to many a recipe, with *Butternut mussel stew* (page 22), *Pumpkin and Swiss cheese mash* (page 59) and *Spicy syrup butternut tart* (page 88) to choose from. The crown of all wild mushrooms, the cep, now plumper, fuller and firmer than ever, is delicious with the ripest of Cox's apples upon walnut toasts (page 38). *Green garden soup* (page 28) brings together the very last of the summer vegetables and young curly kale, leeks and new Brussels sprouts.

A fruit that begins to make an understudy appearance, before taking central stage in months to come, is the quince. This is a fruit that lost face among the British many, many years ago. Mrs Beeton, in the nineteenth century, was one of the last food writers still believing in its virtues, with jams, jellies and many more dishes using quince featuring in her works. Shaped like an apple or pear, this fruit, inedible when raw, changes completely – in texture, colour and flavour – once simmered or baked. You'll usually find the pear-shaped quinces on offer, carrying a rich appetizing golden yellow colour that's bound to capture your interest. The great author of *The Three Musketeers*, Alexandre Dumas, mentions in his late masterpiece, *Le Grand Dictionnaire de Cuisine*, that this particular fruit was also used to make *bandoline*, a product designed for making hair glossy – so you can make gel or jelly: the choice is yours.

Also arriving at this time in the fruit world are fresh figs, with celeriac arriving in the vegetable garden and pheasant just finding its true flavour.

So, October rewards us with slightly more hearty ingredients and dishes, but ones which are still able to offer refreshing crisp finishes. Root vegetables become more prominent, Hallowe'en parties need to be prepared for and the misty mornings and colder evenings of later autumn are here.

The last month of this season, November, soon arrives and with it comes a definite change in cooking. This is a time of gentle bubbling, of many soups and stews. With the sharp frosts of late autumn, the trees are stark and bare and many a garden has its head down – you can almost feel your hands begging to be clutching a mug of hot soup. It is time for baked potatoes and toffee apples to be taking pride of place on the simplest of our menus. Our root vegetables are now at their peak, with carrots, swedes, turnips and parsnips crying out to be taken advantage of. Brussels sprouts are firmer and a richer green than ever, perfect to be rolling in a buttery pan and slightly jumping from a peppery bite.

We now find ourselves having to think and plan just that little bit further ahead, bearing in mind that pots of this and that need lots of care, attention and time. During this season the clocks go back and, in the same spirit, our classic cooking methods of old come to the fore. You'll find examples of these in the pages that follow, with softly poached beef fillets, roast game and a very slowly roasted shoulder of pork, sitting amongst many other cookery techniques and tastes.

The season of autumn, with its falling leaves and tones of orange and brown, offers a new market to us after the summer months. Remember, the purpose of this book is to excite your thoughts and tastes through the darker months of the year, and to help remind you and create an awareness of the ever-increasing great British flavours available to us. I hope these recipes will at least provide you with new ideas, or perhaps just a reminder of how the product in hand will benefit from a simple touch. Autumn daylight may well be disappearing, but new flavours are just beginning.

Serves 4 as a starter
- 2 medium beetroots
- salt and pepper
- 4 medium carrots
- 4 medium parsnips
- 2 tablespoons olive or cooking oil
- 6 fresh walnuts, shelled
- 100g (4oz) mixed salad leaves (see below)

For the vinaigrette
- 1 heaped teaspoon Dijon mustard
- 100ml (3½fl oz) soured cream
- 2 tablespoons sherry vinegar or red wine vinegar
- 100ml (3½fl oz) walnut oil, plus extra for drizzling (optional)

Roast carrot and parsnip salad with soured cream, beetroot and walnut vinaigrette

This salad is a wonderful mid-autumn and winter starter. Endless varieties of root vegetables can be added, with turnips, celeriac and swedes amongst them. Preparation alone can, however, become a bit of a chore. Whenever I've bothered to include a lot, I feel I should have been serving most of them with the main course. So here I'm sticking to just three – two pointed root vegetables with beetroot to add its natural piquancy. The carrots and parsnips are just quartered lengthwise and roasted to a succulent finish with a slight caramelized edge. The creamy beetroot-rippled vinaigrette stands alongside to enhance the dish.

Between the months of September and October, walnuts are at their ripest and best. It is important that walnuts are eaten as soon as possible after buying to prevent their natural oils from becoming rancid, and for them to offer the finest of nutty flavours.

As far as lettuces are concerned, at this time of the year a lot will be imported, but home-grown still provide enough, with rocket, curly endive, corn salad, mizuna and oakleaf all holding until late November.

Method Preheat the oven to 200°C/400°F/Gas 6. To cook the beetroots, trim the stalk, not cutting the root to prevent the beetroot from bleeding its juices. Place the beetroots in a small saucepan, cover with cold water and add a pinch of salt. Bring to a rapid simmer and cook for 50–60 minutes, until tender. Rather than piercing them to check their tenderness, lift the beetroots from the water and gently pull at the skin with your thumb. If the skin feels loose and is easy to remove, the beetroots are ready to be drained and left to cool.

While the beetroots are cooking, peel the carrots and parsnips, trim away the top stalk and quarter lengthwise, to produce sharp sticks. The central core of the parsnips can also be trimmed away, should they appear to be woody. The vegetables can be roasted from absolutely raw, but I often find a short blanching produces a creamier centre. To do so, plunge the carrots into boiling salted water. After 2 minutes add the parsnips and cook for a further 2 minutes. At this point, spoon the carrots and parsnips on to a kitchen cloth or paper, and leave to cool. The vegetables will still be very firm, but with their rawness removed.

Preheat a roasting tray on top of the stove, adding the olive or cooking oil. Add the carrots and parsnips and fry on all sides until well coloured. Season with salt and pepper. Place the roasting tray in the preheated oven and cook for 15–20 minutes, turning the vegetables from time to time, until they are becoming crispy. Remove the vegetables from the oven and season with salt and pepper. These are going to be best served very warm, rather than piping hot.

While the carrots and parsnips are roasting, cut the beetroots into 5mm (¼in) dice or grate coarsely.

To make the dressing, whisk together the mustard, soured cream and vinegar. The oil can now be trickled in as you whisk, allowing it to emulsify with the cream. Should the dressing be too thick, simply loosen with a little water. Season with salt and pepper. You may only need half to two-thirds of the dressing; any left over can be kept in the fridge for several days to be used with other salads.

Once the beetroot is diced, mix half with the dressing and this will create a pink, rippled effect. If the beetroot is grated, any juices can be added to the dressing, also providing a suitable rippled effect.

Arrange the carrots and parsnips in a rustic fashion on 4 serving plates, sprinkling with the remaining diced beetroots. If using grated beetroots, simply divide between the plates, spooning a base on which to place the vegetables. Break the walnut halves into pieces and mix them with the salad leaves, then drizzle with extra walnut oil, if liked. Season with salt and pepper and sprinkle on top of the carrots and parsnips. Spoon over and around with the beetroot and soured cream dressing to finish.

● *A teaspoon of soft dark brown sugar and a knob of butter can be added to the vegetables 10 minutes before they have finished cooking. This will leave a slight bitter-sweet edge to the roasted flavour.*

● *The shelled walnuts can be blanched for 1 minute in boiling water, and the bitter skin scraped away while they are still warm. This is a bit of a fiddly, time-consuming job that is not really essential, but does give a cleaner finish and flavour.*

Serves 4
- 450g (1lb) swedes
- 450g (1lb) carrots
- salt and pepper
- 3–4 tablespoons milk (or single cream for a richer finish)
- pinch of ground cinnamon or mace
- 50g (2oz) butter
- 1 tablespoon flaked almonds, toasted to a light golden brown
- squeeze of lemon juice (optional)

Swede and carrot mash with nut-brown almonds

Mashed swedes can tend to absorb far too much water, still managing to hold texture but losing most of their flavour. It is with this in mind that the carrots are added here, offering a lot more density and sweetness. Of course, this is not a new combination; I'm told this particular marriage was once called stump. Apparently, this dish from the North of England could also include potatoes and, in different regions, even parsnips, turnips and leeks.

The nut-brown butter and almonds are my personal extra. Once mashed, the vegetables are spooned with the sizzling nut-brown butter and toasted flaked almonds (whole blanched almonds can also be used, if sliced thinly). The nuttiness from both helps balance the sweet flavour of the vegetables.

Method Cut the swedes and carrots into rough 2.5cm (1in) dice. Place the chopped vegetables in a saucepan and cover them with boiling water from the kettle. Add a good pinch of salt and simmer for 20–25 minutes, until completely tender. Drain in a colander, return them to the saucepan and stir over a low heat as they dry, to remove excess moisture.

Mash the swedes and carrots, adding the milk or cream to loosen slightly, season with salt and a pinch of cinnamon or mace and a generous twist of pepper, stirring in half of the butter. (For a super-smooth finish, they can be puréed in a food processor.) Spoon the mash into a warmed vegetable dish.

Melt the remaining butter in a small frying pan. Once bubbling, add the almonds and continue to cook the butter until it reaches a nut-brown stage. Add a squeeze of lemon juice, if using, and spoon the almond butter over the finished dish.

● *This mash will accompany virtually all of the autumn and winter meat dishes included in the book.*

● *A generous tablespoon or two of wholegrain mustard can also be added to this recipe for a warmer finished flavour. Chopped chives are another extra worth adding.*

**Serves 8 as a starter
or 6 as a main course**
- 8 medium–large parsnips
- 4 tablespoons olive or
  groundnut oil
- knob of butter
- salt and pepper
- flour, for dusting

- 675g (1½lb) *Quick puff pastry*
  (page 203, or bought)
- 3 large onions
- 6–8 sage leaves, chopped
- 175–225g (6–8oz) soft or semi-
  soft goat's or sheep's cheese
- freshly grated nutmeg
- 1 egg, beaten

For the cream sauce (optional)
- 2 tablespoons sherry vinegar
- 200ml (7fl oz) *Vegetable stock*
  (page 197) or *Instant stock*
  (page 194)
- 3 tablespoons whipping cream
- squeeze of lemon juice
- 3 tablespoons hazelnut or
  walnut oil

Roast parsnip, sage, onion and cheese pie

This pie is assembled in a very French manner, resulting in a *pithiviers* finish. *Pithiviers* is a French pastry cake, classically consisting of two rounds of puff pastry sandwiching and encasing frangipane (a sweet almond filling). It is purely the shape we're borrowing here, which does make it very simple indeed – you just have to arrange and cover it, without shaping it into moulds. A late-autumn/winter dish, this takes full advantage of the sweet parsnip, helped by a roasted edge.

As for the cheese, a British goat's or sheep's cheese, soft or semi-soft, would be just perfect. One that is particularly suitable is the Innes Button, a small goat's cheese, weighing just 50g (2oz), from Staffordshire. With a very creamy texture it has an almond edge to its taste, with honey and a taste of tangerine also happening, all of which suit parsnips. For this recipe, at least three, if not four, of these cheeses will be needed.

I've included a cream sauce here, which does go very well with the pie, but is certainly not essential.

Method Preheat the oven to 200°C/400°F/Gas 6. Cut the parsnips into 13cm (5in) lengths, measuring from the points rather than the large tops. The measured pieces can now each be quartered lengthwise and the woody centre cores cut away. The remaining tops can also be quartered, cored and trimmed.

Heat half of the oil in a roasting tray. Place all of the parsnips in the tray and fry over a moderate heat until golden brown on all sides. Add the knob of butter. Place the tray into the preheated oven and roast for 12–15 minutes, until the parsnips are tender. Remove the parsnips from the tray, season them with salt and pepper, and leave to cool. Increase the oven temperature to 220°C/425°F/Gas 7.

On a floured surface, roll a third of the pastry into a 28–30cm (11–12in) round. Place the round on a large baking tray lined with greaseproof or parchment paper and chill to rest.

Slice the onions into thin rings and separate them. Heat the remaining oil in a large saucepan and fry the onion rings over a moderately high heat, until tender, and allow them to take on a light colour. Season and leave to cool. Once cold, add the chopped sage.

The cheese, if soft, may not need to have its outer skin removed first, but semi-soft cheeses often do. If necessary, trim away any such hard outer skin, being careful not to waste any of the soft centre.

Lay the measured parsnip pieces on the pastry round with the points all meeting in the centre, leaving a 2.5cm (1in) border clear. This naturally forms a neat circle. If they are packed tightly, all of the pieces can be used. Sprinkle with freshly grated nutmeg, spoon a third of the sage onions on top, with most placed towards the centre. Slice or crumble the cheese and scatter on top of the onions. The remaining small pieces of parsnip can now be packed into the centre. Finish these with a little nutmeg. Top and surround the central parsnips with the remaining onion, to produce a slightly domed finish.

Brush the border of exposed pastry with the beaten egg and roll the large piece of puff pastry on a floured surface into a circle slightly larger than the first. Roll this loosely on the rolling pin and unroll it over the parsnip base. Firmly press the edges of the pastry together and chill for 20 minutes to set. To give a neat finish, place a large flan ring or glass bowl over the pastry and trim, leaving a 2 2.5cm (¾ 1in) border. Classically a *pithiviers* has the pastry top scored with the point of a small knife in curved lines from the centre to produce a spiral pattern. This is not essential, but is very effective once baked. Brush the top with the egg, not allowing the egg wash to drop around the sides as this will result in an uneven rising of the pastry.

Bake in the preheated oven for 30–35 minutes, until golden brown and ready to serve, the cheese having softened and melted all over the parsnips.

If serving the pie with the cream sauce, boil the sherry vinegar to reduce by half, then add the stock. Return to the boil and allow to reduce by half again. Add the cream and simmer for a few minutes. Flavour the sauce with the lemon juice and salt and pepper, then whisk in the nut oil. The sauce is ready to serve with the pie.

**Serves 4–6 as a starter
or 3 as a main course**
- 2kg (4½lb) mussels
- 2 onions, finely chopped (saving all trimmings)
- 2 large garlic cloves
- 150ml (¼ pint) white wine
- 1 medium butternut squash
- 3 tablespoons olive oil
- salt and pepper
- 50g (2oz) butter
- 1 tablespoon chopped curly parsley
- 1 tablespoon chopped chives
- 1 tablespoon chopped chervil

Butternut mussel stew

When autumn arrives so do pumpkin and winter squash. These wonderful vegetables are so often ignored or forgotten, yet hold so many possibilities within their culinary repertoires. Whether roasted, sautéed, puréed or simply made into soups, they rarely disappoint.

Here the giant pear-shaped butternut is combined with very meaty mussels, the two flavours complementing each other perfectly, in a loose soup-style brothy stew, suitable for a starter, lunch or full supper dish. As with all mussel dishes, crusty bread to mop up the juices is the perfect accompaniment.

Method Although mussels can often be found pre-cleaned, it is imperative that they are all cleaned again to ensure they are totally free of any impurities.

Place them in a sinkful of cold water and scrape off any barnacles and hairy beards. If any mussels are slightly open, a short sharp tap should make them close. Any that don't close should be discarded. You may also find one or two that are particularly heavy. If so, I recommend these also be discarded, as they are more than likely full of sand. Once cleaned and rinsed, the mussels are ready to cook.

Place the onion trimmings in a large saucepan. Roughly chop one of the garlic cloves and add it to the pan along with the white wine and 750ml (1¼ pints) water. Bring to a simmer and cook for 10–15 minutes.

Meanwhile, prepare the butternut squash. Cut it in half lengthwise, scoop out the seeds and threads and cut each half into thirds or quarters. Cut away the skin, then chop the flesh into 1cm (½in) pieces.

Bring the white wine liquor to the boil, add the mussels and cover tightly with a lid. The mussels will take just a few minutes to open. To ensure even cooking, shake the pan from time to time, or spoon the mussels around.

Once they have all opened, strain the mussels into a colander, collecting the liquor and juices in a saucepan or bowl below. Strain the cooking liquor through a fine sieve and return it to a simmer. Taste the mussel stock for strength. If it is a little shallow in flavour, continue to simmer and reduce slightly to increase the total flavour strength, not allowing it to become over-powerful and mask the butternut.

Heat the olive oil in a large saucepan and add the onions and diced squash. Crush the remaining garlic clove and add it to the pan. Fry these vegetables on a fairly high heat, allowing them just to begin to soften and colour.

After a few minutes, add the stock and bring to a simmer, then cook for about 15 minutes, until the squash has become tender.

While this is cooking, remove the mussels from their shells, discarding any that haven't opened.

Add the mussels to the butternut squash stew, allowing it to simmer gently to warm them through. Season the stew very carefully with salt, if needed, and a generous twist of pepper. Stir in the butter and herbs and the stew is ready to serve.

Serves 6

- 1kg (2¼lb) pumpkin
- 1 teaspoon finely grated orange zest
- 1 large onion, finely chopped
- 1 large carrot, cut into small rough dice
- 1 teaspoon caster sugar
- 900ml (1½ pints) *Vegetable stock* (page 197) or *Chicken* or *Instant stock* (page 194)
- 150ml (¼ pint) crème fraîche or single cream (if preferred without cream, simply use more stock)
- 50g (2oz) butter, to finish (optional)
- salt and pepper

Pumpkin soup

Pumpkins run for quite a season, finding their prime in the month of October. In November, however, a good thick soup is more than welcome at the family table, or perhaps even to keep our hands warm in large mugs on Guy Fawkes' Night. The orange zest here is not just relating to the colour of the pumpkin. Without taking over, its citrus fruit flavour tends to lift and enhance the overall taste of the soup.

Method Cut away the skin and seeds from the pumpkin, cut the flesh into a rough 2cm (¾in) dice, then place in a saucepan with the orange zest, chopped onion, carrot, sugar and stock. Bring to a simmer and cook fairly rapidly for 20 minutes.

The soup can now be blitzed in a liquidizer to a smooth consistency. If slightly grainy, strain through a sieve. Return the soup to a simmer, whisking in the cream, and butter, if using. Check for seasoning with salt and pepper to finish.

- *Large croûtons of bread cubes fried in butter eat very well with this soup.*

**Serves 4 as a starter
or 2 as a main course**

- 450g (1lb) courgettes
- 4 tablespoons olive oil
- salt and pepper
- 6 eggs
- 1 tablespoon chopped chives
- large knob of butter
- 75g (3oz) Beenleigh Blue cheese, crumbled

Beenleigh Blue and courgette egg cake

Beenleigh Blue is a blue Devonshire unpasteurized ewe's-milk cheese. It has quite a rich robust flavour and is normally available from September to February. The British courgettes are with us from mid-summer to mid-autumn, and so September does feel a good time to enjoy this dish. However, this recipe can be put together throughout the year, with plenty of alternative blue cheeses, like Stilton and Roquefort, available and with imported courgettes to match.

The finished cake resembles a potato and onion Spanish omelette. Good crispy bacon works well as an accompaniment. If you are serving this as a starter or vegetarian main course, a small salad of leaves and soft red peppers will not disappoint.

Method Cut the courgettes into thin slices – if possible, cut them into thin julienne strips (spaghetti-style) using a mandolin slicer. Alternatively, simply shred/grate in a food processor.

Heat 2 tablespoons of the olive oil in a 28cm (11in) diameter frying pan, preferably non-stick. Once hot, fry the courgettes for a minute or two, until beginning to soften and taking on a little colour. Season with salt and pepper, and remove the pan from the heat.

Fork the eggs together in a large bowl, adding the chopped chives and knob of butter. Now add the courgettes, spooning the mix in well, to spread the vegetables and warmth evenly.

Preheat a grill to hot. Spoon the remaining olive oil into the frying pan, swirling to cover the whole pan, and return to the heat. Pour the courgette egg mix into the frying pan and cook on a medium heat, moving the mixture with a fork or spatula to ensure an even cooking. As the egg warms it will begin to thicken. After a few minutes, lower the temperature, allowing the mix to set on the base, leaving a thickened but still soft centre and top.

Crumble the cheese across the top and finish under the preheated grill until melted and golden brown. The courgette egg cake is now ready to serve hot or just warm.

● *It is nice to present the cake on the table while still in the pan. This provides a rustic homely feel to the dish.*

● *Extra blue cheese can be sprinkled on top for a creamier and richer finish.*

**Serves 4 as an accompaniment
or 2 as a main course**
- 1 large or 2 small cauliflowers, divided into small florets
- 2 medium carrots
- 1 onion
- 4 tablespoons olive oil
- 1 bay leaf
- sprig of thyme
- 150ml (¼ pint) white wine
- salt and pepper
- juice of ½ lemon
- 75g (3oz) butter
- 2 garlic cloves, finely crushed
- pinch of caster sugar
- 1 heaped tablespoon roughly chopped parsley

Cauliflower casserole

Cauliflower is a member of the same brassica family as cabbage, kale, kohlrabi, broccoli and Brussels sprouts. The differences among them have come about from the thousands of years of cultivation and selective propagation. This particular vegetable was developed by the Arabs during the Middle Ages, but was not highly regarded in Europe until the eighteenth century. The cauliflower can be found today in three basic colours, white, green and purple.

The growers say the best time to enjoy cauliflower is during the autumn, and it is indeed exceptionally good at this time of the year, but there are also the Lincolnshire cauliflowers which join us in spring.

This casserole mixes tender cauliflower florets with carrots and onions, binding them all with a loose cooking liquor enhanced by a garlic butter and some chopped parsley. The dish goes well with many roast and braised meat dishes and fish. It also stands well on its own as a vegetarian stew, to be mopped up with crusty bread.

Method Cook the cauliflower florets in boiling salted water for 5–6 minutes, until completely tender, with just the slightest of bites. Drain in a colander and leave to stand until all excess steam has lifted. This releases the water from the vegetable.

Cut the carrots into very thin slices. For a more attractive presentation, carrots can first be 'grooved' in five or six lines, using a canelle cutter, from top to bottom. This will produce slices with a floral face. Slice the onion into thin rings.

Heat the olive oil in a flameproof braising pot on top of the stove. Add the carrots, onion, bay leaf and thyme, and cook slowly until the vegetables are tender and beginning to take on a little colour.

At this point, add the white wine and bring to the boil. Simmer the wine to reduce it by two-thirds, then add 150ml (¼ pint) of water. Season with salt, pepper and the lemon juice. Simmer gently for 5 minutes, allowing the water to take on the other flavours.

While these vegetables are cooking, melt 25g (1oz) of the butter in a frying pan. Add the cauliflower florets and cook on a fairly low heat, the butter bubbling and heating the florets, while they begin to take on a light golden brown colour. Season with salt and pepper.

Mix together the remaining butter with the crushed garlic. Add the coloured cauliflower to the carrot and onion liquor, along with the pinch of sugar and garlic butter, stirring to emulsify. Sprinkle with the chopped parsley and the dish is ready to be served straight from the pan.

Serves 4–6
- 1 small aubergine
- salt and pepper
- 2 medium courgettes
- 1 large red pepper
- 1 large green pepper
- 2 small red onions
- olive oil and butter, for frying and brushing
- 1 garlic clove
- 2 plum tomatoes, quartered and deseeded

For the Parmesan cream
- 2 eggs, plus 1 egg yolk (optional)
- 300ml (½ pint) milk
- 150ml (¼ pint) double cream
- 4 tablespoons Parmesan cheese, finely grated

Early autumn Provençale bake

From September until about mid-October you can find the ingredients required here. The combination is very much along the lines of ratatouille, utilizing these flavours during their last weeks. The list of vegetables is purely a guideline and any of them can stand alone within the Parmesan cream. Basically, it is a quiche-style recipe without the pastry case – a 25cm (10in) ovenproof ceramic fluted flan dish takes its place. Serve the warm bake as an accompaniment to other foods or as a main dish. Grilled chicken breasts or gammon steaks go very well with it, as does a good early autumn salad.

Method Cut the aubergine into 2.5cm (1in) dice and place the pieces in a colander. Sprinkle with a level teaspoon of salt, mix it in well and leave to stand for 30 minutes. This will draw the bitter juices from the vegetable. After the 30 minutes, the aubergine should not need to be rinsed as the salt will purely have seasoned it; if you are a little unsure, quickly rinse and dry on a kitchen cloth. While salting the aubergine, preheat the oven to 170°C/325°F/Gas 3 and cut the remaining vegetables.

Slice the courgettes into 2.5cm (1in) pieces, preferably at an angle to provide a neat oval pointed shape. Split the red and green peppers, then cut each half into four or five strips and trim away the seeds and stalk, maintaining their curved edge (the stalk can be left on for a more rustic finish). Cut each red onion into eight wedges.

Heat a little olive oil in a large frying pan. Once it is hot, fry the aubergine pieces for just 2 minutes, allowing them to take on a fried edge. Remove and return to the colander or place on a tray lined with kitchen paper. Sauté the courgette pieces in a similar fashion, cooking for an extra 2–3 minutes, until they have just a light golden-brown finish, season with salt and pepper, and transfer to the tray.

Fry the peppers in olive oil, or brush with butter and placed under a preheated grill. These strips need only be gently softened, so cook for just a few minutes. Lastly, grill, fry or bake the onions, season with salt and pepper and brush with butter. The onions will take a little longer to soften, so cook them for 8–10 minutes.

While the onions are cooking, make the Parmesan cream. Whisk together the eggs and egg yolk, if using (this will enrich the finished flavour), adding the milk and cream. The Parmesan cheese can all be added or just add 3 tablespoons, reserving the remainder to sprinkle on top during the last 5 minutes of cooking. Season with salt and pepper.

Split the garlic clove and rub the flan dish (see above) liberally with both halves. Brush the dish with butter, then spoon in the softened vegetables and tomatoes. Pour the Parmesan cream over and bake in the preheated oven for 35–40 minutes until just set. Once cooked, remove from the oven and allow to rest for 5–10 minutes before serving.

● *The garlic halves can be crushed and added to the cream for an even more Provençale finish.*

● *Chopped fresh herbs can also be added to the filling.*

Serves 6–8

- 100g (4oz) small Brussels sprouts
- 100g (4oz) curly kale
- 100g (4oz) runner beans
- 100g (4oz) courgettes
- 3 tablespoons olive oil
- 1 onion, thinly sliced
- 2 celery sticks, thinly sliced

- 2 garlic cloves, thinly sliced or crushed
- 1.25 litres (2 pints) *Vegetable stock* (page 197) or *Instant stock* (page 194) or water
- 1 small leek, thinly sliced
- salt and pepper
- knob of butter (optional)
- 2 egg yolks (optional)

- 4 tablespoons double or whipping cream (optional)
- 1 tablespoon chopped chives
- 1 tablespoon picked chervil leaves
- 6–8 slices of French bread about 2cm (¾in) thick (optional)

Green garden soup

It's mid-autumn and there are now green vegetables joining us – young curly kale, with leeks and Brussels sprouts only in their second month and still not quite at their prime. Courgettes, runner beans and celery are in their final run, as far as home-grown are concerned.

This soup is a good excuse to bring them all together, but if some are not available, there are one or two others which could happily take their place – broccoli and spinach offer rich green flavours.

The only other vegetable ingredients are onion and garlic, just to 'spike up' the finished flavour, with a couple of herbs for added essence. Included in the recipe, as an optional extra, is a combination of egg yolk and cream. This is a rich thickening agent usually referred to in culinary terms as a liaison. It can only be added just before serving, as reboiling will scramble it. Without this, the soup can be enjoyed purely as a broth.

Another optional extra is a slice of French bread placed in the bowl before ladling in the soup. The liquid-soaked bread offers an additional texture to enjoy.

Method To prepare the vegetables, remove the bases of the stalks and outside leaves from the sprouts and halve each sprout. Pick the curly kale leaves from the stalks, washing and tearing the leaves into bite-sized pieces. Remove the outside strings from the runner beans and finely shred the beans. Halve the courgettes lengthwise and cut into thin slices. This whole process can be achieved well in advance of making the soup.

Warm the olive oil in a large saucepan. Add the sliced onion, celery and garlic and cook for 5–6 minutes, until beginning to soften. Add the stock or water and bring to a simmer.

After 5 minutes of simmering, increase the heat to bring the stock to the boil. Now it's time to add the vegetables – first add the sprouts and after a minute the curly kale. These will now both need 3 minutes before adding all the remaining vegetables – runner beans, courgettes and leek – and cooking for a further 3–4 minutes, until all are tender.

Season the soup with salt and a generous twist of pepper, and add the knob of butter, if using. If slightly thickening with the liaison, mix together the egg yolks and cream. Add a ladle of the soup liquor to this and mix well. Remove the soup from the heat and pour the liaison mix into the soup as you stir, slightly thickening and enriching the end result. Add the two herbs and the soup is ready to serve. Place a slice of bread, if using, into each bowl before ladling the soup over.

Serves 6
- butter, for greasing
- flour, for dusting
- 350g (12oz) *Quick puff* or *Shortcrust pastry* (page 203) or 225g (8oz) for one large flan
- 2 sweetcorn cobs, husks removed
- 2 eggs, plus 1 egg yolk
- 175ml (6fl oz) double or whipping cream
- salt and black pepper

For the dressing
- 2 apples, preferably Russets
- squeeze of lemon juice
- 3 tablespoons olive oil
- 3 tablespoons walnut oil
- 1 small red onion, finely chopped
- 10 walnut halves, broken into smaller pieces
- 1 tablespoon cider vinegar
- ½ teaspoon caster sugar
- 1 tablespoon chopped chives

Savoury sweetcorn custard tarts with an apple and walnut dressing

This recipe needs little introduction, with all of these flavours being in season together. Sweetcorn is at its prime between August and September, rolling on into October, so it's during this last month that I prefer to make this dish. The last of the sweetcorn is helped along with these other crisp flavours – together with a very generous twist of black pepper for extra bite.

This recipe is for six individual tartlets, but one 20cm (8in) flan ring can be used (it must be at least 2cm/¾in deep). It is also possible simply to place all of these ingredients into the tart case, together with one or two others, like the red onion and chives that here are included in the dressing, to create a seasonal sweetcorn quiche.

Method Lightly butter and flour six individual tartlet rings, about 9cm (3½in) in diameter. Roll out the pastry thinly on a floured surface and divide it into six pieces. Line each tartlet case, leaving any excess pastry hanging over the edge. Line each pastry case with a round of greaseproof paper and fill with baking beans or rice. Chill on a greased baking tray for 20–30 minutes to allow the pastry to rest.

Preheat the oven to 200°C/400°F/Gas 6. Bake the pastry in the oven for 20 minutes. Remove the greaseproof paper and beans, and return the tarts to the oven for a further 3 minutes. This helps to set the base of the pastry. Remove from the oven and allow to cool, then trim off the excess pastry. Reduce the oven temperature to 180°C/350°F/Gas 4.

Cook the sweetcorn cobs whole in boiling water (without salt as this tends to toughen the kernels), for 15 minutes, then remove from the pan and allow to cool. The kernels can be eased off with the help of a fork. Alternatively you can remove the kernels before cooking. Stand each cob upright on a chopping board and, with a sharp knife, slice against the cob to release the kernels. Turn the cob and continue until all the kernels have been removed. Now cook the kernels for just 5 minutes in boiling water, drain well and sprinkle into the tart cases.

To make the savoury custard, beat together the eggs and egg yolk, then beat in the cream. Season with a good pinch of salt and a very generous twist of black pepper for a spicy finish. Pour over the sweetcorn, in each of the six pastry cases, then bake in the cooler, preheated oven for 15–20 minutes until only just set. Remove the tarts from the oven and leave to relax and cool slightly for about 10 minutes, then remove the tartlet rings.

While the tarts rest, prepare the dressing. Peel and quarter the apples, removing the cores. Cut the apples into 5mm (¼in) dice, adding a squeeze of lemon juice to prevent them discolouring.

To finish the dressing, warm the oils with the red onion. Remove from the heat and add the walnuts, apples, cider vinegar, sugar and chives. Season with salt and pepper and spoon the dressing around the tartlets.

● *A level teaspoon of Dijon or wholegrain mustard can be whisked into the oil for a more fiery finish to the dressing. A tablespoon or two of crème fraîche or soured cream can be added to the dressing or simply drizzled around the tarts.*

- 12 Swiss chard stalks
- juice of ½ lemon
- salt and pepper
- 3 sweet red peppers
- olive oil, for frying
- 2 knobs of butter, plus extra for greasing
- 2 red onions, sliced

- 175g (6oz) mascarpone cheese
- 50g (2oz) Parmesan cheese, finely grated
- 1 egg, plus 1 egg yolk

For the crumble topping
- 3 slices of thick white or granary bread, preferably 24–48 hours old
- 8 basil leaves, torn into small pieces
- 1 teaspoon torn tarragon leaves
- 1 teaspoon chopped parsley
- 1 teaspoon chopped chives
- 25g (1oz) butter
- 1 small garlic clove, crushed

Swiss chard and sweet red pepper mascarpone crumble

Swiss chard can be found most of the year, but does particularly well during the months of August and September. There's also the beautiful ruby chard which, although its colour is lost during cooking, struggles to find its way into our kitchens during autumn months.

Within the recipe for *Swiss chard cheese pie* (page 32), only the vegetable's leaves are used. Here we use purely the celery-like stalks, mixed with sweet red pepper and a smooth mascarpone cream, enhanced with the addition of Parmesan cheese. The Swiss chard leaves can be put to use and cooked in butter, as you would spinach, to accompany another meal. The crumble topping offers a garlic and fresh herb finish, and all of these flavours together will suit the first of our autumn months, September.

If serving as a vegetarian main course, all the dish needs is a mixed leaf salad with a red wine vinegar dressing to finish it off. The crumble also eats particularly well with roast chicken or grilled chicken breasts.

Method Preheat the oven to 200°C/400°F/Gas 6. Should the chard stalks be large and quite tough, it's best to peel away the fine membrane on each side. Cut the stalks into 5cm (2in) pieces and place them in a bowl of water acidulated with the lemon juice to prevent any discoloration. To cook the chard, plunge the pieces into rapidly boiling salted water and simmer for 10 minutes, until just tender. Drain in a colander and allow to cool.

To prepare the peppers, halve and quarter each one, removing the stalk and seeds, then cut each quarter into two or three thick strips. Heat 2 tablespoons of olive oil in a large frying pan. Once hot, add the pepper strips and fry on a medium heat for 6–7 minutes, until becoming tender. Transfer to a large bowl.

Return the pan to the heat and warm a tablespoon of olive oil. Add the pieces of chard and fry for a few minutes, until approaching golden brown. Add a knob of butter, increase the heat and allow the butter to reach a nut-brown stage. Add the chard to the peppers and repeat the frying process with the red onion slices.

Once all these vegetables are together in the bowl, season with salt and pepper. Mix the mascarpone, Parmesan, egg and egg yolk, then season with salt and pepper. Stir this into the vegetables and spoon into a greased 1.5 litre (2½ pint) ovenproof dish.

To make the crumble topping, remove the crusts from the bread slices, then blitz them in a food processor to a rough crumb consistency. Transfer the crumbs to a bowl and stir in the herbs. Melt the butter in a saucepan with the crushed garlic, until beginning to bubble. Season the crumbs with salt and pepper and pour the butter over. Stir the butter into the crumbs, keeping them quite loose.

Sprinkle the crumbs over the chard and sweet pepper mascarpone, then bake in the preheated oven for 15–20 minutes, until golden brown and bubbling. If white crumbs have been used and are not well coloured in the oven, simply finish under a preheated grill. The crumble is ready to serve.

**Serves 6–8 as a starter
or 4–6 as a main course**

- 1kg (2¼lb) unpicked Swiss chard (450g/1lb picked leaves are needed for a full pie filling; if the leaves are too small 1.3kg/3lb unpicked chard will be needed)
- salt and pepper
- iced water
- knob of butter
- 2 tablespoons finely chopped shallots

- 2 eggs
- 50g (2oz) Parmesan cheese, finely grated
- freshly grated nutmeg
- 6–8 thin slices of Swiss Gruyère cheese, about 75–100g (3–4oz)
- 150ml (¼ pint) crème fraîche (optional)
- 1 tablespoon chopped chives (optional)
- 1 level teaspoon Dijon or wholegrain mustard (optional)

For the olive oil pastry
- 225g (8oz) plain flour, plus extra for dusting
- pinch of salt
- 1 egg
- 3 tablespoons lukewarm water or milk
- 3 tablespoons olive oil, plus extra for brushing

Swiss chard cheese pie

Swiss chard is a green-leafed vegetable of the beet family which is rather similar to spinach. The advantage it has over similar greens is that the stalks of the young vegetable can also be cooked, offering a celery-like finish, or shredded raw for a salad.

With this recipe it is purely the leaves we shall be using, flavouring them with some shallots for an extra bite, and Parmesan cheese for enrichment. The pastry has a texture similar to shortcrust with the addition of olive oil to lend a stronger finished flavour that is welcomed by both the chard and the cheese.

Method To make the pastry, sift the flour and salt into a bowl. Add the egg, water or milk and olive oil, and spoon the ingredients together. Once they are beginning to amalgamate, work the mix well by hand to a soft dough. Mixing the dough to this stage can be achieved by simply placing all of the ingredients in a food processor. After just 30–60 seconds the mix is ready to finish by hand to a smooth texture. It is now best to cover and chill the pastry for at least 1 hour to let it rest well.

While the pastry is resting, pick the chard leaves for the filling from the stalks (as mentioned above these can be cooked separately, using them as you would sea kale or celery). Wash the leaves, tear them into smaller pieces and blanch them in rapidly boiling salted water for a few minutes until tender. Drain the chard and refresh in iced water. This will instantly stop the cooking and also retain the rich green colour.

Once chilled, remove the leaves from the iced water and squeeze to release excess water. Melt the knob of butter in a small saucepan and, once bubbling, add the shallots. Cook gently for 5 minutes, without allowing them to colour, until tender. Leave to cool.

Roll just over half of the pastry on a floured surface into a 25cm (10in) diameter circle. Roll this on to the rolling pin, place on a very lightly oiled baking tray and chill once more, letting it rest for 10–15 minutes. Preheat the oven to 190°C/375°F/Gas 5.

While the pastry is resting, fork the eggs together and add them to the chard, along with the shallots and Parmesan. Season to taste with salt, pepper and nutmeg. Spoon the chard mixture onto the pastry base, packing it fairly firmly and leaving a 1cm (½in) clear border around the edge. Roll the remaining pastry into a slightly larger disc to cover the pie. Once placed on top, the edges can be trimmed for a neater finish or left for a more rustic touch. Lightly flouring your fingers, crimp the border together, press with a fork or twist over to give a rope-effect finish. Brush the pie with olive oil and bake in the preheated oven for 25–30 minutes, until crispy and golden brown.

For the cheesy finish, preheat a hot grill and lay the Gruyère slices on top to cover. Place under the preheated grill until bubbling and melted. The pie is ready to serve. If using the crème fraîche, mix with the chives and mustard, then season with salt and pepper and offer as an accompaniment to the pie.

● *The Swiss cheese can also be included in the filling, dividing the chard into two layers, sandwiching the cheese slices in between.*

**Serves 4 as a starter
or side dish**
- 1 medium celeriac
- 2 Russet apples
- salt and pepper
- 1 small shallot, very finely chopped
- 18 walnut halves, roughly chopped
- 100–150ml (3½fl oz–¼ pint) crème fraîche
- squeeze of lemon juice
- 1 heaped teaspoon Dijon mustard
- 1–2 tablespoons red wine vinegar
- 2 tablespoons olive oil
- 2 tablespoons walnut oil
- 2 celery sticks, cut into 5mm (¼in) dice
- handful of washed rocket leaves or watercress sprigs (optional)

Waldorf salad

This is a classic salad that they say was devised at New York's Waldorf Astoria hotel back in the 1890s. The original version contained just apples, celery and mayonnaise, with the chopped walnuts being added at a later date.

Salad is a word that carries a very summery image – lots of mixed leaves with tomatoes, cucumbers, spring onions and more. But salads can adopt many guises, taking advantage of almost all ingredients. The Waldorf is without question an autumn speciality, particularly for the months of October and November, when all of its prime ingredients are home-grown.

This version is slightly different from the original. Celeriac takes the lead role, an alternative that has been used many a time, with the mayonnaise being replaced by crème fraîche for a lighter and fresher finish. The apples are Russets, although more or less any can be used, but it was apparently the Russet that was chosen for the original. The beauty of this apple is its quite distinctive juicy sweetness and nutty edge.

For an extra dressing, diced celery is bound with oil, red wine vinegar and a touch of mustard to offer a contrasting finish. If available, a handful of rocket leaves will help finish the dish. If none is around, a good few sprigs of watercress will be just fine.

Method Cut away the celeriac's tough skin, then chop the root into 5mm (¼in) dice or slice it into spaghetti-like strips. This can be made easy by simply halving the celeriac and cutting into thin strips on a mandolin slicer. Once cut, add a squeeze of lemon juice and mix it in well.

Quarter the apples, cutting away the core and seeds, then peel each quarter. This helps retain the natural shape of the apple. Once peeled, cut each piece into thin slices and add them to the celeriac. Season with salt and pepper.

Rinse the chopped shallot under cold water, shaking away any excess. This removes the raw bitterness, leaving a slightly more subtle finish. Add the shallot to the celeriac and apples along with the walnuts. Stir in 100ml (3½fl oz) of the crème fraîche to bind the flavours. If a slightly looser consistency is preferred, add the remainder. Season with salt, pepper and lemon juice.

To make the dressing, whisk together the mustard and a tablespoon of red wine vinegar. Whisk in the two oils and season with salt and pepper. The remaining tablespoon of vinegar can be added for a sharper bite. Mix the diced celery into the dressing.

To serve, divide the Waldorf salad between the plates and spoon over the celery and red wine vinaigrette. A few rocket leaves (or watercress sprigs) can now be arranged on top, and drizzled with just a drop or two of the vinaigrette.

Serves 6 as a starter or snack

- 225g (8oz) wild or cultivated mushrooms (see page 200)
- 1 leek
- 25g (1oz) butter
- 1 garlic clove, crushed to a paste
- salt and pepper
- 200ml (7fl oz) double cream
- 75g (3oz) Gruyère cheese, grated
- 6 eggs

Mushroom and leek egg baked pots

It is autumn and the wild mushrooms and leeks have arrived. The choice of wild mushrooms is quite extravagant, with ceps, chanterelles, black *trompettes*, shiitake and *mousserons* all on offer. As autumn leads into late November, the variety available begins to dwindle, while leeks become even more predominant. So it is really early to mid-autumn that will offer both.

The egg baked pots can work equally well with chestnut mushrooms, a mushroom that offers a much fuller flavour and firmer texture than basic buttons, or perhaps oyster mushrooms, which were once naturally wild but are now cultivated 'wild', available throughout the year. The quantity of mushrooms listed above will suit all of these fungi, and, if deciding on wild, mixed bags are available, or you can buy them loose as a selection, or feature just one variety.

Method Preheat the oven to 200°C/400°F/Gas 6. If using wild mushrooms, simply rinse and trim them as explained on page 200. For cultivated mushrooms, simply wipe or rinse and trim the stalks, then slice.

Split the leek in half lengthwise, removing the outside layer. The halves can now be rinsed, releasing any grit caught between the layers. Trim the stalk and green tops, then slice thinly.

Heat half of the butter in a large frying pan. Once hot and bubbling, add the mushrooms and crushed garlic, and fry over a high heat for just a minute or two, to tenderize rather than completely cook through. Season with salt and pepper and drain in a sieve or colander.

Wipe the pan clean and melt the remaining butter. Once bubbling, add the sliced leek and cook again on a fairly high heat for a few minutes, until it is approaching a tender stage. Season with salt and pepper and drain in a colander.

While the mushrooms and leeks are cooling, place a baking tray in the oven to warm through. Divide half of the cream between six size-1 ramekins. Mix together the mushrooms and leeks and divide these between the pots. Sprinkle each with the grated cheese, then crack an egg on top. Season the remaining cream with salt and pepper, and pour over each of the eggs.

Place the pots on the warmed baking tray in the preheated oven and cook for 15 minutes, until golden brown. At this stage the eggs will still be soft, continuing to cook once removed from the oven. For a firmer finish, cook for a further 3–5 minutes. The pots are now ready to serve, eating very well with crusty bread or thick toast.

- *The finished presentation is very rustic and homely looking; this is certainly not a 'designer' dish. The true focus is purely in the overall finished flavour.*

- *A little olive oil can be drizzled on top before serving; mix this with some chopped mixed herbs for extra taste.*

Serves 4
- 450g (1lb) *Quick puff pastry* (page 203, or bought variety – frozen or fresh can be purchased, usually in 450g/1lb blocks)
- flour, for dusting
- 1 egg, beaten
- 450g (1lb) button mushrooms
- 2 onions, very finely chopped
- 1 teaspoon marjoram or thyme leaves
- salt and pepper
- 450g (1lb) mixed wild mushrooms (see page 200 for different varieties)
- large knob of butter, plus extra for greasing
- 2 garlic cloves, crushed
- 6 rindless rashers of streaky bacon
- 1 tablespoon roughly chopped curly parsley
- 50–100g (2–4oz) blue cheese, crumbled
- 150ml (¼ pint) crème fraîche

Mixed mushroom and bacon pie with melted blue cheese crème fraîche

The mixed mushrooms basically consist of simple button mushrooms, making more of a stuffing base, along with a variety of wild mushrooms that are at their most abundant during our autumn months, in particular October.

There was a time when wild mushrooms were only to be found in restaurants, unless you happened to have time for a visit to Harrods. They were a food of luxury, something that hadn't really changed since the pharaohs of Egypt became so intrigued with their delicious flavour that it was decided that wild mushrooms were fit only for royalty.

Fungi have been growing since prehistoric times and have been used by us for hundreds of years, often in the preparation of beverages and medicines. 'Mushroom' was first recorded as a word in the English language in the ninth century, coming from the French word *mousseron*, which nowadays applies only to one of the small wild mushrooms, in season mostly during the summer months leading into autumn.

This recipe is a 'flat' pie, not using any pie dish or flan case. It is simply a rectangle of puff pastry, topped with the button mushroom stuffing, followed by the sautéed wild mushrooms and bacon rashers. The juices from the bacon bleed into the mushrooms, giving them a very distinctive flavour. Smoked or green unsmoked bacon can be used; the smoked can, however, sometimes become a little too overpowering for the distinctive wild mushroom flavours.

Today packs of mixed wild mushrooms can be found in most supermarkets. As for the blue cheese, it's up to you – Stilton, Roquefort, Cashel Blue, Beenleigh or blue Wensleydale can all be used. I've suggested 50–100g (2–4oz), allowing you to decide the strength that suits your palate.

This recipe will feed four very comfortably as a main course, with a large bowl of buttered curly kale served separately (which eats particularly well with the blue cheese crème fraîche). By the way, you'll have quite a delicious vegetarian dish if you omit the bacon.

Method Grease a baking sheet. Cut a third of the puff pastry and on a floured surface roll this thinly into a rectangle, measuring about 30 × 25cm (12 × 8in). Lay this on the greased baking sheet, prick the base with a fork and brush with the beaten egg. Roll the remaining pastry into a rectangle slightly bigger than the first to provide the excess required to cover the mushroom topping. This piece of pastry will also be thicker, to give a lighter, more 'puffed' finish, while the thinner base will be crispier. Place on a tray and chill for 30 minutes with the base.

Quarter the button mushrooms, then place in a food processor and blitz to reasonably small pieces. Place in a large shallow saucepan with the chopped onions and marjoram or thyme and cook on a low-to-medium heat. As the mushrooms warm, their natural juices will be released, creating a stew. Increase the heat and continue to cook until the mushrooms and onions are virtually dry. Season with salt and pepper and leave to cool on a clean tea towel to absorb any remaining liquor.

The wild mushrooms will need to have their stalks

trimmed and scraped, or perhaps just torn, before being rinsed and left to dry on a kitchen cloth or paper. If ceps are being used, just the stalks will need trimming, and if they are not too dirty, just wipe them before slicing.

Melt the knob of butter in a frying pan over a high heat. Once bubbling and almost at the nut-brown stage, add the mushrooms with the crushed garlic. Fry quickly for just a minute or two to take away their rawness. Season with salt and pepper, then drain in a colander and leave to cool on kitchen paper.

The bacon rashers are best rolled between sheets of cling film to extend their length to at least 25cm (10in), just the right size for this dish.

To build the pie, remove the two pastry rectangles from the fridge. Add the chopped parsley to the button mushrooms and spread these along the centre of the smaller rectangle, leaving a 2.5cm (1in) clean border all around. Spoon the wild mushrooms on top, then lay the 6 rashers of bacon lengthwise on top of them, slightly overlapping.

Now fold the remaining rectangle of puff pastry in half from the long side. At the fold, using scissors or a sharp knife, cut strips about 1cm (½in) apart, leaving a 2.5cm (1in) border at either end and at the outer edge. Brush around the border of the 'pie' base with egg, then place the folded sheet on one side and open up and seal to the other side. The central cuts will release any steam and also finish the dish with a French *jalousie* dessert presentation. The sealed edges can now be pressed together to produce a rustic finish, or pinched by hand or marked with a fork. It is also not essential to

trim the pastry for a very neat edge as a ragged look often quite suits this home-made pie. Chill for 15–20 minutes. Preheat the oven to 200°C/400°F/Gas 6.

Brush the pastry with more of the egg and bake in the oven for 30–35 minutes, until crispy. For maximum colour, rebrush the pie with egg 15 minutes before the end of the cooking time.

While it is baking, mix the crumbled blue cheese with half of the crème fraîche and warm the two together, allowing the cheese to melt. Add the remaining crème fraîche and season with a twist of pepper. The baked pie and warm blue cheese crème fraîche are now ready to serve.

● *Half, or all, of the wild mushrooms can be replaced with sliced and sautéed chestnut mushrooms, which offer a nutty finish, also making this a year-round dish.*

● *A heaped teaspoon of chopped chives can be added to the crème fraîche.*

Serves 4

- 8 ceps (12 if small)
- 4 slices of walnut bread, about 2cm (¾in) thick
- knob of butter, plus extra for spreading (optional)
- 2 Cox's Orange Pippin apples
- 1–2 tablespoons walnut or groundnut oil

For the dressing

- 4 tablespoons fromage frais
- 2 tablespoons vinegar (white wine, red wine or sherry)
- 1 teaspoon Dijon mustard
- salt and pepper
- 1 tablespoon chopped chives

Sautéed cep mushrooms and Cox's apples on walnut toasts

This recipe is a very simple starter or snack dish using two very 'in season' ingredients. Cep mushrooms join us in the summer and carry through to the autumn and early winter very well. This particular mushroom is one of the finest, with a strong meaty texture and a flavour that more than matches it. Should ceps not be available, the chestnut mushroom – not a wild mushroom, but one that is available throughout the year – has a good nutty taste.

The Cox's apple carries the title 'the king of English apples', probably because of its flavour and quite rich, creamy consistency, with a juicy, sweet, nutty edge and enough acidity to work through all three.

The balance between the mushrooms and apples is helped by the walnut bread toasts and the fromage frais and chive dressing. The toasts can be simply toasted or buttered and pan-fried for a richer finish. Fromage frais is a soft, fresh, unripened cheese, made from skimmed milk and beaten to a smooth consistency. Almost all fromage frais has zero fat content and is mostly packed and marketed like yoghurt. With the help of vinegar, mustard and chives, it blends well with the ceps and apples. Fresh salad leaves can also be added to the recipe, garnishing the finished dish.

Method Wipe the ceps clean with a damp cloth and trim the bases of the stalks. Cut the mushrooms into 5mm (¼in) thick slices.

The walnut bread can be toasted at the last moment, while you sauté the mushrooms. If pan-frying, first butter both sides of the bread. Warm a frying pan and sauté the slices of bread to a golden brown on both sides. Keep warm to one side.

Quarter the apples, then peel and cut away the core with a small paring knife. Cut each quarter into three, providing six slices per portion.

Heat the oil in the frying pan and, once hot, fry the mushrooms for a few minutes on each side, to a rich golden brown. While the mushrooms are sautéeing, make the dressing by mixing the fromage frais with the vinegar and mustard, and seasoning with salt and pepper. Add the chives just before serving.

Once the ceps are ready, season with salt and pepper, and add the sliced apples and the knob of butter, if using. Stir for just a minute to warm the apples through before spooning them over the toasts. The dish can now be finished by drizzling the dressing over and around.

Serves 4 as a main course

- 6 celery sticks
- 25g (1oz) butter
- 2 tablespoons groundnut oil
- 1 x 1.5kg (3¼lb) brill, dark side skinned, head removed, trimmed of fins and tail and cut into 4 portions
- flour, for dusting
- salt and pepper
- 200ml (7fl oz) cider
- 3 apples, peeled (red apples need not be peeled)
- sprinkling of caster sugar
- 1–2 tablespoons calvados (optional)
- 2–3 tablespoons crème fraîche
- 1 heaped teaspoon torn flatleaf parsley or tarragon (optional)

Brill on the bone with celery, cider and apples

Brill is the understudy to 'the king of all flat fish', turbot. Less expensive to buy, it is not too less exciting to eat. This is a fish that will adapt to all cooking methods, whether on or off the bone. It is rare to find one bigger than perhaps 3.5kg (8lb) in weight; for four good-sized portions a 1.5kg (3¼lb) fish will be perfect. This weight takes into account the head and fins still to be removed, and the weight of the bone to be left in the fish.

Celery and apples are readily available during the earliest of the autumn months (having been around throughout summer too). October will offer a wider range of apples, with the early Windsor (quite juicy with a honeyed edge), Egremont Russet (with its famous nutty flavour) and Cox's Orange Pippin (Britain's most popular, also nutty with extra sweetness) all filling the greengrocers' shelves.

The brill is cooked in two stages. Stage one is frying it on one side only; stage two is poach-baking on top of the celery and cider in the oven. The fish takes on the cider flavour, releasing some of its juices into the alcohol, to create a stock with which to finish the lightly creamed liquor.

Method Preheat the oven to 190°C/375°F/Gas 5. Wash the celery sticks, pulling away the stringy fibres attached (or simply peeling) for a more tender finish. Cut the sticks into 5mm–1cm (¼–½in) dice. Melt half of the butter in a large shallow ovenproof pan and add the celery. Cook over a gentle heat for a few minutes until the pieces are just beginning to soften.

In a separate frying pan, heat the groundnut oil.

Lightly dust the skin side of the brill steaks with flour and season with salt. Place the fish in the hot oil, skin-side down, and fry over a moderate heat for about 5 minutes, until golden brown. Season the skinned side of the flesh with salt and pepper while still in the pan, then place the steaks on top of the celery, fried-side up.

Pour the cider into the pan around the celery and bring to a simmer, then place in the preheated oven, and bake for 8–10 minutes, until the fish is cooked through.

While the fish is cooking, cut each of the apples into eight wedges, removing the central core from each piece. Melt the remaining butter in a non-stick frying pan. Once bubbling, fry the pieces of apple quickly to a golden brown, turning each and repeating the same process on the other side. This will take just a minute or two, as Russet apples in particular soften very quickly. Once coloured on both sides, sprinkle with a little caster sugar and baste with the butter to give a slightly caramelized finish. If using, the calvados can now be added, and reduced until dry. Keep warm to one side.

Remove the brill steaks from the pan and keep warm. Bring the cider and celery to the boil, allowing the cider to reduce by half to two-thirds. Stir in 2 tablespoons of the crème fraîche – for a silkier, creamier finish add the remaining tablespoon. Season with salt and pepper. The torn parsley or tarragon leaves can now also be added, if using.

Divide the baked brill between four plates, fried-side up, along with the creamy cider celery. Garnish each with five or six apple wedges and the dish is complete.

- 2 x 450–675g (1–1½lb) Dover soles, heads and dark skin removed
- 100g (4oz) *mousseron* mushrooms
- 1 large or 2 small courgettes, cut into 5mm (¼in) dice
- salt and pepper
- plain flour, for coating
- 2 tablespoons olive oil
- 40g (1½oz) butter, plus a large knob and extra for greasing
- 1 lemon
- 1 large garlic clove, finely crushed (2 cloves for garlic lovers)

Dover sole meunière with garlic mousseron mushrooms and courgettes

Dover sole has a texture that is unique amongst flat fish. At times I've even found it to be too tough, if caught and cooked on the same day. The flesh needs a relaxing period, making way for a quite heavenly flavour and feel. Two to three days since the fish last swam is about perfect.

During early autumn all the three main ingredients of this dish are around, home-grown courgettes slowly coming to the end of their season, with the small *mousseron* mushrooms in the same situation.

The *mousseron* has quite a rich, strong flavour for such a small mushroom. Should you find it unavailable, a straightforward button mushroom can be used, or towards October you could try many more of the wild mushroom varieties, with chanterelles, *trompettes-de-la-mort* and ceps in abundance.

This must be one of the simplest recipes in the book – pan-fried sole with quickly sautéed courgettes, which just happen to love garlic, with wild mushrooms and a squeeze of lemon. I've kept the recipe for just two portions, but it can be doubled, though I would then suggest grilling rather than trying to find four frying pans.

Method With any flat fish, I like to keep on the white skin. This can become almost crispy, and it also protects the flesh, keeping it moist during cooking. To remove the dark skin, simply make a cut at the tail and scrape a little of the skin away. Once enough is free to get a grip on, pull it towards the head. This skin will come away cleanly. The white skin must be scraped clean of all scales. Cut away the side fins and trim the tail. The head can now also be cut away if it hasn't already been removed. Any roe sitting in the fish can easily be pushed towards the head and pulled away. Now just wash away any blood lying along the main bone and the fish is ready to cook.

The *mousseron* mushrooms are sometimes found without stalks; if so, simply wipe clean with a damp cloth or rinse quickly in cold water, then dry on a kitchen cloth.

The courgettes can be fried from raw, but to speed up their cooking process it is best to blanch the diced vegetables quickly in boiling salted water. As soon as the water returns to the boil, drain in a colander and allow to cool naturally. This enriches their green skin colour, leaving a deeper finish.

To fry the soles, lightly flour the white skin side of the fish and season with salt only. Heat the olive oil in a large frying pan (or two smaller pans). Place the fish in the pan, floured-side down, and fry for 5–6 minutes, until golden brown. Add the knob of butter, season the flesh side of the fish with salt and pepper and turn them over in the pan. Continue to fry for a further 5 minutes, basting the fish with butter from the pan. Finish with a squeeze of lemon juice from half of the lemon.

To grill, butter a baking tray and season with salt and pepper. Lay the soles, skin-side up, on the tray, buttering their presentation side and seasoning with salt only. Place under a preheated grill and cook for 8–10 minutes until golden brown. Finish with lemon juice as above.

When there is just a minute or two left of cooking time for the fish, fry the mushrooms and courgettes. Melt the butter in a frying pan. Once bubbling, add the courgettes and fry on a reasonably high heat, allowing them to take on a little colour. Add the mushrooms and garlic and continue to fry for a further 30–60 seconds.

At this point the cooked soles should be presented on hot plates. Season the mushrooms and courgettes with salt and pepper. When just approaching the nut-brown stage, sizzling vigorously, squeeze the remaining lemon juice into the butter and spoon over the Dover soles.

● *The ultimate accompaniment to this dish is classic creamy* Mashed potatoes *(page 198).*

● *Chopped parsley and tarragon, a mixed teaspoon of the two, can be added to the butter with the lemon juice at the last moment.*

Serves 4

- 10 salsify sticks
- juice of 1½ lemons (or 2 tablespoons white wine vinegar)
- 4 x 275–350g (10–12oz) skate wings, skinned (as usually found in the fishmongers)
- flour, for dusting
- salt and pepper
- 2 tablespoons olive oil
- large knob of butter, plus extra for greasing
- 100–150ml (3½fl oz–¼ pint) crème fraîche
- 1 level teaspoon Dijon mustard (optional)
- squeeze of lemon juice
- 1 tablespoon chopped parsley

For the mushrooms

- 450g (1lb) mushrooms (if using wild mushrooms refer to page 200 for cleaning)
- 40g (1½oz) butter

For the red wine liquor

- 2 tablespoons finely chopped shallots
- 1 garlic clove, crushed
- 1 bottle of red wine
- 2–3 sugar cubes

Wing of skate with creamed salsify and red wine mushrooms

Skate is an all-year-round fish that just happens to be at its best during our autumn, happily coinciding with the salsify and mushrooms. The ribbed-textured wing is roasted, while the mushrooms are finished in a red wine liquor and the off-white sticks of salsify are flavoured with cream.

Here I don't specify any particular type of mushroom. There are plenty of wild or cultivated to choose from and standard buttons, cups or chestnuts can be used as well.

Method Preheat the oven to 200°C/400°F/Gas 6. It is best, whenever peeling salsify, to wear rubber gloves and use a swivel peeler. This prevents being covered in too much dirt and permits reasonably stress-free peeling. To peel, place the salsify on a chopping board, peeling in long strips as you would asparagus. Once each stick has been peeled, place it in a large bowl of cold water acidulated with a third of the lemon juice or 1 tablespoon of the vinegar. Once all are peeled, each stick can be cut in two or three. Rinse and place in a saucepan with fresh cold water and the remaining lemon juice or vinegar. Bring to a simmer and cook for 10–12 minutes, 15 minutes being the maximum time required. Once cooked, remove the salsify from the pan and leave to drain and cool in a colander.

To make the red wine liquor, place the chopped shallots and crushed garlic in a saucepan, and pour over the red wine. Bring to a rapid simmer, and allow the wine to reduce by two-thirds to three-quarters, until slightly thickening. Add 2 sugar cubes and stir them into the wine. The sugar removes the wine's bitterness and

slightly thickens the liquor. The last cube can also be added for a slightly sweeter finished flavour.

It is best to colour the skate wings one or two at a time. To do so, lightly flour the presentation side of the fish and season with salt only. Heat 1 tablespoon of the olive oil in a large frying pan. Place the fish in the pan, floured-side down. Fry for 5 minutes until golden brown, then season with salt and pepper. Remove the fish, transferring to a greased baking tray. Wipe the pan clean before repeating the same process with the remaining skate wings. Roast the fish in the preheated oven for 8 minutes until tender.

While the skate is roasting, heat the remaining olive oil in a non-stick frying pan. Gently fry the salsify, adding the knob of butter, until the sticks just begin to colour. Season with salt and pepper.

Mix together 100ml (3½fl oz) of the crème fraîche with the Dijon mustard, if using. For a creamier finish, add the remaining crème fraîche. Add a squeeze of lemon juice, and season with salt and pepper. This can now be spooned into the pan with the salsify, removing it from the heat, or simply spooned over the sticks once presented on the plate.

While the salsify are colouring, fry the mushrooms. Heat the butter in a frying pan. Once sizzling, add the mushrooms and sauté for 2–3 minutes, until golden brown and tender. Season with salt and pepper.

To serve, present the skate wings on large warm plates, placing piles of the creamy salsify alongside. Spoon the mushrooms around the skate, finishing with the shallot red wine liquor and chopped parsley.

- 4 (not too big) fennel bulbs
- salt and pepper
- 4 medium red onions
- 25g (1oz) butter, plus extra for frying and greasing
- 6 tablespoons olive oil
- 1 tablespoon red wine vinegar
- 75–100g (3–4oz) Parmesan cheese, finely grated
- 4 x 175g (6oz) cod fillet portions, skin left on and pin bones removed (page 11)
- flour, for dusting

Fried cod with a Florence fennel and red onion Parmesan bake

Florence fennel is a vegetable that should be taken full advantage of. It has been with us through the summer and continues to hold its own during these slightly colder months of autumn. Its aniseed flavour can be appreciated in two totally different forms – raw, just lifted with a lemon juice (or balsamic vinegar) and olive oil dressing, or cooked until tender, with a more subtle finish that stands alone and works well with both fish and meat. The fish, fennel and red onions are finished here with a baked Parmesan topping – few ingredients, lots of flavour.

Method Preheat the oven to 200°C/400°F/Gas 6. Cut away the top stalks from the fennel, and trim the base. Any damaged outside layers should also be removed, leaving very attractive, round bulbs. Now quarter each from top to bottom. Cook the fennel in rapidly simmering, salted water, covering with greaseproof paper to ensure each piece stays submerged. Simmer for 12–15 minutes, before removing the fennel pieces and draining in a colander.

Cut each red onion into six wedges, then gently fry in a large knob of butter for a few minutes, until beginning to soften.

In a small bowl, mix together 4 tablespoons of the olive oil and the red wine vinegar. Place the red onions in a separate bowl, season well with salt and pepper, and add the dressing. Leave to stand for 15 minutes, stirring from time to time. Arrange the red onions and fennel (squeezing these gently to release unwanted water), rustic style, in a greased ovenproof dish, and

pour over any remaining dressing. Dot with the butter and sprinkle with the Parmesan (the more you use, the richer the finish).

Bake in the preheated oven for 20 minutes until the Parmesan is golden brown. During the baking, fry the cod fillets. Heat the remaining olive oil in a frying pan. Season the cod fillets with salt and pepper, and lightly dust the skin side with flour. Place the fish, skin-side down, in the pan and cook on a medium heat for 8 minutes. At this point, turn the fish, adding a knob of butter, and continue to cook for a further 2 minutes. Remove the pan from the heat and leave the fish to continue cooking for a further 2–3 minutes.

The fish can now be presented on plates, each drizzled with any butter from the pan. Offer the Parmesan-baked fennel and red onion at the table with the fish.

- *Almost any other fish – sea bass, turbot, skate, salmon and more – will eat well with the fennel and red onions.*

- *A wedge of lemon is a simple and perfect accompaniment for this dish.*

Serves 4

- 150g (5oz) button onions, peeled
- 2 medium celeriac
- 25g (1oz) butter, plus an extra knob and more for brushing
- salt and pepper
- 2 tablespoons olive oil
- 100g (4oz) piece of streaky bacon or diced pancetta
- 200ml (7fl oz) *Chicken* or *Instant stock* (page 194)
- 4 x 175–225g (6–8oz) cod fillet portions, skin left on and pin bones removed (page 11)
- flour, for dusting
- 2 tablespoons cooking oil
- 1 tablespoon roughly chopped curly parsley

Roast cod with braised celeriac, button onions and bacon

Celeriac is closely related to celery, with a similar flavour but holding a nutty edge. Although not the most attractive of vegetables, this rugged round tuber root is slowly but surely becoming more popular. The texture suits roasting and puréeing particularly well, also sautéeing like potatoes. The celeriac season runs through autumn and winter – it can even be found in early spring.

This recipe uses celeriac in place of potato in a classic French dish. *Pommes au lard* is basically quartered or diced potatoes with button onions and fried bacon pieces, baked in the oven with chicken stock to moisten the dish. The potatoes absorb the flavour of the stock, enhanced by the onions and bacon. This is exactly how the celeriac chunks react. The meaty, nutty, savoury flavour accompanies the cod fillet very well, the fish keeping its own 'meaty' texture, with enough flavour to hold its own.

Method Preheat the oven to 220°C/425°F/Gas 7. Place the button onions in a small saucepan of cold water and bring to a simmer, then cook for a few minutes. Strain and leave to cool. This short cooking takes away the raw onion flavour and they begin to tenderize.

Cut away the outer skin from the celeriac and chop the flesh into 2.5cm (1in) dice. Melt the butter in a large frying pan and, once bubbling, add the celeriac. Fry gently for just 2 minutes, season with salt and pepper and transfer to a large bowl.

Add a drop of the olive oil into the pan and increase the heat. Cut the bacon into 5mm–1cm (¼–½in) dice and fry the bacon or pancetta in the hot oil for a few minutes, until golden brown. Add to the celeriac and wipe the frying pan clean.

Split the button onions in half and heat the remaining olive oil in the frying pan. Sear the onion halves to a rich golden brown, cut-side down, turn them and continue to fry for a further minute or two. Season with salt and pepper, and add to the celeriac.

Mix the celeriac, onion and bacon, and spoon into a suitable earthenware or Pyrex dish (approximately 25 × 18 × 4cm/10 × 7 × 1½in). Bring the stock to the boil and pour it over the vegetables. Place in the preheated oven and bake for 40–45 minutes until golden brown and tender. Turn the oven off, leaving the dish in it, so the celeriac can relax and keep warm while you are cooking the cod fillets.

Season both sides of each fillet with salt and only the flesh side with pepper, before dusting the skin side with flour. Heat the cooking oil in a frying pan and, once hot, place the fish in, skin-side down. Cook on a medium heat for 10 minutes, then turn the fish over in the pan and remove from the heat. Leave to stand for 2–3 minutes. The residual heat in the pan will continue the cooking process, without imparting a dry, leathery texture to the fish.

To finish, sprinkle the chopped parsley over the celeriac and divide between the plates, along with the cod fillets, brushing each fillet with a little butter.

- *Halibut, John Dory and salmon also eat well with the celeriac, onions and bacon.*

Serves 4 as a main course
- 25g (1oz) butter
- 4 x 175g (6oz) sea bream fillets, scaled and pin bones removed (page 11)
- sea salt and pepper
- 2 large shallots, sliced into thin rings
- 2 tablespoons white wine vinegar

- 100ml (3½fl oz) white wine
- juice of 1 orange
- juice 1 lemon
- pinch of caster sugar
- 6 black peppercorns
- 2 tablespoons olive oil
- 1 teaspoon picked and torn tarragon leaves

For the fennel chips
- 2–3 medium bulbs of fennel
- oil, for deep-frying

For the batter
- 300ml (½ pint) cider (or sweet cider for a less acidic bite)
- 175g (6oz) self-raising flour, plus extra for coating, sifted

Salt and vinegar sea bream with fennel chips

Sea bream is a fish, very much like the snapper, which comes in many guises, a lot of different varieties all falling under the same name. The three most common are the red, black and gilt-head sea bream. The latter are the finest, known in France as the *daurade royale*. All three of these types are available in this country, with the black available between July and December, and the red and gilt-head generally both found between June and February. Small bream (350g/12oz) are best left whole: simply gut and scale them before use. I prefer to buy slightly larger fish, towards 600g (1lb 6oz), as this will provide two good-sized fillets around 175g (6oz). Bought scaled and bone-free from the fishmonger, they need no other attention. Any of the sea bream mentioned can be used in this recipe; if unavailable, red snapper can fill the spot.

Fish, chips and vinegar go back a long way. Here the concept is similar, with batter and chips both included, and a warm court-bouillon, reduced into a sauce, served to accompany the steamed/poached fish. The chips are thin wedges of fennel, still with us from the summer, dipped in a cider batter and deep-fried until crisp and golden.

Method Preheat the oven to 180°C/350°F/Gas 4 and a deep-fat fryer to 180°C/350°F. Using a small knob of the measured butter, grease a roasting tray or baking dish large enough to hold the four fish fillets. Season with a twist of pepper and a few sea salt flakes. Separate the shallot rings and scatter them across. Mix together the white wine vinegar, white wine, orange and lemon juice, caster sugar and black peppercorns, along with 100ml

(3½fl oz) water. Place the fillets on top of the shallots and pour the liquor over. Bring to a very gentle simmer, until just giving off a little steam. Cover with foil and bake in the preheated oven for 8–10 minutes until the fillets are just firm to the touch.

While the fish is steam-poaching, prepare the fennel. Trim them of their stalk tops and remove any bruised outside layers. Halve each bulb lengthwise and cut these halves into 5mm (¼in) wedges. Season with salt and pepper.

To make the batter, whisk the cider into the sifted flour. Lightly flour a handful of the fennel wedges, dip each into the batter and place in the preheated deep-fat fryer. Cook until golden brown, drain, season with salt and keep warm in the oven while continuing to fry the rest.

Once cooked, remove the sea bream from the oven and tray and keep the fillets warm to one side. Reduce the oven temperature to 140°C/275°F/Gas 1, using it purely as a 'hot cupboard' for the fish and fennel chips while making the sauce. Transfer the bream court-bouillon to a saucepan, bring it to the boil and reduce by half. Whisk in the olive oil, remaining butter and torn tarragon leaves, then season with salt and pepper if necessary.

To serve, place the sea bream fillets on warmed plates, pouring any excess fish juices into the sauce. Sprinkle a few sea salt flakes over each fillet. Arrange stacks of fennel chips beside (or offer them separately) and spoon the sauce over the fish fillets.

● *The fennel chips are also nice to serve as a snack or starter, with* Mayonnaise *(page 198 or bought).*

Serves 4 as a starter
- 1 large or 2 medium parsnips, quartered
- salt and pepper
- 2 apples (Cox's, James Grieve or Laxton's Superb all work well), peeled and cored
- squeeze of lime juice
- 1 tablespoon hazelnut oil
- 15g (½oz) butter, plus extra for greasing and brushing

- 4 x 275–350g (10–12oz) herrings, scaled, filleted and trimmed (see below)

For the dressing
- 1 teaspoon wholegrain mustard
- 1 tablespoon white wine vinegar
- pinch of caster sugar
- 1–2 tablespoons crème fraîche (optional)
- 3 tablespoons olive oil

- 3 tablespoons hazelnut oil
- 4–6 cooked chestnuts (page 201), chopped
- 1 tablespoon chopped chives (or cut into 1cm/½in lengths)

Grilled herring fillets with stir-fried parsnips and apples and a mustard nut dressing

Herrings and mustard sauce have often shared happy times together, with apples also finding their way into the story every now and again. The herring, with its distinctive flavour and moist texture, is a totally underrated and often ignored fish. It is possibly the fiddly cleaning, and sometimes eating, if they are served whole, that are to blame.

Bought scaled and filleted, the fillets should need very little extra preparation. If placed skin-side down on a chopping board, any remaining bones and 'sinews' connected to the belly flap can be scraped away, leaving the fillets totally clean. Any tiny bones still embedded in the flesh will virtually disintegrate during the cooking. An autumn catch will provide you with plump fish, with the parsnip and apple accompaniments also reaching their prime.

The nut dressing is a combination of hazelnut oil and chopped chestnuts, with the wholegrain mustard and chives adding a sweet, peppery, onion edge.

Method To make the dressing, mix together the mustard, vinegar, caster sugar and crème fraîche, if using (the extra tablespoon will give a creamier finish). Pour the oils slowly into the mix, whisking continuously. Once all the oils are added, season with salt and pepper. The chopped chestnuts and chives can be stirred in just before serving.

Remove the woody central core from the parsnip quarters, then cut each quarter into rough 1cm (½in) dice. Plunge the diced parsnips into boiling salted water. When it has returned to the boil, drain the parsnips in a colander and leave to cool naturally. Dice the apples to a similar size and squeeze the lime juice over them. This maintains their natural colour while offering a citrus bite.

Preheat a grill to hot. Heat the hazelnut oil in a wok or frying pan. Once hot, add the blanched parsnips and fry them over a moderate heat for 4–5 minutes, until just tender. Increase the heat and add the butter and apples. Quickly fry for a further minute or two, then season with salt and pepper.

While the parsnips are cooking, grease a baking tray and season it with salt and pepper. Place the herring fillets on the tray, skin-side up. Brush each with butter and season with salt and pepper. Place under the preheated grill and cook for a few minutes (5–6 maximum), until just approaching a firm touch. Stir the chestnuts and chives into the dressing. Arrange the herring fillets on warm plates with the stir-fry and finish with the dressing.

- *Mackerel also eats very well with the parsnips and apples.*

- *A few grains of coarse sea salt can be used to season the skin side of the fillets.*

**Serves 4 as a starter
or 2 as a main course**
- 6–8 sardines, scaled and filleted (12–16 fillets)
- olive oil, for brushing
- coarse sea salt and pepper
- 175g (6oz) *Quick puff pastry* (page 203, or bought)
- flour, for dusting

- large knob of butter, plus extra for greasing and brushing
- 2 large onions, thinly sliced
- 1 large or 2 small bulbs of fennel
- good squeeze of lemon juice
- 8 black olives, stoned
- milk, for brushing

For the fennel butter sauce (optional)
- 1 tablespoon crème fraîche or whipping cream
- 50g (2oz) butter
- squeeze of lemon juice
- 1 teaspoon chopped fennel tops or dill

Grilled sardine, fennel, onion and black olive tart

Sardines have been with us since the summer (they are particularly good barbecued), continuing through the winter months. Fennel is now coming to an end in late autumn, hence our taking advantage of its flavour while it's still with us.

The tart is made in a rectangular form, very much like a sort of one-layered savoury *mille-feuilles*. This is a very simple starter to put together (it can also make a main course for two sardine fans), with just the fennel, onions and olives baked on the puff pastry strip, before topping with the sardine fillets.

The fresh sardines need to be scaled, gutted and filleted. Your fishmonger can do this, but it's reasonably easy to do at home. Run the fish under cold water while you push the scales off and away. Then remove the head and this will show you exactly where to sit the blade of a sharp filleting knife. Cut along the bone confidently and the fillet will come away in one movement. Turn the fish over and repeat the same cut. Scrape away the gut and bones, rinse and pat dry. Any fine pin bones will virtually disintegrate during the cooking.

Method Lay the sardine fillets on a greased and seasoned baking tray. Brush the fillets with olive oil and season with coarse sea salt and a twist of pepper. Chill until needed.

On a lightly floured surface, roll the puff pastry into a long thin rectangle, approximately 25–30 × 10cm (10–12 × 4in). Transfer the pastry to a buttered baking tray. This can now be left as it is for a rustic uneven finish, or trimmed for a neater shape. Prick the strip of pastry with a fork and chill.

Preheat the oven to 200°C/400°F/Gas 6. Heat the knob of butter in a large frying pan. Once bubbling, add the onions and fry them over a fairly high heat, until softened and a rich golden brown. Season with salt and pepper and leave to cool.

Trim the fennel tops, saving any sprigs for the sauce, if you are making it. Split the fennel bulbs in half, removing any bruised outside layers, along with the central core. Now shred the halves finely, cutting across the bulbs. Place the cut fennel in a saucepan and add a good squeeze of lemon juice. Top with 250ml (9fl oz) of water and bring to a simmer. Gently simmer for 10 minutes until just becoming tender. Strain the fennel, collecting all of the flavoured liquor if you are making the sauce.

Spoon the cooked and cooled onions on to the pastry, leaving a 1cm (½in) clear border on all sides. Cut the olives into quarters and sprinkle these over the onions. Spoon the drained fennel on top of the onions and season with salt and pepper, then brush with a little butter. Brush the pastry with milk and bake in the preheated oven for 15 minutes.

If you are making the butter sauce, warm the fennel liquor and add the crème fraîche or cream and the butter. Whisk to a smooth consistency, seasoning with salt and pepper and a squeeze of lemon juice. Just before serving, add the chopped fennel tops or dill.

During the last few minutes of cooking the tart, place the sardines under a preheated grill and cook for just 3–5 minutes, until tender.

To serve, lay the sardine fillets on top of the tart, offering the fennel sauce, if using.

Serves 4

- 2 teaspoons white peppercorns
- 4 x 175g (6oz) tuna fish steaks, ideally blue fin (see below)
- 15g (½oz) butter, plus an extra knob for the tuna
- 8 sticks of forced rhubarb cut into 2.5cm (1in) chunks (saving any trimmings)
- 1–2 tablespoons caster sugar
- ½–1 teaspoon balsamic vinegar, preferably aged
- cooking oil
- sea salt

Seared peppered tuna fish with sharp rhubarb sticks

The main seasonal item here is the first of the indoor-forced rhubarb. Growers call it champagne rhubarb, and that it is too. Each of the pink stalks is tender and slim, and not in need of too much of a sweet helping hand. Cooking champagne rhubarb needs only a little time, tenderizing quite quickly with a finished flavour that really does fall within the champagne category.

Tuna fish can be found more or less throughout the year, but it's the blue fin tuna, probably the best of all tuna, that finds itself in our markets at this time of the year. It is not a cheap fish, but then nothing in the premier league is. For a main course, only 175g (6oz) portions are needed, bearing in mind that this will eat as tender and clean as a fillet steak.

The tuna and rhubarb both have rich flavours, and their partners – white peppercorns for the tuna and balsamic vinegar for the rhubarb – both help to create an exciting combination as well as a balanced overall taste.

Method Crush the white peppercorns to a texture slightly larger than milled pepper, then pat this on to just one side of each tuna steak. These can now be chilled while the rhubarb is being prepared and cooked.

Melt the butter in a large saucepan and add the rhubarb pieces, 1 tablespoon of the sugar and 6 tablespoons of water. Cover and bring to a gentle simmer, then cook for just a few minutes until tender. Carefully spoon the rhubarb chunks from the liquor and keep to one side.

Chop any reserved trimmings into rough small dice and add to the liquor. Bring to a simmer and cook gently for a few minutes, mashing the rhubarb to thicken the liquor. Purée the liquor to thicken (if it is still too loose, simply increase the heat and reduce further). Strain through a sieve, then add ½ teaspoon of vinegar and taste for a sharp acidic bite. The remaining vinegar can be added if needed for a sharper bite and the extra tablespoon of sugar for a slightly sweeter finish.

While the syrup is simmering, heat a tablespoon of cooking oil in a frying pan and, once hot, place the tuna fish, peppered-side down, in the pan. Cook for 2 minutes, turn the fillets and add the knob of butter to the pan. Continue to cook for a further 2 minutes, basting frequently with the butter. Season with sea salt.

Spoon the warm rhubarb chunks on to warm plates, drizzle with the sharp syrup and present the tuna fish next to them.

- *Simple steamed new potatoes will eat very well with this dish.*

- 2 medium or 4 small beetroots
- 300ml (½ pint) red wine
- 150ml (¼ pint) red wine vinegar
- salt and pepper
- 4 rashers of smoked streaky bacon
- 350g (12oz) whites of leeks, diced
- 2 knobs of butter
- 125ml (4fl oz) milk
- 125ml (4fl oz) single cream
- 2 x 550–675g (1¼–1½lb) red mullets, scaled, filleted and pin bones removed (page 11)
- 2 tablespoons olive oil
- flour, for dusting

Pan-fried red mullet with red wine beetroot, crispy bacon and creamed white leeks

All three of the main ingredients here will be found throughout the months of autumn. The mullet, beetroots and leeks all fair well during such an unpredictable time. The complete dish is remarkably simple, the real interest to be found in the amazing combination of flavours, all complementing one another. The beetroots are cooked in red wine and red wine vinegar, which might indicate something quite sharp and acidic, but which in fact leaves a quite sweet, moreish piquancy. To cut into this taste we have the leek purée, which is almost like the French classic *soubise* – a purée of onions. Here the leeks – whites only – take the place of the onion, and are cooked in milk and cream before being blitzed to a smooth finish. The flavours of the leeks and the beetroot accompany red mullet well, with the bacon lending a slightly smoky accent to all three. The red wine liquor can be used two or three times, getting stronger each time.

Method Top and tail the beetroots, taking care not to cut into the flesh, otherwise the beets will bleed their juices. Place the beetroots in a small saucepan along with the red wine, 600ml (1 pint) of water, the vinegar and ¼ teaspoon of salt. Bring to a simmer and cook for 1 hour. Remove the pan from the heat and leave to cool in the liquor before peeling. The beetroots can now be stored in the liquor until needed, serving them just warm.

While the beetroots are simmering, preheat the oven to 200°C/400°F/Gas 6. Crisp the bacon by laying the rashers on a baking tray and covering them with another tray. This will keep them completely flat and crisp. Place in the preheated oven and bake for 20 minutes. At this point, remove the top tray and pour away any excess fat from the rashers. If not yet crisp, simply return the bacon to the oven, without covering, and bake for a further 5–10 minutes. Once deep golden and crisp, the rashers can be left to cool on a wire rack.

To cook the leeks, melt one of the knobs of butter in a saucepan. Add the diced leek whites and cook on a low heat for a few minutes, until just beginning to soften. Add the milk and cream and bring to a simmer, cooking for 5–6 minutes, until completely tender. The cream will possibly begin to curdle, but this will have no effect on the finished consistency. Now purée the leeks in a liquidizer, until completely smooth, and season with salt and pepper.

To cook the fish, heat the olive oil in a frying pan. Lightly dust the skin side of the mullets with flour, then season with salt on both sides and pepper on the filleted side only. Place the fillets, skin-side down, in the pan and cook on a medium/hot heat for 5–6 minutes without moving the fish. If undisturbed, no heat will be lost and the skin will become crispy. Add the remaining knob of butter, then turn the fillets over in the pan and remove from the heat. The residual heat will continue to cook the fish, leaving a soft and succulent texture to the flesh.

While cooking the fish, slice or cut the beetroots into wedges. Serve these just warm, barely reheated in a drop or two of their own liquor, seasoned again with salt and pepper. The leek white purée can also be warmed.

Spoon a pool of leek purée on to each plate, topping with the red mullet fillets. A pile of beetroot wedges can be stacked to the side, finishing with the crispy bacon.

Serves 4

- 2 medium leeks
- 900g (2lb) mussels
- 100ml (3½fl oz) white wine
- 1 teaspoon flour
- 1 teaspoon butter, plus 2 large knobs and extra for greasing and brushing
- salt and pepper
- 4 x 175g (6oz) halibut fillet portions, skinned
- coarse sea salt
- 4 tablespoons double cream
- squeeze of lemon juice

Steamed halibut with leek tagliatelle and mussels

Halibut can sometimes be found as quite 'beautifully grotesque'-sized beasts, with a weight exceeding 200kg (approximately 440lb). A flat fish, the halibut suits virtually all cooking techniques – baking, poaching, braising, frying – but steaming is the process used here, leaving the fillets with a very real, natural taste. Adding a different edge are our two seasonal friends, leeks and mussels. Both are available throughout the autumn and winter, both also having worked with one another many times before. The 'tagliatelle' is actually the leeks, cut into long, 1cm (½in) thick strips. Once tender, these are bound with the mussels and their lightly creamed liquor.

Method Trim the coarse green top of the leeks (approximately 2.5cm/1in) and the stalks from the base of each leek. Split lengthwise, discarding the first tough outer layer. The leeks can now be well rinsed, to remove any grit, before cutting each one lengthwise into 1cm (½in) thick strips.

Wash the mussels well in plenty of cold water, scraping away any barnacles and beards, and discarding any mussels that don't close on being tapped or are heavy. Drain. Heat the white wine in a large saucepan. Once boiling, add the mussels and cover with a lid. These will now take just 4–5 minutes to cook. During the cooking process, shake the pan, with the lid on, or stir from time to time, to ensure an even cooking. Drain in a colander, saving all of the juices. The mussels can now be picked from the shells, keeping them to one side.

Strain the cooking liquor through a fine sieve to remove any grit, then bring it to a simmer. Mix together the teaspoon of flour and the teaspoon of butter. This is *beurre-manié*, or 'kneaded butter'. When added to warm sauces, the melting butter helps the flour find its way evenly into the liquor, thickening as it does so. Once the mussel liquor is simmering, whisk in the *beurre-manié*, return to a simmer and cook for a few minutes.

Butter four small squares of greaseproof paper, season with salt and pepper and place a halibut fillet on top of each. Season the presentation side with coarse sea salt only and place the fish in a steamer above rapidly simmering water. The fillets will now take 8–10 minutes to cook.

While the fish steams, the mussel sauce and leeks can be finished. Add the cream to the sauce and check the seasoning, before adding a squeeze of lemon juice. Whisk in a large knob of butter to finish.

Melt another large knob of butter in a large pan and add 2 tablespoons of water. Once bubbling, add the leeks and cover, removing the lid and stirring from time to time. After 5 minutes the leeks will be tender. Season with salt and pepper.

To serve, warm the mussels gently in the cream sauce. Remove the halibut fillets from the steamer, place one on each warm plate and brush with butter. Spoon the mussels next to the halibut and top with a pile of the leek tagliatelle. Spoon any of the remaining sauce over and around the leeks. The dish is ready to serve.

● *The leeks can be added to the cream sauce with the mussels. Spoon between plates or bowls and finish with the steamed fish.*

Serves 4 as a very generous starter or as a main course

- 50g (2oz) butter, plus an extra knob
- 1 onion, sliced
- 2kg (4½lb) fresh mussels, cleaned (see below)
- 150ml (¼ pint) white wine
- 1 level teaspoon plain flour
- 2 tablespoons finely chopped shallot or onion
- 225g (8oz) button mushrooms, sliced
- 2 egg yolks
- 100ml (3½fl oz) double cream
- 1 tablespoon roughly chopped parsley
- 1 heaped teaspoon torn tarragon leaves
- salt and pepper
- squeeze of lemon juice

Mussels bonne femme

Mussels are generally 'in season' between the months of September and March, but it is said that the months of October and November will offer the best. Mussels sold are virtually all cultured by a technique founded by the French well over 500 years ago. It was the Dutch, however, who introduced the bags of well scrubbed mussels. It's still a good idea to wash them in plenty of cold water, scraping away any barnacles and pulling away the beards (byssus). It's with these beards that the mussels attach themselves to rocks, poles, ropes, etc. If any mussels are slightly open, a short sharp tap should make them close. Any that don't close should be discarded, along with any that are particularly heavy. Once cleaned, they are ready to cook.

The term *bonne femme* is generally used of a fish dish, usually of sole, which I was first taught during my college years. It basically means with a white wine cream sauce flavoured with mushrooms, shallots and parsley, everything being glazed under the grill. All of these flavours are to be included here, with the addition of fresh tarragon.

Wild mushrooms are also in season right now and can be used in place of the buttons. Any of the varieties will work, so a mixed bag would be fine. If you're looking to feature just one, ceps or chanterelles would be my first choice. All I tend to eat with a dish like this is lots of crusty bread.

Method Melt a third of the butter in a large saucepan and add the sliced onion. Cook for a minute or two, then add the mussels and white wine. Place a lid on top and cook over a fierce heat, turning the mussels from time to time, until they have all opened. This will literally take just a few minutes once the liquor is boiling. Any mussels that refuse to open should be discarded. Drain the mussels in a colander, saving all of the juices.

Strain the saved liquor through a fine sieve into a saucepan and bring to a simmer. Mix another third of the butter with the flour to make a *beurre-manié*, before whisking it into the liquor. This will thicken the sauce to a coating consistency. If still too thin, mix the remaining third of butter with a little more flour and add to the liquor. Cook the sauce on a very low heat for 3–4 minutes to cook out the flour flavour.

The mussels can now be removed from their shells, and any remaining beards can be pulled away. Preheat a grill to hot.

Melt the knob of butter in a large frying pan and add the chopped shallot or onion. Cook on a fairly high heat for 2–3 minutes, then add the mushrooms, frying for a further few minutes.

Mix the mushrooms with the mussels and spoon them into a large ceramic flan dish or ovenproof bowl. Add the egg yolks to the double cream and lightly whip to soft peaks. Stir the parsley and tarragon into the mussel sauce, seasoning with salt, pepper and the lemon juice. Fold in the whipped egg cream.

Spoon the sauce over the mussels, and finish under the preheated grill until a light golden brown. The dish is now ready to serve, with lots of bread and a glass of chilled, crisp white wine.

Serves 4
- 4 lamb shanks
- salt and pepper
- 2–3 tablespoons cooking oil
- large knob of butter
- 2 onions, each cut into 6 wedges
- 2 carrots, cut into 1cm (½in) slices
- 3 celery sticks, cut into 1cm (½in) slices

- 4 garlic cloves
- generous sprig of thyme
- 2 bay leaves
- juice of 2 oranges and rind of 1 orange
- 1 bottle of full-bodied red wine
- generous pinch of demerara sugar
- cornflour or arrowroot, for thickening (optional)

For the pumpkin
- 1kg (2¼lb) pumpkin, skinned and deseeded
- large knob of butter
- 1 heaped tablespoon finely chopped shallot
- freshly grated nutmeg
- 100ml (3½fl oz) whipping or double cream (optional)
- 50–75g (2–3oz) Gruyère cheese, grated

Braised lamb shanks with pumpkin and Swiss cheese mash

The shank of lamb is a cut taken from the leg that can be quite awesome in appearance, purely in terms of its sheer size. However, almost 50 per cent of it is bone and it is not such a hard task to cook it by very slow braising, producing a sublime melting culinary experience.

In this recipe, oranges and red wine are added to the cooking liquor, both working very well with lamb, the meat already being quite sweet. The seasonal edge to this dish is to be found in the pumpkin. Although it is with us through quite a few months, it is during October and November that the pumpkin is at its best. Here it is cooked until just softened, then coarsely mashed and gratinéed with Swiss cheese.

Method Preheat the oven to 160°C/325°F/Gas 3. Season the lamb shanks with salt and pepper. Heat the cooking oil in a large frying or roasting pan. When at a medium heat, place the shanks in the pan and slowly fry until golden brown all over. This will take up to 15–20 minutes, and a good percentage of the lamb fat will have been released. Remove the joints from the pan and keep to one side, discarding the lamb fat once cooled.

Melt the knob of butter in a braising pot large enough to cook the shanks. Place the cut vegetables, garlic cloves, thyme and bay leaves in the pot. Cook over a moderate heat for 10–15 minutes, until the vegetables are beginning to soften. At this point, add the orange juice, rind, red wine, 600ml (1 pint) of water and the sugar. Bring to a simmer. Add the lamb shanks to the pot, cover with a lid and place in the preheated oven. The secret to good shanks of lamb is to cook them very

slowly for 2–3 hours, depending on their size. It's always best to check after every 30 minutes, turning and basting the joints, and checking their tenderness. This will quite easily be identified by applying slight pressure by hand or with a spoon – the meat should give, almost wanting to fall off the bone. During the cooking time, should the simmering process be too lively, simply reduce the temperature of the oven. After 2 hours have a good check. If still slightly firm, leave for a further 30–60 minutes to achieve a perfect 'carve with a spoon' texture.

Once cooked, carefully lift the shanks from the pot and keep warm to one side. Strain the liquor through a sieve. If you wish to serve the vegetables, garlic and herbs, they can be kept warm with the lamb. Bring the liquor to a simmer, continually skimming away any fat content and impurities. The liquor can now be served as thin or thick as you wish. It is important to taste as it simmers and reduces; if too strong, the lamb flavour can be lost behind the over-strong wine reduction. If you feel the flavour is right, but a thicker consistency would be preferred, mix a little water with a teaspoon or two of cornflour or arrowroot, and whisk this into the sauce a few drops at a time until the right consistency is achieved. Whichever you prefer, it's always a good idea to boil and reduce 100ml (3½fl oz) of the cooking liquor to a thicker syrupy stage. This can then be brushed over the warmed lamb just before serving to give a shiny finish. Return the shanks to the sauce (the vegetables can also be added or microwaved) and warm through for 10–15 minutes.

While the shanks are braising in the oven, the pumpkin can be cooked. Cut it into rough 2.5cm (1in) dice. Melt the butter in a large saucepan and, once bubbling, add the pumpkin pieces and the shallot. Cook on a medium heat for a good few minutes to start the cooking process without colouring. Add 4 tablespoons of water and cover with a lid. Cook very gently, stirring from time to time, for 15–20 minutes, until the pumpkin is tender. If a lot of liquid is created within the pot, drain the pumpkin in a colander before returning it to the pan to be mashed. This liquor can now be discarded, or boiled in a separate pan and reduced to a thick syrupy consistency. This will intensify its flavour, and it can be added to the finished mash. Remove the saucepan from the heat and mash the pumpkin, as coarsely or as fine as you wish. Season with salt, pepper and grated nutmeg. If using the cream, this can be mixed into the mash or spooned over the pumpkin once in a suitable serving dish.

To finish, preheat a grill to hot. Sprinkle the grated Gruyère cheese over the top of the pumpkin and gratinée under the preheated grill until golden brown. The lamb shanks can now be presented on plates or in bowls, with the vegetables, garlic and orange rind, if serving them. Spoon some of the lamb sauce over, offering the pumpkin mash separately.

● *When simmering and reducing the lamb cooking liquor, it is best not to allow it to reduce by more than half. At this point the flavour will be full enough, needing just a little arrowroot, cornflour or instant gravy granules or powder (using a gravy thickener will also add a depth of colour to the finished sauce) to thicken if preferred. Should the sauce be lacking its orange bite, 100–150ml (3½fl oz–¼ pint) of extra orange juice can be boiled and reduced to a syrup, enlivening the finished result.*

● *Orange segments can be cut into two or three pieces, and added to the finished sauce, along with a teaspoon or two of finely chopped chives, to give the sauce a different edge.*

Serves 4

- 1 x 1.75kg (4lb) free-range chicken
- 1 lemon, halved
- 75g (3oz) butter
- 4 sprigs of rosemary
- coarse sea salt and pepper

For the pumpkin pancakes (makes approximately 8–12)

- 450g (1lb) pumpkin, skinned, deseeded and cut into 2.5cm (1in) dice
- 3–4 tablespoons plain flour, sifted
- 2 eggs, plus 1 egg white
- cooking oil
- 2 knobs of butter

Roast lemon water chicken with pumpkin pancakes

The pumpkin featured in this recipe is the orange Hallowe'en variety we all know and recognize. A number of squash varieties can also be used, particularly the acorn, butternut and gem. Pumpkins and squash begin to arrive in late summer and are with us through to late autumn. It's at this point that the vegetables are stored, holding their own through the winter. For an autumn or winter night, this dish features well. The chicken is just roasted with a squeeze of lemon juice until golden and crispy. The water is added to the roasting tray for the last 20 minutes in the oven to collect all of the flavours from the tray to trickle over the carved bird. The pancakes can be made and fried while the chicken is roasting.

Method Preheat the oven to 220°C/425°F/Gas 7. Place the chicken in a roasting tray and rub one half of the lemon all over it. Brush two-thirds of the butter over the bird, then squeeze the remaining juice from both lemon halves all over and place the squeezed citrus fruits into the cavity of the chicken along with two sprigs of the rosemary. Sit the other two sprigs on top of the bird. Season liberally with the coarse sea salt and pepper and place into the preheated oven.

Cook for 20 minutes, then reduce the oven temperature to 190°C/375°F/Gas 5. Continue to roast the chicken, basting from time to time, for another 20 minutes. At this point, pour 150ml (¼ pint) of hot water from a kettle into the roasting tray. This will begin to loosen all of the residue in the tray, and mellow the sharp lemon bite. Continue to roast the bird, without basting, for a further 20 minutes. Remove the chicken

from the oven and leave to rest while still in the roasting tray, which will continue to collect any juices released while the bird relaxes.

While the chicken is roasting and resting, the pumpkin can be cooked. There are several methods to choose from: steaming or boiling until tender (approximately 15–20 minutes), or stewing slowly in a large knob of butter in a covered pan. Once cooked, by whichever method, spoon the pumpkin into a colander and allow to drain. Then purée the pumpkin in a food processor until smooth. If the purée still has a watery consistency, spoon it into a saucepan and stir on a low heat until thickened. Leave to cool.

Mix the flour, eggs and egg white into the cooled purée and season with salt and pepper.

To cook the pancakes, warm a large frying pan, preferably non-stick, over a low heat. Pour a trickle of cooking oil into the pan and add a knob of butter. Pour a spoonful of the mix into the pan, cooking three or four pancakes at a time, and fry for a few minutes, until the top is beginning to set and the base is golden brown. Using a palette knife or kitchen slice, turn the 'cakes' and continue to fry for a further 2–3 minutes. Once cooked, place the pancakes on a baking tray and keep warm to one side while continuing to cook the rest.

Carve the chicken on a chopping board, collecting any juices and adding them to the roasting tray. Warm the roasting tray on top of the stove, stirring in the remaining butter. The pancakes and carved bird can now be plated with the rich lemon water juices strained over each portion of chicken.

Serves 6
- 2 x 1.5kg (3¼lb) chickens, preferably corn-fed
- 4 tablespoons olive oil
- salt and pepper, plus coarse sea salt
- 25–50g (1–2oz) butter

For the sweetcorn
- 6–8 sweetcorn cobs, husks removed
- 15 button onions, peeled
- 1 tablespoon olive or cooking oil
- 50g (2oz) butter
- 175g (6oz) streaky bacon or pancetta, cut into 5mm–1cm (¼–½in) dice
- 2–3 Little Gem lettuces, shredded
- pinch of sugar

Chicken sauté with sweetcorn à la Française

Sauté is a culinary term translated from the French *sauter*, meaning 'to jump'. It is this technique we're applying to the chicken pieces, here making them 'jump about' the pan, in bubbling, nutty brown butter. Most sauté dishes are then accompanied by a sauce made in the sauté pan once the main ingredient is cooked and tender. In this recipe there is no sauce, just the buttery chicken helped along by the soft sweetcorn.

Home-grown corn on the cob joins us in August, enjoying its short spell until mid-October. Here I'm adapting the corn to a garden pea dish. *Petits pois à la Française* is a classic combination of sweetened peas, onions and lettuce, all bound with a slightly thickened and silky cooking liquor. An extra I've added is fried bacon, giving a little more body. This style and garnish suits the sweetcorn just perfectly, particularly when playing a supporting role to chicken (or pork). I don't think this dish needs another thing, apart from lots of crusty bread to mop up the juices. It's just two large bowls on the table, one with chicken, the other with sweetcorn.

You'll notice I'm using two 1.5kg (3¼lb) chickens here for six portions. The two birds cut into 16 pieces of chicken, which is plenty to go round, some being lucky with three pieces to enjoy. One large 1.75kg (4lb) bird can be used for just four portions; alternatively you could sauté four chicken legs.

Method Preheat the oven to 200°C/400°F/Gas 6. Cut each chicken into eight pieces, first removing the legs and splitting them into drumsticks and thighs, then cutting each breast off the bone and dividing into two. The carcasses can now be discarded or frozen to use for stocks at a later date.

To prepare the sweetcorn garnish, cook the cobs in boiling water for 10–15 minutes, until tender, and then drain. Release the kernels by easing them off with a fork. Alternatively you can remove the kernels before cooking. Stand each raw cob on a chopping board and, using a sharp knife, cut against the cob from top to bottom to release the kernels. Continue this process until all are free. These can now be cooked in boiling water for just 5 minutes until tender, then drained and left to cool. Save 150ml (¼ pint) of the cooking water to finish the dish. It is important, whenever cooking sweetcorn, not to salt the water, as this does tend to toughen the kernels.

Place the button onions in a saucepan of cold water and bring to a simmer. Cook for 5 minutes, then drain and allow the onions to cool. This starts their cooking process, also removing the raw onion flavour. Once cold, halve them and fry them in the olive or cooking oil, until golden brown on the flat side only. Keep the onions to one side ready to add to the sweetcorn. A simpler alternative is to cook the onions in the water until completely tender, up to 10 minutes, before leaving to cool. Once halved, the onions can simply be reheated with the sweetcorn.

To sauté the chickens, heat half of the olive oil in a large frying pan (this may have to be done in two stages). Season the chicken pieces with salt and pepper. Add the chicken leg pieces to the pan, skin-side down. Sauté on a reasonably high heat, turning and allowing the pieces to become a rich golden brown. Transfer to a roasting tray and place in the preheated oven. Fry the breast pieces in the remaining olive oil until golden brown, then add them to the roasting tray with the butter. The chicken will now need 12–15 minutes in the oven to complete the cooking.

While the chicken is roasting, finish the sweetcorn. Heat a knob of the butter in a large frying pan. Once hot and bubbling, add the diced bacon or pancetta and sauté for a few minutes, until golden brown. Add the button onions, if wishing to increase their colour, and continue to fry for a further 5–6 minutes, until heated through. Warm the cooked sweetcorn in a large saucepan (adding the halved onion pieces if a more natural finish is preferred) with the saved cooking water, placing a lid on top to create steam. Once hot, add the shredded lettuce, allow it to soften, and stir in the bacon, onions, a pinch of sugar and the remaining butter. Season with salt and pepper, and transfer to a serving dish.

Remove the chicken pieces from the oven, baste with the butter in the pan and sprinkle with coarse sea salt. Present the two dishes, drizzling the chicken with any butter and juices left in the pan.

● A quick chicken stock can be made with which to finish the dish, replacing the sweetcorn cooking liquor. If you wish to do this, chop the carcasses quite small, quickly rinsing off any excess blood. Place the pieces in a saucepan and cover with 600ml (1 pint) of cold water. Bring to a simmer, skimming off any impurities, and cook for 30 minutes, then increase the heat and reduce by half. Strain.

Serves 4

- 75g (3oz) walnuts, preferably skinned
- 100g (4oz) butter, plus 2 extra knobs for the apples and the courgettes
- 2 teaspoons brandy (optional)
- salt and pepper
- 1 x 1.75kg (4lb) free-range chicken
- pinch of freshly grated nutmeg
- 2 tablespoons cooking oil
- 3 onions, sliced
- 450g (1lb) apples
- 300ml (½ pint) dry cider
- 550g (1¼lb) courgettes
- 1 tablespoon oil, preferably walnut oil
- 1 teaspoon picked thyme
- 1 tablespoon chopped flatleaf parsley (optional)

Roast walnut chicken with cider, apples, onions and thyme courgettes

The title of this recipe has a real wintry feel. This dish is quite simple, however, without over-rich gravies, roast potatoes and lots of veg. In early autumn, courgettes are still sublime, and should be totally taken advantage of. Here they're just sautéed and then rolled in thyme with a knob of butter. You will also be lucky with early British walnuts and apples in September.

Method Preheat the oven to 220°C/425°F/Gas 7. To skin the walnuts, simply cook them in boiling water for 3 minutes. Remove the pan from the stove, leave them in the water and, taking one out at a time, scrape them while still warm. This takes just a few minutes, leaving you with a less bitter and more tender component to the dish. Chop the skinned walnuts reasonably finely, leaving just a slight rustic edge. Mix the nuts with the butter and brandy, if using, and season with salt and pepper.

Carefully ease the skin from the chicken breasts, creating enough space to cover the breasts entirely with the butter. Push and spread the butter over the breasts under the skin, saving 25g (1oz) for later. Fold the skin back under the neck and secure with a cocktail stick. Season the bird with salt, pepper and nutmeg. Heat the cooking oil in a large braising pot or saucepan and quickly fry the chicken until golden brown on all sides. Remove the bird and keep to one side.

Fry the onions in the pan, cooking for 6–8 minutes until well coloured, then remove from the pan. While the onions are frying, peel, quarter and core the apples. Add a knob of butter to the pan and fry the apples on a fairly high heat for just a few minutes, allowing them to colour.

At this point return the onions to the pan, adding the cider and 100ml (3½fl oz) water. Bring to the boil and reduce by half.

Sit the chicken on top of the onions and apples, cover with a lid or foil and place in the preheated oven, pot-roasting for 1 hour. For the final 20 minutes, remove the lid to allow the chicken to brown well. Remove the cooked bird from the pot, cover and leave to rest.

While the chicken is resting, cook the courgettes. If using young and small courgettes, just wash and cut into 1cm (½in) thick slices at a slight angle. If large, split lengthwise into halves or quarters, then cut in the same way. These can now be blanched for 30 seconds in boiling salted water, and then drained in a colander. Warm the walnut or other oil in a large frying pan. Add the courgettes and fry well for 5–6 minutes, until tender and with a golden edge. Add a knob of butter and the thyme, and season with salt and pepper.

While the courgettes are cooking, carefully strain the onions and apples from the cider stock, keeping them to one side. Boil the liquor to reduce it, if necessary, for a stronger flavour. Add the remaining walnut butter, whisking it in well, and add the chopped parsley, if using.

Carve the chicken, offering half a leg and half a breast per portion. Divide the soft onions and apples between the plates, top with the chicken pieces and spoon the sauce around. Serve the courgettes separately.

● *When pre-blanching the courgettes, it is best simply to drain and not refresh in iced water. Any extra moisture will steam off, leaving them dry to fry.*

Serves 4

- 450–675g (1–1½lb) curly kale (or spinach)
- salt and pepper
- iced water (optional)
- 2 large knobs of butter
- 4 x 175–225g (6–8oz) pieces of venison loin, trimmed
- 1 tablespoon groundnut oil

For the sauce

- 50g (2oz) shallots, sliced
- 8 black peppercorns, crushed
- 6 juniper berries, crushed
- 1 bay leaf
- 4 tablespoons red wine vinegar
- 300ml (½ pint) full-bodied red wine
- 300ml (½ pint) *Game stock* (page 195) or tinned game or beef consommé
- 1 teaspoon plain flour
- 1 teaspoon butter
- 1 level tablespoon redcurrant jelly

For the fig tarts

- 225g (8oz) *Quick puff pastry* (page 203, or bought)
- flour, for dusting
- 25g (1oz) butter, plus extra for greasing
- 6 figs, halved lengthwise
- 2 tablespoons groundnut oil
- 1 egg, beaten
- 4 teaspoons demerara sugar
- black pepper

Roast loin of venison with savoury fig tarts

Venison carries a double bonus: it happens to offer such a distinctive gamey flavour, that can be controlled by hanging, and it is also one of the healthiest and most nutritious foods available. It may well be a 'red' meat, but it is lower in fat, higher in protein, richer in vitamins and minerals, and contains fewer calories than most other red and white meats.

There are five or six species of deer available in the UK, but the finest to choose from are the roe or fallow deer. In France the roe (*chevreuil*) is considered the ultimate. This is the youngest and usually most tender, but I also feel the fallow stands as its equal. The meat's title – venison – applies to all deer once killed, including the elk, moose and reindeer of America.

For roasting, the best cut is the saddle, the leanest of loins with a moist succulent finish. The haunch (leg) adapts well to most cooking methods, as does the boned and rolled shoulder (the shoulder can also be slow-roasted until well done). Other cheaper cuts are perfect for slow stewing and braising.

The roe and fallow deer are both in open season in England from 1 November to the end of February. In Scotland, from where most of our venison comes, the roe season runs from 21 October to 31 March, and the fallow from 21 October to 15 February. The beauty of these two types of venison is that they need very little hanging and maturing. If cooked particularly young with no hanging, the meat will still be very tender with a beefy flavour, enhanced with a gamey punch. After 7 days of hanging, the gamey flavour improves, and after 14 days, a more distinctive taste will be found. So, as

mentioned, you can be in command of the gamey strength.

This recipe gently roasts the loin and serves it with a savoury fig tart. November is the perfect time for venison and figs to work together. Figs are at their prime, with young venison available from Scotland and the first of the English. The tarts are peppered and cooked until slightly caramelized, to enhance their crisp, savoury-sweet, pepper-fruit flavour. The venison itself will then sit happily alongside, on a spoonful of buttered curly kale and red wine game sauce.

Method The sauce and kale can be prepared well in advance of serving the dish. To make the sauce, place the shallots, peppercorns, juniper berries and bay leaf in a saucepan with the red wine vinegar. Bring to the boil and allow to reduce until almost dry. Add the red wine, return to the boil and reduce by two-thirds. Add the game stock or tinned consommé, return to the boil and reduce by a third. The depth of flavour will have increased, producing a loose broth consistency. Mix together the flour and butter, then whisk this into the broth, which will thicken as it regains its temperature. Simmer gently for a few minutes to cook away the raw flour taste. Whisk in the redcurrant jelly, allowing it to melt into the sauce. This adds an extra flavour to accompany the venison, also giving the sauce a glossy shine. Adjust the seasoning with a pinch of salt and strain through a fine sieve. Reheat before serving.

Remove the thick stalks from the curly kale leaves. Rinse them and tear into smaller pieces. To cook in advance, blanch the leaves in boiling salted water for 3–4 minutes until tender, refresh in iced water and drain in a colander. Lightly squeeze off excess water and season with salt and pepper, then melt a large knob of butter and pour it over the leaves. These can now be reheated in the microwave when needed. Alternatively, the kale can be cooked while the roasted venison is resting. Melt the butter in a large saucepan with a few tablespoons of water. Once it is bubbling, add the washed torn leaves, stir, season and cover with a lid to create steam. Cook for 5–6 minutes, stirring from time to time, until tender. The kale is now ready to serve. If offering spinach, halve the cooking times.

To prepare the tarts, preheat the oven to 200°C/400°F/Gas 6. On a floured surface roll the puff pastry very thinly into a rectangle large enough to provide four smaller rectangles, each approximately 13 × 7.5cm (5 × 3in). Place the pastries on a lightly greased baking tray, prick each lightly with a fork and chill. Lightly dust the cut side of each fig with a little flour. Heat the oil in a large frying pan and, once hot, quickly fry the fig halves, floured-side down, to a golden brown. This literally takes seconds to achieve. Remove the fruits from the pan and leave to cool. Brush the pastries well with the beaten egg and place three fig halves, cut-side up, top to tail on each rectangle. Dot with the butter, and sprinkle each tart with a teaspoon of demerara sugar and a good twist of black pepper. Bake the tarts in the preheated oven for 15–20 minutes, until the pastry is crisp and the figs tender.

While the tarts are baking, roast the venison. Heat the groundnut oil and remaining butter in a roasting tray on top of the stove. Once sizzling, season the pieces of meat with salt and pepper and place them in the tray. Fry for a few minutes, until well coloured on all sides. Place the venison in the preheated oven and roast for 8 minutes for a medium-rare finish or 10–12 minutes for medium (well done will need 15–20 minutes), turning each piece over halfway through the chosen cooking time. Remove the roasted loins from the oven and tray and leave to rest for 6–8 minutes.

To serve the venison dish, spoon the cooked kale in a rectangular shape on one side of the plate and place a fig tart by its side. Pour a spoonful or two of the warmed sauce over and around the curly kale. Carve the loins into round slices and present them overlapping on top of the kale.

● *Port, between 3 tablespoons and 100ml (3½fl oz) depending on strength preferred, can be boiled and reduced by two-thirds, before adding to the sauce for a classic finish.*

Serves 4
- 4 oven-ready partridges, preferably red-legged, barded with a thin slice of back fat or rasher of bacon
- 2 tablespoons groundnut oil
- large knob of butter

For the sauce
- 2 teaspoons butter
- 2 shallots, finely chopped, or 2 tablespoons chopped onion

- 1 garlic clove, halved
- sprig of thyme, plus extra to cook with the vegetables
- 2 tablespoons red wine vinegar
- pinch of caster sugar
- 300ml (½ pint) full-bodied red wine
- 300ml (½ pint) *Game stock* (page 195), *Chicken* or *Instant stock* (page 194), or tinned game or beef consommé
- 1 teaspoon plain flour
- salt and pepper

For the vegetables
- 2 medium potatoes, preferably Romano or Desirée, peeled
- 4 small parsnips, peeled and quartered
- 2 medium carrots, peeled
- 2 turnips, peeled
- 1 small swede (or ½ large), peeled
- 1 small celeriac (or ½ large), peeled
- 6 tablespoons groundnut or vegetable oil
- large knob of butter

Roast partridge with roasted root vegetables

The partridge was once, during the 1800s, our most common of game birds. It would seem that over the years, being highly susceptible to modern farming techniques, it has become much harder to find, particularly our own British grey variety. This is smaller than the French red-legged, first introduced to Britain in the seventeenth century, but does have a fuller and better flavour. Both the grey and red-legged are available from 1 September to 1 February. The best time to enjoy their rich flavour is during the autumn months, when the birds are younger and their meat more tender. Although having said the grey partridge is of a better quality, I'd suggest you go for the red-legged, as these are bigger – just one a portion is ideal – still with a very good flavour.

As accompaniments, we have simple roasted root vegetables, including carrots, swedes, turnips, parsnips and celeriac. It's not essential to include all of these – choose as few or many as you wish. Another vegetable used is the potato, just roasted like the rest, but first cut lengthwise to create a plinth on which the partridge can sit.

The partridges are 'barded' with back fat. This is the process of tying a thin layer of fat across the breast to protect the meat from drying out during roasting – a self-basting technique. Most such birds will come with this already in place, but if not, a rasher of bacon can be used in this way or the bird can be left unprotected.

Method The sauce can be made in advance. Melt half the butter in a small saucepan. Once bubbling, add the chopped shallots or onion, garlic and sprig of thyme and fry to a light golden brown. Add the red wine vinegar and reduce quickly until almost dry. Sprinkle with the caster sugar and add the red wine. Bring to the boil and allow to reduce by two-thirds. Add the stock or consommé and reduce by just a third. If condensed consommé is being used, it won't need to be reduced. Mix together the flour and remaining butter and whisk it into the sauce. Cook for a few minutes, season with salt and pepper, then strain through a fine sieve. The sauce is now ready to be reheated before serving.

The vegetables can all also be prepared in advance. First cut the potatoes lengthwise and trim the domed side for a neater and slightly flatter finish. This will help to provide a stable platform for the birds. Keep them in water until ready to cook. Quarter the small parsnips lengthwise, then cut out their central core if it feels too woody in texture. Halve or quarter the carrots lengthwise, cutting each at an angle into two or three sharp sticks. Treat the turnips like apples, cutting each into 8–12 wedges, providing plenty to go round. The swede and celeriac are best cut through the middle to provide two round discs from each. These can now also be cut into wedges like the turnips.

Preheat the oven to 200°C/400°F/Gas 6. All of the potatoes and vegetables can be roasted from raw. Some can also be pre-blanched in boiling water to begin their cooking, offering a softer finish to their centres.

If wishing to follow this route, place the potatoes in boiling water and return to the boil, then simmer for 5 minutes, drain and allow to cool naturally. Plunge the carrots and swede into boiling water, cooking also for 5 minutes, then drain and leave to cool. The parsnips, turnips and celeriac are best roasted from raw. Blanched or raw, the roasting time will remain the same.

Heat 2 tablespoons of the oil in a small roasting tray and fry the potatoes (first drying them well if soaked in water) to a light golden brown on both sides. Season with a pinch of salt, place the tray in the preheated oven and roast for 25–30 minutes.

Heat the remaining oil in another large roasting tray and add all of the remaining vegetables. Fry for a few minutes to allow the vegetables to take on a slightly 'roasted' colour, then add a few sprigs of thyme and season with salt and pepper. Roast these with the potatoes for 20–25 minutes, until tender. During this time, turn the vegetables once or twice to ensure even colouring.

To prepare the partridges, season them with salt and pepper, heat the groundnut oil in a roasting pan and fry the birds on one side over a moderate heat, until golden brown. Turn the birds to colour on the other side, then fry and colour breast-side down.

Stand the birds on their backs in the pan, breast-side up, add the butter and, once bubbling, baste the birds and put them in the oven. If the potatoes and vegetables are cooked at this stage they can be removed, ready to put back in the oven and heat through while the

partridges are resting. Roast the birds for a minimum of 8 minutes for a rare finish, or cook for 12–15 minutes for a more medium touch. Remove the partridges from the oven and tray, and leave them to rest for 5–10 minutes, breast-side down. (This enables any juices to find their way back into the meat.)

The rested partridges can be untied and the barding or bacon fat removed. The skin can be left on or removed as wished. Cut away the legs, then the breasts, following the natural breastbone line with a sharp knife. The cutting does take a few minutes and, if necessary, the legs and breasts can be quickly warmed through in the oven while the potatoes and vegetables are served.

Place the potatoes in the centre of the plates and scatter the other vegetables around with a sprig or two of the cooked thyme. Rather than overcrowd the plate, any extra can be offered separately. Place the partridge breasts side by side on top of the potatoes with the legs on either side, the drumsticks meeting towards the front to re-create the shape of the bird. Strain the warmed sauce again, if necessary, then pour around and over the vegetables before serving.

● *An optional enhancer is to chop the back carcasses of the birds roughly when removing them from the bone. These can then be added to the sauce, allowing it to simmer softly while presenting the potatoes, vegetables and birds on plates. The sauce can then be strained quickly and poured around, holding a more distinctive partridge flavour.*

Serves 8–10

- 1 rabbit (domestic, approximately 1.5kg/3½lb)
- 450g (1lb) pork belly, boneless
- 2 tablespoons olive oil
- salt and pepper
- 1 large onion, finely chopped
- 2 bay leaves
- sprig of thyme
- 2–3 strips of lemon rind
- 300ml (½ pint) *Chicken stock* (page 194) or water

For the rhubarb and mustard soured cream

- 225g (8oz) forced rhubarb, cut into 1cm (½in) pieces
- 1 teaspoon caster sugar
- 1 tablespoon Dijon or wholegrain mustard
- 150ml (¼ pint) soured cream

Rabbit and pork pot with a rhubarb and mustard soured cream

Domestic rabbits are available throughout the year, but do have a suggested season between the months of August and February. From September to November, the rabbit is said to be at its prime. Unlike wild rabbit, the domestic needs no hanging time to help develop flavour and tenderize, particularly when made oven-ready at the age of three months. The meat is usually cooked in very much the same way as many a chicken or pork dish. The legs and saddle suit a simple roast; the shoulders (legs also) are good in a casserole or pâté.

In this recipe a whole rabbit is used, cooked slowly with pork belly. When completely tender, the two meats are shredded and flavoured. The result is a very coarse pâté-style dish, the pork fat content acting as the preservative, ready to eat with lots of toast.

As an accompaniment to help offset this rich flavour, we have a purée of forced rhubarb, which joins us in November. The sharp, slightly sweetened rhubarb flavour is warmed by either wholegrain or Dijon mustard and bound with thick soured cream.

Method Preheat the oven to 120°C/250°F/Gas ½. Divide the rabbit, separating the shoulders, saddle and legs (I'm sure your butcher will do this for you). Remove the rind from the pork belly, keeping it to one side, and cut the belly into 2.5cm (1in) dice.

Heat the olive oil in a suitable large ovenproof braising pan, add the pork dice and cook on a low heat, allowing the fat to be released and the pork to colour slightly. This will take a good 15–20 minutes.

Using a slotted spoon, remove the pork pieces from the pan. Season the rabbit with salt and pepper, and lightly colour it in the pork fat left in the pan. Once it is sealed, return the pork to the pan, along with the chopped onion, bay leaves, thyme and lemon rind. Add the chicken stock or water and bring to a simmer. Arrange the pork rind on top of the meats (this prevents them from becoming dry, also releasing any remaining fat content) and cover the pan with a tight-fitting lid. Place in the preheated oven and cook slowly for 2½ hours.

Take the meats from the oven, leaving them in the pot to cool slightly until comfortable to handle. Remove the rabbit meat from the bone, shredding or tearing into thin strands. Shred the pork pieces with a knife or fork, and mix with the rabbit. Drain the cooking liquor through a sieve, removing the bay leaves, thyme and lemon rind. Add the onion to the meats, along with the strained liquor and fat. Season with salt and pepper, then spoon into a suitable 1.25 litre (2 pint) pot or terrine. The shredded meat pot can now be chilled for several hours until set.

While the meats are chilling, make the rhubarb and mustard soured cream. Place the rhubarb pieces in a saucepan with 2 tablespoons of water. Cover with a lid and cook on a moderate heat for 8–10 minutes, until the pieces have become tender. Add the caster sugar and cook uncovered, stirring from time to time, to a thick pulp. Leave to cool. Mix together the mustard and soured cream with the cooled rhubarb. Season with salt and pepper and the cream is ready.

The rabbit and pork pot will now eat at its best with lots of toast, helped along with the accompanying cream.

● *The meats, once shredded and chilled, will keep for several days. To extend their life span, melt 100g (4oz) of pork lard and, as it begins to cool and thicken, pour it over the meats and place in the fridge to set. Providing the pot is completely covered (more fat may be needed), this will now have at least a fortnight's shelf-life. The pork fat, when set, scrapes away quite easily.*

● *Ramekins can also be used in which to set the meats for individual portions.*

Serves 4

- 1.25kg (2½lb) boned and rolled shoulder of pork, rind scored
- cooking oil, for brushing
- salt and pepper
- 3 jacket potatoes
- 50g (2oz) butter, plus extra for greasing
- 1 large onion, finely chopped
- 2 large Bramley apples, peeled and cored
- 2 teaspoons demerara sugar
- 1 head of celery, stringy fibres removed
- 300ml (½ pint) sweet cider
- 450ml (¾ pint) *Chicken* or *Instant stock* (page 194)
- 6–8 sage leaves, chopped

Slow-roast shoulder of pork with a celery, Bramley apple and potato pot

All three main features in this dish have a long affinity with one another – apples and pork, celery and apples, and now the three together. This is an autumn dish through and through, with the Bramleys and celery in abundance. These fruits and vegetables are cooked slowly together, sitting on the potato, absorbing each other's flavours, ready to accompany a 4-hour, slow-roasting of pork.

The advantage of choosing a shoulder of pork when slow-roasting is that it tends to carry a reasonable quantity of fat, self-basting as it cooks and maintaining a moist finish. After 4 hours the meat is ready to be virtually carved with a spoon, eating well with the soft, overcooked celery, bound with what is almost a Bramley apple sauce. For slow cooking, a larger piece of pork than usual needs to be purchased. This will then provide plenty of meat to share between four.

Method Preheat the oven to 160°C/325°F/Gas 3. When purchasing the pork, ask the butcher if it's possible to have a few pork bones on which to place the meat. This will prevent the joint from becoming stuck and burnt to the base of a roasting tray, over such a long cooking time. If bones are unavailable, use a small wire rack. Oil the pork skin and sprinkle liberally with salt. Place the joint on the bones or wire rack in the roasting tray and begin the slow roast in the preheated oven. This can now be left to roast for 1 hour before basting with any pork fat collected under the meat. Continue to roast, basting once more after the second hour. From here, I prefer not to baste, just leaving the joint to self-baste with the fat layer between the skin and meat. This helps the skin to crisp well, becoming crunchy crackling.

While the pork is roasting, prepare the celery, Bramley apple and potato pot. This will also be baked at the low temperature with the pork, needing 1½ hours before the celery is as tender as butter to eat. Place the jacket potatoes in a large saucepan, cover with cold water and add a generous pinch of salt. Bring to a simmer and cook for just 5 minutes, then remove the potatoes from the pan. Once cool enough to handle, peel the potatoes and cut each into 1cm (½in) thick slices. Grease a large ovenproof dish with butter and season it with salt and pepper. Lay the potato slices in the dish, overlapping if necessary, topping with the chopped onion and seasoning with salt and pepper. Slice the Bramley apples into similar thick round slices, lay them across the top and sprinkle with the demerara sugar. Cut the celery into 7.5–10cm (3–4in) pieces and place across the top. Season with salt and pepper.

Stir together 150ml (¼ pint) of the cider with 150ml (¼ pint) of the stock and pour over the celery. Dot with 25g (1oz) of the butter, cover with a lid or foil and place in the oven 1½ hours before the pork is due to be finished. After the first hour the lid can be removed, allowing the celery to take on a little colour, or it can be left to serve as it is.

Once the pork is cooked, remove from the oven and leave to rest for 15 minutes. This provides a little extra cooking time for the celery, should it be needed, also relaxing the meat ready to be carved (or broken) with a spoon.

Pour away any excess fat from the roasting tray and heat the tray on the stove. Add the remaining cider and boil to reduce by two-thirds. Add the remaining stock and boil to reduce by half. This now leaves a well-flavoured liquor to support the moistness of the pork. The remaining butter can be whisked in for a slightly silky finish before checking for seasoning and straining through a fine sieve, and then adding the chopped sage.

Remove the crackling from the pork, breaking it into pieces to serve. The meat can now be divided into portions, offering the crackling pieces and sage and cider liquor along with the celery, Bramley apple and potato pot.

● *For a more golden finish to the cooked celery, Bramley apple and potato pot, brush it with butter and colour under a preheated grill.*

Serves 4

- 4 x 175–225g (6–8oz) gammon steaks
- olive oil, for brushing

For the gnocchi

- 1 medium butternut squash
- 1 large Maris Piper or Desirée potato, pierced with a knife
- knob of butter (optional), plus extra for greasing
- 175g (6oz) plain flour, plus extra for dusting
- 1 egg
- salt and pepper
- freshly grated nutmeg

- 50g (2oz) Parmesan cheese, grated (optional)
- 2–3 tablespoons olive oil (optional)

For the sage sauce

- juice of 1 orange
- 1 shallot, finely chopped
- 50g (2oz) butter
- 4 sage leaves, chopped

Grilled gammon steaks with butternut squash gnocchi and sage

Gnocchi is Italian for 'dumplings', and they can be made in different ways, from semolina, choux pastry or potato. Here the butternut squash is the most predominant flavour, with potato helping as a back-up and binder. This particular squash is with us throughout the autumn, offering a quite densely packed texture and carrying a sweet and nutty, buttery flavour. For the gnocchi, it is best to bake the butternut through in the oven, along with the potato. This will prevent the vegetable, which has a naturally high moisture content, from absorbing any more water.

Gammon steaks currently seem to have quite a bad 'school dinner' image. Fairly recently I was served one of these steaks, not quite sure what to expect, but what I did receive was a wonderful piece of meat, so moist and tender, without being over-salty, as so many had been in my past experience. To complement the gammon and gnocchi is a sage butter. Orange juice is also included, just to enhance the two main features of meat and dumplings.

Method Preheat the oven to 200°C/400°F/Gas 6. Prepare the gnocchi: halve the squash lengthwise, deseed and cut each half into three wedges. Loosely wrap these and the potato in buttered aluminium foil. Place on a baking tray and cook in the preheated oven for 1–1¼ hours, until tender. Remove both from the oven, leave for 10–15 minutes to rest and cool slightly, then scoop both from their skins. Mash the vegetables separately or pass them through a potato ricer. Once mashed, the butternut squash can be squeezed in a very fine sieve or muslin cloth, to get rid of as much excess moisture as possible. Drain this into a saucepan. The quantity of purée remaining will be approximately 150g (5oz), with the juice measuring 300–450ml (½–¾ pint). Boil the juice to reduce by three-quarters, leaving approximately 100ml (3½fl oz) of finished liquor with a richer flavour. This will be used to make the orange and sage butter sauce, spreading the butternut flavour further into the complete dish.

While both of the purées are still warm, mix them together, adding the flour and egg, then season with salt, pepper and nutmeg. The Parmesan can now also be added to the mix, if using, or saved to sprinkle over the gnocchi once cooked and ready to serve. Knead into a pliable dough on a floured surface. This can now be divided into two. Roll each into a long thin cylinder and cut each into 16–20 pieces, ready to roll into balls. This will provide 8–10 gnocchi per serving.

Bring a large pan of water to the boil. Add the gnocchi, just a handful or two at a time, and cook for 2–3 minutes, until the pieces all rise to the surface. Remove the dumplings with a slotted spoon, transfer them to a bowl of iced water and leave to refresh for just a few minutes, before removing and patting dry on kitchen paper. Repeat the same process until all are cooked.

Season the gammon steaks with pepper and brush with olive oil. Preheat a large griddle plate or a grill. Trim the rind of the gammons to prevent the steaks from curling as they cook. Grill the steaks for 6–7 minutes on each side.

While the gammon is cooking, make the sage sauce. Mix the orange juice with the shallot in a saucepan and bring to the boil. Cook for a few minutes until the juice has reduced by half. Add the reduced butternut squash liquor and bring it to a simmer, then whisk in the butter just before serving. Season with salt and pepper, adding the chopped sage at the last moment. This provides enough liquor to help loosen the gnocchi.

Fry the gnocchi in the olive oil with a knob of butter, to warm them through and give them a golden finish, or just microwave them with the knob of butter until heated through. Either way, they can be sprinkled with the Parmesan, if using (if you have not added it to the mix) and gratinéed to a golden brown under a hot grill if a crisper edge is preferred.

Divide the finished gnocchi between four plates (or place them in one large serving bowl). Place the gammon steaks on the plates and trickle the sage sauce over and around the gnocchi.

● *For a creamy finish, a tablespoon of whipping cream can be added to the sauce before whisking in the butter.*

Serves 4–6

- 1 small swede, peeled
- 1–2 medium turnips, peeled
- 1 large or 2 medium carrots, peeled
- 2 celery sticks, peeled
- 1–2 parsnips, peeled and quartered, with the central core removed
- 2 medium potatoes, peeled
- ¼ Savoy cabbage
- 12 button onions, peeled
- 1.2 litres (2 pints) *Beef stock* (page 195) or *Instant stock* (page 194) or tinned beef consommé
- 2 bay leaves
- large sprig of thyme
- salt and pepper
- 4–6 x 175g (6oz) beef fillet steaks (preferably taken from the central fillet to ensure equal portions), trimmed of all sinews
- knob of butter (optional)
- 1 tablespoon chopped parsley

Poached beef fillet with lots of vegetables

It's mid-to-late autumn, winter is very close and there are plenty of our root vegetables to choose from. With this recipe it's not what you actually choose, so much as taking advantage of as many flavours as possible.

As you can see, glancing at the ingredients list, there are lots of vegetables to warrant the title of this dish. It is, in fact, a reasonably quick recipe, with the meat, potatoes and abundance of vegetables simply poached and all appearing from the one pot. In France this style of dish is known as *à la ficelle*, which literally translates as 'on a string', as each beef fillet is tied with string to help retain its neat round shape. Enough string is usually left to tie the meat to the saucepan handle, making it a lot simpler when lifting the fillets from the pot, but a slotted spoon is more than adequate for the job.

Method Cut the swede, turnips, carrots, celery and parsnips into rough 2cm (¾in) dice or into baton-shaped sticks about 5cm (2in) long and 5mm (¼in) thick. They don't need to be perfectly neat, or exactly that size, but making all of them similar in size helps ensure even cooking. Cut the potatoes into rough 2cm (¾in) chunks and shred the cabbage into strips of about 5mm (¼in).

Place the button onions in a small saucepan and cover with water. Bring to a simmer, then refresh in cold water. Repeat this process twice more to help remove the raw onion flavour and begin their cooking.

Place the potatoes, carrots, celery, swede and blanched onions into a large saucepan or braising pot, and cover them with the stock or consommé. Add the bay leaves and thyme and bring to a simmer. Once at simmering point, cook the vegetables gently for 10–15 minutes (10 minutes will be plenty if they are cut into sticks), adding the turnips and parsnips after the first 5 minutes when the other vegetables are becoming tender. Season with salt and pepper.

While the vegetables are simmering, tie the beef fillets loosely to help retain their round shape. Season each with salt and pepper. After the first 10–15 minutes of cooking the vegetables as above, lower the beef into the stock. It is now very important to allow the pot to be at a slight murmuring simmer only; any more and the beef will become toughened. About 8 minutes of poaching will cook the beef to a rare stage, 10 minutes for medium rare; for well done, at least 20–25 minutes of poaching will be needed, so in this case it is best to add the beef to the pot with the vegetables. Add the cabbage for the last 4–5 minutes of poaching. As the beef cooks, spoon away any impurities that may rise to the surface. By the time the beef is cooked, the vegetables will have reached an 'overcooked' stage, making them even more tender.

To serve, lift the beef fillets from the pot and remove the string. Add a knob of butter to the vegetables, if you wish, before spooning into bowls. Place the beef fillets in the centre of each bowl, ladling the cooking liquor over and sprinkling with chopped parsley.

● *Any remaining vegetables and stock can be served as a vegetable broth the following day, or liquidized into a puréed vegetable soup.*

fruit and puddings

Serves 4

- 4 small quince (approximately 175g/6oz each) or 2 large
- ½ lemon
- 100g (4oz) clear honey
- 300ml (½ pint) sweet cider
- 4 strips of orange rind
- 5cm (2in) piece of cinnamon stick
- 1 vanilla pod
- 25g (1oz) icing sugar
- 150ml (¼ pint) double cream
- 225g (8oz) raspberries

Baked cider, cinnamon and honey quince with raspberries and sweet vanilla cream

Home-grown quince can be found, but are not produced on a commercial basis. This yellow-golden fruit, originally from western Asia, is closely related to apples and pears. Quinces are either pear- or apple-shaped, according to variety. First choice is the pear-shaped, as these tend to be richer and sweeter, turning a delightful shade of pink once cooked. Ripe quinces will have a wonderful flavour and a rich golden colour. With a high pectin content, the quince is perfect for marmalade and jellies, as well as various puddings and savouries; indeed sweetened quince is traditionally served with roasted pheasant and many more game dishes.

The relationship of the quince to the apple and pear is what led to the idea for this dish. Cider with apples or pears is always a winner, with honey usually happily involved. Raspberries are still around in October and these red berries provide a slightly bitter contrast to the sweet honey syrup. The sweet vanilla cream can become an optional extra – you could just serve pouring cream or a dollop of crème fraîche.

Method Preheat the oven to 190°C/375°F/Gas 5. Peel the quince and halve them. Remove the core and seeds using a teaspoon. This is not essential, as once cooked and served, cutting around the core is simple enough. Rub each of the quince halves with the lemon half to prevent any discoloration. Place the fruits, cored-side up, in a roasting tray. Whisk together the honey and sweet cider and, once totally combined, pour over the quince halves. Add the orange rind and cinnamon stick to the tray. Split the vanilla pod and scrape out the seeds, keeping them for flavouring the cream. You can also add the scraped pod to the tray for an extra spicy edge. Cover the tray with foil and bake in the preheated oven for 40 minutes.

At the end of this time, remove the foil, baste the fruits generously and return them to the oven uncovered. Continue cooking for another 40 minutes until tender. During this time, baste the quince occasionally until golden brown, with the honey cider also becoming syrupy. Once cooked, remove the quince from the oven and leave to cool until just warm.

In a bowl, mix the vanilla seeds and icing sugar with the double cream. Whip this to soft-peak stage, just creamy enough to hold its own shape. The warm quince can now be served drizzled with the syrupy cider honey, finishing with the raspberries and sweet vanilla cream.

Serves 6
- 150g (5oz) plain flour, sifted
- 2 eggs, plus 1 egg white
- 200–300ml (7fl oz–½ pint) milk
- vegetable oil, for greasing

For the damsons
- 1kg (2¼lb) damsons, stoned (see below)
- 275g (10oz) caster sugar
- pinch of ground cinnamon
- 150–300ml (¼–½ pint) double cream (extra-thick is even better)
- 1–2 heaped tablespoons icing sugar, plus extra for dusting

Stewed damson yorkies with lashings of sweet cream

Damsons are the small blue-black plums in season from late summer to, in a good year, late autumn; in September they are guaranteed. Traditionally you will find these stony little beasts in the pie dish or jam pot, hidden beneath the skiing slopes of caster sugar needed to calm their acid bite.

Home-made damson tarts are a great treat, which is what I have for you here, but instead of a pastry case, I use a Yorkshire pud batter. The individual soufflé rings of this Sunday favourite surround a collection of tender sweet fruits ready to be coated in thick luxurious double cream – pure indulgence.

A couple of pointers: one, the batter needs a minimum of 1–2 hours' rest before baking. For the ultimate result, make the batter 24 hours in advance – you will not be disappointed. Two, the damsons can be halved, and their large pip cut away with the point of a small knife (alternatively, use an olive stoner, which works providing the fruits are not rock-hard).

Method Whisk together in a bowl the flour, eggs, egg white and 200ml (7fl oz) of the milk. The consistency should be one that coats the back of a spoon. If too thick, add the remaining milk. The batter can now be left to rest for a minimum of 1 hour (preferably chilled for 24 hours). If only 200ml (7fl oz) of the milk has been added, you may find that, after resting, the batter has congealed and needs the last 100ml (3½fl oz).

Preheat the oven to 220°C/425°F/Gas 7. Oil six individual 10cm (4in) flan tins generously and place them on a baking tray. Preheat in the oven to very hot.

Fill each mould with the batter until almost full and bake for 25–30 minutes (if using one large flan tin, 45–60 minutes will be needed). The puddings will have risen, ready for serving and filling with the fruits.

While the Yorkshire puddings are baking, place the stoned damsons, sugar, cinnamon and 4 tablespoons of water in a large saucepan. Cover with a lid and poach over a gentle heat, stirring carefully from time to time, for 12–15 minutes, until the fruits are tender. If particularly under-ripe, an extra 5–10 minutes may be needed. Should a lot of water and juices have been released, a high quantity of syrup will have been created. If too loose and watery, strain the fruits in a colander sitting above a clean saucepan. The syrup can now be simmered rapidly, to reduce it to a coating consistency. The fruits can now be returned to the pan, spooning the syrup over them.

In a bowl, whisk together the preferred quantity of cream and icing sugar and whip until the cream has thickened but is still pourable. Extra-thick cream will not need to be whisked; just spoon sugar through it. Present the Yorkshire puddings in bowls or plates, filling each with the poached damsons and offering the sweet cream to spoon over.

● *If damsons are unavailable, ordinary plums can be used, halved, stoned and cut into quarters. These can now be cooked as above.*

Serves 4–6

- 12 plums, halved and stoned
- 75g (3oz) caster sugar
- knob of butter

For the sponge topping

- 100g (4oz) butter, plus extra for brushing
- 100g (4oz) caster sugar
- finely grated zest of 1 small lemon
- finely grated zest of 1 small orange
- generous pinch of ground cinnamon (optional)
- 2 eggs, beaten
- 225g (8oz) self-raising flour, sifted
- 2 tablespoons milk
- 1 tablespoon demerara sugar, for sprinkling
- pouring cream or *Crème Anglaise* (page 204), to serve

Baked plum pudding

Imported plums are available throughout the year. As far as home-grown are concerned, we have the Victoria, which joins us in mid-to-late summer, reaching its best in early autumn. This particular plum has a sweet, juicy flavour, and can be easily recognized by its red/yellow colour. Another joining us at this time is Marjorie's Seedling, a large, blue-black variety, which again has a rich flavour.

This dessert is very simple to make, the plums lightly warmed with the butter and sugar, before being topped with the citrus sponge mix. Once baked, the plums have softened amongst their own sweet juices, with the baked sponge topping enhancing the lemon and orange flavours. This pudding is best cooked in a 1 litre (1¾ pint) ovenproof clear glass dish, which shows off the bubbling plums sizzling in their own juices.

Method Preheat the oven 180°C/350°F/Gas 4. The plum halves can be mixed with the sugar and a little water, and baked from raw. I prefer, however, to begin their cooking process gently. I find this helps release their juices and produce maximum flavour. To do so, melt the knob of butter in a large saucepan. Once bubbling, add the plum halves, cut-side down, and cook on a medium heat for just a few minutes, then add the caster sugar. Continue to cook for just a further minute or two, before adding 4 tablespoons of water. Transfer the plums and juices to the pudding dish and leave to cool.

To make the sponge, beat together the butter and caster sugar until pale and creamy. Add the grated lemon and orange zest, along with the cinnamon,

if using. Pour the beaten eggs into the bowl and mix slowly until all are added. Fold in the flour gently, followed by the milk. Alternatively, this mix can be made by placing all the ingredients in a food processor and blitzing to a smooth consistency. Lightly butter the rim of the plum dish, then spoon and spread the sponge mixture on top and sprinkle with the demerara sugar.

Place the dish on a baking tray and cook in the preheated oven for 55–60 minutes, until the sponge top has become golden brown and crispy. To check the sponge is completely cooked through, pierce with a skewer and leave for 10 seconds before removing. The skewer should come away clean without any uncooked pudding mix attached. If not quite ready, return to the oven and continue to bake for a further 10–15 minutes.

The baked plum pudding is now ready to serve, accompanied by pouring cream or crème Anglaise.

● *Should the plums be slightly under-ripe, the caster sugar quantity can be increased to 100g (4oz) to compensate.*

● *Many other fruits can be cooked beneath the sponge, such as rhubarb, blackberries and apples or pears.*

Serves 4–6

For the meringues
- 2 egg whites
- 100g (4oz) caster sugar

For the cider apples
- 150ml (¼ pint) sweet cider
- 50g (2oz) sugar
- 3 apples, preferably Discovery, Katy or Spartan

For the blackberry cream
- 350g (12oz) blackberries (slightly over-ripe if possible)
- 50g (2oz) caster sugar
- 1 vanilla pod, split, or a few drops of vanilla essence (optional)
- 300ml (½ pint) double or whipping cream

Blackberry Eton mess with cider apples

'Eton mess' obviously takes its name from the public school, where the dessert was created to celebrate King George III's birthday, the 'mess' simply describing how it is presented. Eton mess has assumed many guises over the years with ice-cream, soft cream cheese, lots of fruits and different styled meringues all playing a part. I prefer using meringue, cream and fruit – this is probably the simplest variation, which can so often be the best.

The berries normally chosen are strawberries or raspberries; here it is a summer/autumn cousin of the two, the blackberry. Blackberries do not normally appear until August, running through to October. The apple also joins us in the autumn, with many varieties available from September onwards. The apples to use for the most perfect of flavours are Discovery, Katy or Spartan. All three are red-skinned, with a touch of strawberry within their crisp, slightly acidic juiciness.

Method Preheat the oven to 120°C/250°F/Gas ¼. First make the meringues. Using a scrupulously clean bowl and whisk (an electric hand whisk or mixer will offer the best results), beat the egg whites until very stiff. Add half of the caster sugar and continue to beat until smooth and thickened. Add the remaining sugar and continue to whisk to stiff peaks. Spoon the meringue in small dollops on to a baking tray lined with parchment paper, not worrying about shape or quantity, as these will be broken to mix with the blackberry cream. Bake the meringues in the preheated oven for 2 hours, then switch the oven off and leave the meringues in it for 30 minutes while it cools.

While the meringues are baking, prepare the apples.

First, bring the cider and sugar to the boil. Peel and quarter the apples, removing the core. Cut the quarters in half, providing eight wedges per apple. Place these in the cider and bring back to a simmer. Cook for 1–2 minutes, until the apples are tender. Remove from the cider and keep to one side. Boil the syrup until reduced by a third to a half, giving a syrupy consistency. Leave to cool.

To make the blackberry cream, place the blackberries and caster sugar in a saucepan and lightly warm over a gentle heat to soften the berries. Should the sugar begin to caramelize, loosen it with a tablespoon or two of water. Once the blackberries are tender but not completely broken down, remove the pan from the heat. Lightly crush the fruits with a fork, keeping a rough texture throughout. Leave to cool.

Break the cooked meringues into pieces; if not completely dry throughout, this will provide a toffee-like cream. If using, scrape the inside of the vanilla pod into the cream, or add the vanilla essence, and whip to soft peaks. Three-quarters of the forked blackberries can now be spooned in, and the remainder saved to trickle around. Fold the broken meringues into the blackberry cream, also saving a spoonful or two for sprinkling over.

To serve, divide the apple wedges between the plates, and spoon the blackberry meringue cream on top. Sprinkle with the reserved meringue and trickle the reserved forked blackberries and the cider syrup over or around. The Eton mess is ready to serve.

● *A few of the softened blackberries can be left whole as a garnish.*

- 225g (8oz) self-raising flour, plus extra for dusting
- 1 teaspoon baking powder
- pinch of salt
- 50g (2oz) caster sugar
- 75g (3oz) butter, slightly softened, plus extra for greasing
- 50g (2oz) chopped walnuts
- approximately 125ml (4fl oz) milk
- 1 egg, beaten (optional)

For the orange double cream custard
- 3 egg yolks
- 50g (2oz) caster sugar
- 1 vanilla pod, split (optional)
- 300ml (½ pint) double cream
- finely grated zest of 2 oranges

For the fruits
- knob of butter
- 225g (8oz) blackberries
- 225g (8oz) raspberries
- 2 heaped tablespoons icing sugar

Walnut butter scones with warm blackberries, raspberries and orange double cream custard

In the first month of autumn, blackberries and raspberries are at their best, with walnuts just arriving to join them. To add to this over-indulgence of good produce, topping the whole thing with an orange double cream custard takes on a sort of very attractive obscenity. Very homely, nutty scones have become a complete dessert. If you prefer, the fruits and custard can be omitted, leaving some scones, jam and cream to treat yourself. If nuts are a 'no-no' in your diet, then drop those too.

This dessert can be planned several hours or days ahead, but the scones should be made and eaten when still just warm from the oven, while light, moist and moreish. The custard can also be eaten at its freshest or it can be cooked ahead, ready for rewarming. Serve as a dessert or a complete treat for a Sunday afternoon, or any day for that matter!

Method Preheat the oven to 220°C/425°F/Gas 7 and grease a baking tray. Sift the flour, baking powder and pinch of salt together into a bowl. Stir in the sugar, add the softened butter and rub quickly into the flour to create a fine breadcrumb consistency. Add the chopped walnuts, along with the milk, a spoonful at a time, and mix to a smooth dough. Should the dough seem too dry, add a little more milk, but do not allow it to become sticky. Roll the dough on a lightly floured surface until approximately 2–2.5cm (¾–1in) thick. Using a 5cm (2in) pastry cutter, cut scone shapes from the dough with one sharp tap, not twisting the dough as you cut, as this results in uneven rising.

Brush the scones with the beaten egg for a shiny glaze, or lightly dust them with flour for a matt finish. Place the scones on the greased baking tray and bake towards the top of the preheated oven for 10–12 minutes until golden brown. These are best served just warm.

To make the custard, beat the egg yolks and sugar together in a bowl until well blended. Scrape the insides of the vanilla pod, if using, into the double cream, then add the pod, along with the orange zest. Bring the cream to the boil, then whisk it into the egg yolks and sugar. Place the bowl over a pan of simmering water, the bowl not making contact with the water as this will become too hot and begin to scramble the egg yolks. Keep stirring until the egg yolks have begun to thicken sufficiently to coat the back of a spoon. Remove the bowl from the heat, and take the vanilla pod from the custard. The custard is now ready to serve hot, or leave to cool slightly for a warm finish. The orange zest can be left in or strained before serving. This custard also eats very well cold.

To prepare the fruits, heat the knob of butter in a large frying pan. Once bubbling, add the blackberries and cook on a fairly high heat for 2–3 minutes, then add the raspberries. Continue to cook for a further minute, then add the icing sugar. Roll the fruits quickly in the syrup and loosen with a few tablespoons of water. The syrupy fruits are now ready to serve.

To serve, split the warm walnut scones in half, serving two, three or four halves per portion. Spoon the warmed fruits on top, pouring the custard over and around, or offering it separately.

Serves 8 (minimum)
- 350g (12oz) self-raising flour
- 1 teaspoon baking powder
- 1–2 vanilla pods, split (optional)
- 4 eggs
- 225g (8oz) caster sugar
- 100g (4oz) butter
- finely grated zest and juice of 3 limes
- 8 greengages
- icing or caster sugar, for dusting
- 4 tablespoons ginger syrup, from a jar of stem ginger (optional)
- 300ml (½ pint) full-fat crème fraîche (optional)

Greengage lime cake

The greengage is a member of the plum family, with virtually all of the family – Victoria, Marjorie's Seedling, Excalibur, damsons and more – in season between late July and September. In France, the greengage is known as the Reine-Claude, after the wife of Françoise I. This rich, green, tender fruit became known as the greengage in this country purely by chance. In the early eighteenth century, Sir Thomas Gage received a collection of plants from his brother in France. The gardener, on losing the name tag for this particular fruit, decided to baptize it with a simple combination of its colour and his employer's surname.

The greengage lime cake can be enjoyed simply as a nice wedge of cake helped along by a good pot of tea, a sort of Sunday afternoon affair. Its other advantage is how easily it will heat up in the microwave – when topped with melting vanilla ice-cream, the cake is turned into a quick dessert. Included in the recipe is an optional addition of ginger-syruped crème fraîche, using syrup taken from a jar of stem ginger. An extra squeeze of lime juice can also be added to continue the citrus flavour, the lime and ginger complementing, rather than fighting, one another quite well.

Method Preheat the oven to 180°C/350°F/Gas 4. Line the base and sides of a 22.5cm (9in) loose-bottomed cake tin with buttered parchment paper. Sift together the self-raising flour and baking powder, then scrape the vanilla seeds out of the pods, if using, and add them to the flour, spreading them evenly throughout. Using an electric mixer or electric hand whisk, beat together the eggs and caster sugar until reaching a thick and creamy sabayon stage. Lift the whisk from the mix and, if a thick trail is left, the sabayon is ready. While beating, melt the butter and then leave to cool. Add the lime zest to the flour, then fold it into the whipped eggs and sugar. Stir in the lime juice, along with the melted butter.

Halve and stone the greengages, then cut each half into six wedges. Add two-thirds of the greengages to the cake mix and pour it into the prepared cake tin. Sprinkle with the remainder of the fruits, which will slowly sink into the sponge. Place in the preheated oven and bake for between 1 hour 20 minutes and 1½ hours, until only just cooked through, leaving a slight hint of moistness in the centre.

Remove the cake from the oven and leave to cool for 10 minutes before turning out to stand on a wire rack, then dust it with icing or caster sugar. The cake can now be left to cool completely to enjoy as it is, or served warm as suggested above.

To make the ginger-syruped cream, whip the syrup into the crème fraîche, and offer separately or spoon over each slice of cake.

- *A very sticky topping can be achieved by mixing 3–4 heaped tablespoons of Greengage jam (page 205) with 4–6 tablespoons of water. Warm the two together until a syrupy consistency is reached. This can now be brushed or rustically drizzled over the cake, allowing a little to trickle down the sides.*

- *A slice of the cake topped with the jam eats at its best with dollops of clotted cream.*

Serves 6–8

- butter, for greasing
- 350g (12oz) *Sweet shortcrust pastry* (page 203)
- flour, for dusting
- 600ml (1 pint) milk
- 300ml (½ pint) double or whipping cream
- 1 vanilla pod, split
- 1 tablespoon finely grated lemon or orange zest
- 50g (2oz) caster sugar
- freshly grated nutmeg
- 100g (4oz) Arborio rice
- 225g (8oz) raspberries
- large knob of butter, melted, and extra grated nutmeg; or icing sugar, for dusting (optional)

Raspberry rice pudding flan

Fresh raspberries are still with us, the Scottish variety at its absolute best, the soft red berries absolutely packed with flavour. This particular fruit should be with us until October, dependent on reasonable weather, so this dish has a good 2-month autumn life span.

The rice pudding is slightly different from the traditional, as it uses Arborio rice in place of the usual short-grain pudding rice. This does offer a slightly different texture and flavour, the rice being very absorbent, but each little grain maintains its consistency and texture, leaving us with a sweet risotto finish.

This recipe can be made without the tart case, purely offering the fresh raspberries to accompany the warm creamy pudding. However, the pastry case does offer an extra crisp biscuity bite.

Method Butter a 25cm (10in) flan ring, 4cm (1½in) deep, and place it on a greased baking tray. Roll out the sweet pastry and use to line the flan ring. It is best to leave any excess pastry hanging over the edge; once the tart is cooked, this can be trimmed away, leaving a neat finish. Prick the base of the pastry and chill for 30 minutes. Preheat the oven to 200°C/400°F/Gas 6.

Line the pastry case with greaseproof paper and baking beans or rice, place in the preheated oven and cook for 25 minutes. After this time, remove the beans and paper and return the pastry case to the oven for a further 10–15 minutes to seal the base. Remove from the oven, trim away the excess pastry and leave to cool.

While the pastry case is baking, make the rice pudding. Pour the milk and cream into a suitably sized saucepan, add the split vanilla pod and bring the milk to the boil. Remove the pan from the stove, add the grated lemon or orange zest, the caster sugar and a generous sprinkling of freshly grated nutmeg. Leave to stand and infuse for 10 minutes.

Add the rice to the flavoured milk, return the pan to the heat and bring to a gentle simmer. Stir the rice and cook for 30–35 minutes, until very tender and creamy. Remove the pan from the heat and take out the vanilla pod from the rice.

Arrange the raspberries in the cooked pastry case and spoon over the rice pudding. Leave to relax for 5–6 minutes, then drizzle with the butter, grating over the extra nutmeg. Alternatively, dust liberally with icing sugar and glaze quickly (to a light golden brown) under a preheated hot grill or with a gas gun (page 11), or heat long trussing needles or skewers and press these in lines across the icing-sugar-topped tart. All of these finishes are optional extras, none essential, but all presenting and eating very well. The raspberry rice pudding flan is now ready to serve.

● *For a lighter finish, the cream can be totally omitted, replacing it with an equal quantity of milk. For a richer alternative, the cream can be increased to 450ml (¾ pint), and the milk reduced to the same quantity.*

● *A tablespoon or two of raspberry jam can be spread across the tart case before the fresh fruits are added.*

Serves 8–10

- 1 tablespoon butter, plus extra for greasing
- flour, for dusting
- 225g (8oz) *Sweet shortcrust pastry* (page 203)
- 550g (1¼lb) butternut squash, peeled, deseeded and diced
- 2 eggs, beaten, plus 1 egg yolk
- 75g (3oz) soft light brown sugar
- 1 dessertspoon golden syrup
- 1 dessertspoon treacle
- 1 heaped teaspoon ground mixed spice
- 300ml (½ pint) double cream

Spicy syrup butternut tart

This recipe is a sort of classic in the USA, often finding its way on to the Thanksgiving menu. The usual main feature is pumpkin, but I have found the butternut squash just gives that extra bit of flavour, with a sweet, nutty and almond buttery edge. For an extra nutty finish, toasted chopped or flaked almonds or walnuts can be sprinkled over and dusted with icing sugar just before serving.

Method Butter and lightly flour a 20cm (8in) loose-bottomed flan case and place on a baking tray. Roll the pastry on a lightly floured surface into a large circle before lifting with a rolling pin and unwinding it across the case. Press to fit neatly, leaving any excess pastry hanging over the edge. This can be left attached while pre-baking the tart case, to ensure a neat even edge. Chill the tart case for 30 minutes to relax and set. Preheat the oven to 180°C/350°F/Gas 4.

To make the filling, melt the butter in a large saucepan or roasting tray. If using the saucepan, add the diced squash and cook on a low heat, cover with a lid and stir from time to time. Cook the squash for 20–30 minutes, until tender, then transfer to a colander and allow any excess juices to drain. If using a roasting tray, simply melt the butter in the tray, add the squash and cover with a double layer of foil. Then bake in the preheated oven for the same cooking time until tender, also draining in a colander.

While the squash is cooling, pre-cook the pastry case. Prick the base of the pastry case with a fork and line with greaseproof paper and baking beans or rice. Bake in the preheated oven for 20 minutes, then remove the beans and greaseproof paper. Return the tart case to the oven and bake for a further 5 minutes, then remove from the oven. Leave to rest for 10 minutes. Trim away the excess pastry and brush the pastry case with a little of the beaten egg. Reduce the oven temperature to 160°C/325°F/Gas 3.

Gently squeeze away any excess moisture left in the squash, before pushing it through a sieve into a clean bowl (if blitzed in a food processor, the consistency tends to become too wet and loose). Spoon the sugar, syrup and treacle into the purée, then add the mixed spice, eggs and extra yolk, and the cream. Pour the tart mix into the pre-baked tart case and cook for 35–40 minutes. It's best to check the tart every 15 minutes. If it seems to be over-colouring, cover lightly with foil. Once baked and just set, remove from the oven and leave to cool until just warm.

This eats very well with whipped or pouring cream.

Serves 4–6

- 4 medium Cox's Orange Pippin apples, peeled and quartered
- 8 apricots, halved and stoned
- juice and finely grated zest of ½ lemon
- 1 teaspoon finely grated orange zest
- 2 heaped tablespoons demerara sugar
- pinch of ground cinnamon (optional)
- 150g (5oz) butter, softened, plus extra for greasing
- 2 tablespoons caster sugar
- 350g (12–15 slices) medium-sliced white bread, crusts removed
- caster or icing sugar, for dusting (optional)

Bread and butter apple and apricot pie

This certainly isn't a variation on my favourite bread and butter pudding. Instead it is more of a crumble, with fresh white breadcrumbs replacing the flour. The dessert can also be made as a traditional crumble, with fruits in the dish, topped and baked with the crumbly topping. However, the method I use here turns the dish into more of a pie, lining the base and sides of the tin with half of the crumble mix, before filling it with the fruit and topping with the remaining mix.

Cox's apples are generally in season between September and May. May sees the arrival of apricots on our shelves. Hence the two have a very short 'hello-and-goodbye' relationship during the first month of autumn.

Method Preheat the oven to 220°C/425°F/Gas 7. Slice each of the apple quarters into three pieces, then halve these into chunks. Quarter each apricot half, then mix the two fruits in a bowl with the lemon juice and zest, the orange zest, demerara sugar and cinnamon, if using.

Grease a 20 × 5cm (8 × 2in) flan tin well with the extra butter. Spoon the caster sugar into the tin and shake to coat. Tap off any excess and keep to one side. Place the white bread and butter in a food processor and blitz briefly to create a fine breadcrumb texture. Press half of the crumb mix into the base and sides of the tin, then fill with the apple and apricot mix. Add any caster sugar tapped from the tin to the remaining crumb mix and pack it on top of the fruits.

Bake the pie in the preheated oven for 1 hour 10 minutes, until golden brown and crispy. If using caster sugar or icing sugar for dusting, either can be sprinkled on top once the pie is cooked or 10 minutes before the end of the cooking time. When the pie is cooked, remove from the oven and leave to rest for 10–15 minutes.

The pie is now ready to be served; cut it into wedges or simply spoon it into bowls. The best accompaniments for this dessert are *Crème Anglaise* (page 204) or extra-thick cream.

● *Once cooked, the pie may well be crisp enough to remove from the tin. This is not essential, but does show off its crumbly texture.*

Serves 8–10

For the pastry
- 350g (12oz) plain flour, plus extra for dusting
- pinch of salt
- 175g (6oz) butter, diced, plus extra for greasing
- 75g (3oz) caster or icing sugar, sifted
- 1 egg, beaten, plus 1 egg for brushing
- 2–3 tablespoons milk

For the filling
- 675g (1½lb) Egremont Russet apples
- 1.25kg (2½lb) Bramley's Seedling apples
- large knob of butter
- 75g (3oz) caster sugar (or 100g/4oz for a slightly sweeter finish)
- finely grated zest of 1 orange
- finely grated zest of 1 lemon
- 1 heaped tablespoon semolina

Bramley and Russet apple pie

This classic dessert can take on so many new faces. The old English Bramley apple is normally cooked in a relatively deep pie dish and simply covered with the pastry before baking. This method has found great success, because of its pure simplicity. Another pie-making technique is one that, they say, was introduced to us from America. Basically it consists of the apples totally encased in pastry. There are many other combinations, with the French extra-fine apple tart and the upside-down-baked caramelized *tarte Tatin* amongst them. Here I have chosen a totally encased pie. This does take a little longer to prepare, but, for me, finishes with the best of results. The quantity of apple slices is balanced well with the quantity of crispy pastry within which it is cooked.

The autumn and winter months, particularly October, provide us with a wonderful selection of home-grown apples. Here we use the Bramley's Seedling, which has an established reputation for use in cooking; its piquant bite will never let you down, needing only a slight helping hand with a sprinkling of sugar to counter its sharp cut on the palate. The Egremont Russet is also eating at its absolute prime in October. The flesh is surrounded by a rusty-coloured skin and has a distinctive, nutty, pear-like taste. Texturally the two apples marry very well, and the finished flavour is the best of combinations.

I also like to add finely grated orange and lemon zest. Neither begins to take over, but instead each adds an extra touch. The sweet pastry used here will offer exactly the right quantity to line and top the pie mould,

leaving a crisp finish. For a thicker finish, the quantities can be increased to 450g (1lb) flour, 225g (8oz) butter, 100g (4oz) icing sugar, 1 egg, 50–75ml (2–2½fl oz) milk and a pinch of salt.

Method First make the pastry. Sift together the flour and salt. Rub the diced butter into the flour until the mixture resembles breadcrumbs, before adding the caster or icing sugar. Work the beaten egg into the mix, then slowly add the milk until it just begins to form into a dough. It is always best not to overwork the pastry; if you do, the finished result will lose some of its shortness. Cover and leave to rest in the fridge for 30 minutes.

While the pastry is resting, prepare the apples. Keeping the varieties separate, halve each apple and cut each half into three wedges. Using a paring knife, cut away the skins and cores. The apples can be left as they are or cut once more into thinner wedges, or simply cut in half for a chunkier finish.

Melt the butter in a large saucepan and, once bubbling, add the Russet apples and cook them on a medium heat for 5–6 minutes, then add the Bramleys and the sugar, along with the orange and lemon zest. Continue to cook on a medium heat, turning from time to time, until the apples are beginning to soften. Strain the apples in a colander, collecting all juices in a bowl beneath. Leave to cool.

Preheat the oven to 200°C/400°F/Gas 6. Grease a baking tray and butter and flour a 25 × 4cm (10 × 1½in) flan ring. On a floured surface, roll two-thirds of the pastry into a circle large enough to line the prepared

flan ring. Press the pastry well into the ring, leaving any excess pastry hanging over the edge. Allow to rest in the fridge for 20 minutes.

Line the rested pastry case with greaseproof paper and baking beans or rice. Bake the pastry case in the preheated oven for 25 minutes. Remove the beans and paper, return the case to the oven and continue to bake for a further 5–10 minutes to crisp the base. Remove the case from the oven and carefully cut away the excess pastry hanging over the edge of the ring. Leave to cool. Trimming the case while still warm will prevent the pastry from splitting as it cools and retracts within the ring. Should the pastry have split during its cooking process, simply fill with raw pastry pieces once cold.

Roll a long thin strip from a small piece of the remaining pastry. Beat the remaining egg, brush the edge of the cooked pastry case with a little of it and cover with the thin strip of pastry. This will ensure the pastry lid will stick to the sides and not shrink over the pie. Brush this new edge with egg and brush the base of the case itself. Sprinkle the semolina into the case. This will help absorb excess liquor from the apples, preventing the pastry from becoming too wet. Spoon the apples into the case (the reserved apple syrup can be offered to accompany the finished pie). Roll the remaining pastry into a disc slightly larger than the flan ring. Roll on to the rolling pin and place across the top. Press the edge gently, then trim away any excess. Cut a small cross in the centre of the pastry to release excess steam from the pie. Leave to rest for just 10 minutes. During this short rest period, increase the oven

temperature to 230°C/450°F/Gas 8. Brush the pie with egg and bake for 25–30 minutes, until golden brown. Remove from the oven and leave to relax for 15–20 minutes before removing the ring.

The pie is ready to serve, along with any saved apple syrup. This pie will eat very well with fresh cream, or perhaps *Crème Anglaise* or *Prune and Armagnac custard* (page 204).

● *When peeling and preparing the apples you can place them in acidulated lemon water to help prevent discoloration. It is, however, always best to remove them from the water as soon as possible, so as not to allow the apples to absorb too much.*

● *Ground cinnamon, nutmeg or vanilla seed can also be added to this recipe for a slightly spicy finish.*

● *The sweet pastry can be made in a food processor, simply mixing to the dough stage.*

Serves 4
- 100g (4oz) caster sugar
- 400ml (13fl oz) sweet white wine
- juice and finely grated zest of
  1 lemon
- 2 Cox's Orange Pippin apples
- 3 Comice pears

For the sabayon
- 3 large egg yolks
- 1 vanilla pod, split

Poached apples and pears with a lemon and vanilla sabayon

In the last days of autumn, Cox's Orange Pippin apples are already with us and the sweet and succulent Comice pear is just perfect to enjoy. In this recipe, the fruits are poached in sweet white wine, enhanced with lemon zest. Served trickled with the syrup and whipped cream alone, they will eat beautifully but, although a little more involved, whisking the syrup with egg yolks to a light frothy sabayon stage offers the perfect accompaniment for the simple fruits.

Method First make the syrup for the apples and pears. Spoon the caster sugar into a saucepan and add the sweet white wine and the lemon zest. Bring the syrup to a simmer and cook gently for 5–10 minutes, until the sugar has dissolved, slightly thickening the liquor.

While the syrup is cooking, pour the lemon juice into a bowl. Peel and quarter the apples, cutting away the core carefully with a sharp knife. (When peeling apples and pears, it is always best to peel from 'top to tail', rather than around, as this helps maintain the natural shape of the fruits.) Halve the apple quarters into wedges and place them in the lemon juice to prevent discoloration. Peel and halve the pears, then halve each piece again to provide 12 wedges. If possible, the stalk can be left on, perhaps between two wedges, to give a very natural appearance to some of the quarters. The core can also be carefully removed with a sharp knife, before the fruits are added to the lemon juice.

Once all the fruit is prepared, place all of the wedges into the simmering sweet white wine syrup, along with the lemon juice. Cover the fruits with a small disc of greaseproof paper to ensure they are fully submerged in the syrup. Bring the liquor back to a simmer and cook for 3–5 minutes. Remove the pan from the heat and leave to cool until just warm. While cooling, the fruits will continue to cook, becoming very succulent and tender.

When the fruits are just warm, make the sabayon. Spoon 100ml (3½fl oz) of the syrup into a large bowl and add the egg yolks and seeds scraped from the vanilla pod. Whisk over a saucepan of simmering water (an electric whisk or hand blender with attachment will make life a lot easier). It is important that the water is not in contact with the bowl, as this tends to scramble the egg yolks – the steam created will provide enough warmth on its own. Continue to whisk the ingredients until at least doubled in volume and creating thick ribbons. Remove the bowl from the pan.

Divide the fruits between four bowls, offering four pieces of apples and three of the pears per portion. Drizzle with a spoonful or two of the syrup, finishing the dish with the sabayon.

- *Apple or pear juice (or a mixture of both) can be used in place of the sweet white wine. If so, increase the sugar content of the syrup by 50g (2oz).*

- *The split vanilla pod, if stored in an airtight container with caster sugar, will provide a beautiful vanilla sugar with which to make other sweet dishes.*

- *For a sweeter finish to the sabayon, add 25g of caster sugar along with the egg yolks and vanilla seeds.*

Serves 4
- 5 Conference pears
- 1 large knob of butter, plus extra for greasing and brushing
- 1 tablespoon demerara sugar
- caster sugar, for coating
- whipped or pouring cream, to serve

For the sponge
- 100g (4oz) butter
- 100g (4oz) caster sugar
- finely grated zest of 2 oranges
- 2 eggs
- 100g (4oz) self-raising flour, sifted
- pinch of salt
- 1 level teaspoon freshly grated nutmeg

- 75g (3oz) cooked and peeled chestnuts (page 201), roughly chopped
- 2 tablespoons golden syrup
- 1 teaspoon black treacle

Hot pear and chestnut sponge with roasted Conference halves

The freckled, Russet-apple-look-alike Conference pear usually arrives at the beginning of October, lasting until early spring. It is from this mid-autumn month that chestnuts also begin to appear, particularly those from Spain and Portugal, which are in full flow. Here the sponge is also flavoured with orange zest, which helps the two seasonal tastes to come into their own. For maximum extravagance, a mixture of golden syrup and treacle is allowed to bleed its way into the sponge, leaving a sticky trail of flavour. This recipe makes a good alternative to Christmas pudding.

Method Peel three of the pears, halve and core them, then cut into large, roughly 2cm (¾in) dice. Melt the large knob of butter in a frying pan and, once bubbling, add the demerara sugar. When the sugar begins to caramelize, add the pears and cook quickly until golden brown and beginning to soften. Remove the pears from the pan and leave to cool.

To make the sponge, beat the butter and caster sugar with the orange zest until light and fluffy. Add the eggs, one at a time, until well mixed in. Mix together the flour, salt and nutmeg and beat into the creamy butter, along with the chestnuts.

Work together the golden syrup and treacle, then spoon into a buttered and floured 900ml (1½ pint) pudding basin (preferably plastic). Add a third of the caramelized pears. Stir the remaining pears into the sponge mix and spoon into the pudding bowl.

Cover the bowl with buttered greaseproof paper and foil, then place in a hot steamer and cook for 1¼–1½ hours.

If you don't have a steamer, simply place the bowl in a saucepan, fill with hot water halfway up the bowl, cover with a lid and steam for the same amount of time. Check the level of the water from time to time to make sure it doesn't run dry. If a plastic bowl has been used, it is best to place a small plate or a piece of cardboard in the pan, to prevent it making contact with the bottom of the hot pan.

About 30 minutes before the sponge is due to be ready, prepare the remaining two pears. Preheat the oven to 200°C/400°F/Gas 6. Peel the pears and halve lengthwise, cutting carefully through the stalk and leaving it on for presentation, if possible. Scoop out the core with a coffee spoon or melon baller. Alternatively, leave the pears in their natural shape with the cores left in. Dry the pear halves on kitchen paper, then brush all over with butter and dip in the caster sugar to coat. Place the pears, flat-side down, on a baking sheet.

Bake in the preheated oven for 15 minutes, turn the pears over and baste with any syrup juices. Return them to the oven and continue to roast for a further 5–10 minutes. The pears should now have taken on a rich golden colour. If slightly opaque, finish the colouring process under a preheated grill. Once the sponge is cooked, remove it from the steamer and leave it to stand for 5 minutes before turning it out on to a plate.

To serve, divide the pudding into four portions and garnish each with a roasted pear half, trickling them with any juices. Serve with whipped or pouring cream.

winter

It's winter and the final season of the year is with us. The first of its three months offers frosty starts to our mornings, with the crackling sound of the family fire joining us later in the day. For many of us, daylight hardly shows its face at all, with overcast mornings leading into the return of darkness by four o'clock in the afternoon. These shorter, darker days help nurture the spirit of winter.

December is, however, also the grand finale to the year. Without doubt this month holds a feel of true festivity, building up to the 25th when the real celebrations begin. Christmas is probably the most sociable time of all. It offers many opportunities for bringing family and friends together, with tables of huge feasts featuring the very best from the British winter garden, with our carrots, cabbages, parsnips and Brussels sprouts in peak condition, all showing off their various colours and flavours. Joining these much anticipated side dishes is a selection of imported fruits. The rich colours of tangerines, clementines, pineapples and cranberries furnish the shelves of every greengrocer and supermarket at this time of year, sitting proudly opposite our own slightly muddy root vegetables and gritty leeks, which, with a quick rinse, show how they are now at their absolute best. During those well-wrapped-up shopping trips for such items, the nose picks up the smoky trail of roasted chestnuts, to be enjoyed by the bagful. On the big day itself, however, they will have found their way into the turkey stuffing, or will be rolled in lashings of butter with tender, quite sweet sprouts.

A festive tradition not to be forgotten is Stilton, which sits proudly on the family table, waiting to be scooped out and accompanied by a glass of port. The attractiveness of this particular blue cheese is how easily it adapts to so many dishes. In this chapter the Stilton joins company with roasted figs and Parma ham, all drizzled with a port vinaigrette (page 178). This blend of winter flavours, presented almost in a summery style, makes the perfect start to the Christmas feast.

Amongst the very varied selection of recipes to be found here, there are alternatives to the traditional roast turkey, with *Roast turkey and cranberry Wellington* (page 150), *Crown of roast turkey* (page 147), and even, for a complete change, *Roast leg of pork with sage roast parsnips, apples and prunes* (page 160). There are also desserts, not to replace the very fruity Christmas pudding (the meal just wouldn't be the same without it), but to present to your guests as another option. *Fresh tangerine curd ice-cream with marshmallow meringues and tangerine Grand Marnier syrup* (page 186) is one, and *Cranberry, orange and port jelly with tangerine biscuit fingers* (page 185) another.

The game season continues in December and apples are still with us, one or two from the tree and others from the cold store. Almonds, quince and celeriac, along with plump scallops, turbot and salmon, which all hold a good price at this time, are ready and waiting during this final month of the year. There are also one or two

surprises, with 'exotics', many home-grown, on offer. Kohlrabi, curly kale, Jerusalem artichokes, salsify and kumquats are in evidence, holding quite a prime spot throughout all of the winter months.

As the Christmas festivities draw to a close and the first month of the new year begins, it is time for braised dishes to come into their own. One of my favourites is *Braised Seville orange beef with horseradish dumplings* (page 165). Every feature of this dish tells me that January is here, with not only the stew-and-dumplings element, but also the citrus bite of the short-seasoned Seville orange. Virtually all of the crop of this Spanish orange crosses into English waters, as in Spain it is held in little respect. Not a fruit for eating raw, it comes into its own in many a cooked dish.

So what else does this month bring us? Cod stands us in good stead throughout winter, especially topped with a walnut crust and sitting alongside the smoothest of parsnip purées (page 130). It always seems quite odd that the parsnip thrives on its frost-bitten start to the day. If you manage to come across this root vegetable grown organically, buy as many as you can, and enjoy the pleasure of just pushing away the usually coarse outer skin with your thumb. This is a time to take full advantage of all winter root vegetables – experience the abundance of home-grown Jerusalem artichokes, with kohlrabi and celeriac from British soil still on the market. And whatever else is featured on your 'must have' list, make sure cabbages are there, particularly the Savoy.

And fruits? Well, apples and pears are still available,

as well as citrus fruits, which are performing well, probably reaching their prime in this mid-winter month. And don't forget our attractive, soft, sweet friend from the southern hemisphere – the lychee.

As the days and weeks pass us by, we approach a quieter month for British foods. February is more a follow-on from the previous month, with apples, particularly the Bramley, pears and citrus fruits, the small and easily peelable varieties of orange holding their own with their larger partners, although there are one or two newcomers on offer too. Home-grown forced rhubarb offers its own 'champagne' touch to the close of winter, to celebrate the end of three glorious months. Purple sprouting broccoli is also hitting its peak in February, reminding everybody of its former pole position in the broccoli world.

In this, the coldest of our seasons, we wrap up in plenty of pullovers, thick coats, scarves and gloves, or huddle in front of a roaring fire. And that's just fine by me, for if you're hibernating at home, you're closer than ever to the eager and willing stove.

Serves 6
- butter, for greasing
- flour, for dusting
- 350g (12oz) *Shortcrust pastry* (page 203), or 225g/8oz if making one large tart

For the tart filling
- large knob of butter
- 225g (8oz) carrots, peeled and cut into small rough dice
- 150ml (¼ pint) whipping cream

- 1 egg, plus 1 egg yolk
- salt and pepper

For the kohlrabi
- 5 tablespoons olive oil
- 1 medium–large kohlrabi, peeled and cut into 5mm (¼in) dice
- 100ml (3½fl oz) *Vegetable stock* (page 197) or *Instant stock* (page 194) or water
- 1 heaped tablespoon pine nuts, chopped into halves

- juice of 2 oranges (optional)
- 1 tablespoon white wine vinegar
- 1 teaspoon Dijon mustard (optional)
- generous pinch of sugar
- 1 shallot, finely chopped and rinsed under cold water
- 1–2 tablespoons crème fraîche or soured cream (optional)
- 1 heaped tablespoon picked and torn coriander leaves

Mashed carrot tart with a kohlrabi, pine nut and coriander dressing

Mashed is exactly how the carrot will be before meeting up with the remaining tart ingredients. Using individual tartlet cases is my first choice, each presented as a starter surrounded by the dressing.

Kohlrabi are the trendy-looking round vegetables, sprouting antennas. Once trimmed and peeled, they impersonate the turnip very well, but only in looks. The kohlrabi is more delicate, offering a slightly sweet finish, big enough to take on the pine nut, coriander and carrot.

Method Butter and flour 6 × 7.5–9cm (3–3½in) tartlet cases or a 20cm (8in) case if making one large tart. Roll the pastry thinly on a lightly floured surface and divide it into six pieces, lining each tartlet case and leaving any excess hanging over the edge. Cover the base of each tartlet with a disc of parchment paper and fill with baking beans or rice. Chill for 30 minutes. Preheat the oven to 200°C/400°F/Gas 6.

Bake the pastry cases in the preheated oven for 20 minutes. Remove the paper and beans and return the cases to the oven for a further 5–6 minutes to help set the base of the pastry. Remove the tarts from the oven and allow to cool, then trim away the excess pastry. Reduce the oven temperature to 160°C/325°F/Gas 3.

Melt the knob of butter in a small saucepan and add the chopped carrots. Cover with a lid and cook on a low heat until the carrots have softened. To help this along, a tablespoon or two of water can also be added to create steam. Once softened, pulp the carrots with a potato masher, leaving some lumpy pieces for texture. For the smoothest of finishes, purée in a food processor.

Bring the cream to a simmer and pour over the purée, mixing in well. Whisk in the egg and egg yolk, and season with salt and pepper. Spoon the mixture between the tartlet cases, sit them on a baking tray and bake in the oven for 15–20 minutes (one large tart will need 30–35 minutes), until just set. Remove from the oven and allow to relax for 5–10 minutes before serving.

While the flans are in the oven, cook the kohlrabi. Heat 3 tablespoons of the oil in a saucepan and add the diced kohlrabi, cooking on a medium heat for 5–6 minutes. Add the stock and bring to a gentle simmer. After 5 minutes, increase the heat and allow the stock to boil and reduce by half.

Heat the remaining olive oil in a frying pan and roast the pine nuts to a golden brown, seasoning with salt and pepper. Strain the pine nuts in a sieve, collecting the oil in a bowl below. The kohlrabi can also be strained in the sieve, the oil and juices mixing below.

Boil the orange juice, if using, until reduced by three-quarters. Whisk the orange juice, vinegar, mustard, if using, sugar and shallot into the reserved oil and juices. This can be whisked into the crème fraîche or soured cream, if using, or just use the chosen cream to drizzle over the kohlrabi once presented on the plates.

Place the carrot tarts on to plates. Add the kohlrabi and pine nuts to the dressing, along with the torn coriander leaves. Spoon the dressing around the warm tarts and serve.

● *If the carrot and cream mixture is very loose, two whole eggs will be needed, omitting the egg yolk.*

Serves 4–6

- 1kg (2¼lb) kohlrabi
- salt and pepper
- 8 rashers of streaky bacon, smoked or unsmoked
- 150ml (¼ pint) crème fraîche
- 150ml (¼ pint) single cream
- 2 garlic cloves, crushed (optional)
- butter, for greasing
- 100g (4oz) Gruyère or Cheddar cheese, grated (Parmesan can also be used)

Baked kohlrabi with bacon and cheese

Kohlrabi is sadly not one of the most popular of vegetables in this country, being better appreciated in Europe and further east in India and China. It has a sort of turnip shape with stalks that have decided to sprout from within at random. When it is peeled, the white flesh beneath resembles the flavours of radish and celeriac, with a texture a little like that of water chestnuts. Kohlrabi suits almost all types of cooking – roasting, sautéeing and boiling, with one of the best methods baking *au gratin*, with lots of cream and cheese.

Here I have added rashers of bacon to sit between the layers to provide a contrast of flavour. The bacon can be omitted, leaving this dish totally vegetarian. Spinach or curly kale can also be used as a good central layer of vegetables. I normally serve this dish as an accompaniment to a main course (usually a roast meat), these quantities providing enough for six. It can, however, be served as a neat supper dish for four.

Method Preheat the oven to 160°C/325°F/Gas 3 and a grill to medium. Peel the kohlrabi quite generously to remove the outer skin and reveal the white flesh and cut into 5mm (¼in) thick slices. Cook in boiling salted water for 10 minutes, until just becoming tender. Drain in a colander, leaving excess steam to be released. Grill the bacon until crispy.

Stir together the crème fraîche and single cream, then add the crushed garlic, if using. Season with salt and pepper. Add the kohlrabi slices, mixing them in so all are coated. Layer the slices in a greased shallow 1.25 litre (2 pint) ovenproof dish, sprinkling each layer with the cheese of your choice. Once half have been placed in the dish, lay over the bacon rashers, then continue with the kohlrabi layers. Pour over any remaining cream and sprinkle with the last of the grated cheese. Bake in the preheated oven for 30–40 minutes, until completely tender and bubbling golden brown on top.

- *You can use just crème fraîche or single cream, if you prefer.*

Serves 4
- 450g (1lb) Jerusalem artichokes
- squeeze of lemon juice
- large knob of butter
- 1 tablespoon olive oil
- 1 large onion, finely chopped
- 300ml (½ pint) *Vegetable stock* (page 197) or *Chicken* or *Instant stock* (page 194)
- 300ml (½ pint) milk
- salt and pepper
- 150ml (¼ pint) single cream (optional)
- freshly grated nutmeg
- groundnut oil, for frying

Palestine soup with crispy Jerusalem artichokes

This Palestinian soup is made purely of creamed Jerusalem artichokes. The crispy artichokes accompanying it offer another texture and give a fuller flavour to the finished soup.

The Jerusalem artichoke is a brown-skinned tuber resembling the ginger root. It was named *girasole* by the Italians, meaning 'sunflower', as the vegetable's yellow flower also turns towards the sun; *girasole* became corrupted to 'Jerusalem'. It is not related in any way to the globe artichoke, but its white flesh has a similar nutty, sweet flavour and crunchy texture to that of a raw globe artichoke, hence the latter part of its name. It responds well to most of the treatments given to potatoes – puréeing, roasting and sautéeing.

Jerusalem artichokes are available between the months of October and March, so this soupy recipe is probably best made during the last month of winter, February, to use up the remaining few. Whenever choosing Jerusalem artichokes, it is always best to try to find the smoothest and cleanest available, rather than spend hours cleaning the many over-knobbly ones on the market.

Method Save one large or two smaller artichokes for frying. Scrub or peel the remainder thoroughly, then slice thinly or chop into rough dice. As they are cut, place in a bowl of water acidulated with lemon juice to prevent discoloration.

Melt the knob of butter in a saucepan with the olive oil and add the onion. Cook on a low heat for several minutes, until the onions are beginning to soften without colouring. Drain the artichokes and pat them dry with kitchen paper or a cloth, then add them to the pan with the onion. Cook for 6–8 minutes, then add the stock and milk. Bring to a simmer, season with salt and pepper and cook for 20 minutes, or until the artichokes are well softened. During the simmering of the artichoke soup the milk may take on a curdled consistency; this is due to the artichokes being placed in acidulated water but, once liquidized, a totally smooth finish is regained.

Liquidize the soup in batches until smooth, straining it through a sieve, if necessary, for the creamiest of finishes. Return the soup to a saucepan and warm through, then add the single cream, if using. If the single cream is to be omitted and the soup is too thick, simply loosen with a little more milk. Adjust the seasoning with salt and pepper, and add the freshly grated nutmeg.

To make the Jerusalem artichoke crisps, scrub or peel the reserved artichokes and then slice very thinly, preferably on a mandolin slicer. Dry on a cloth or kitchen paper. Heat 1cm (½in) of groundnut oil in a saucepan or wok. Once hot, fry the slices in batches, until all are crispy and golden brown. Once fried, season with a pinch of salt.

Serve the soup in bowls, topping each with some of the crispy slices.

● *The crispy artichokes are by no means essential. Serving the soup with fresh crusty bread is just as good.*

● *An extra squeeze of lemon juice can be added to the soup once finished, for a slight citrus edge.*

Serves 4

- 15g (½oz) butter, plus a large knob for the onions and extra for greasing
- 15g (½oz) plain flour
- 300ml (½ pint) milk
- 100–150ml (3½fl oz–¼ pint) whipping cream
- salt and pepper
- freshly grated nutmeg
- 1kg (2¼lb) Jerusalem artichokes (unpeeled weight)
- 2 large onions, sliced
- 100g (4oz) Gruyère cheese, grated

Cheese and onion Jerusalem artichoke gratin

Jerusalem artichokes, the slightly knobbly tubers that look a bit like a Pink Fir Apple potato, begin to appear at the beginning of October, quite often lasting until the beginning of March. Gratinéed artichokes are quite classic, normally just sliced raw and seasoned, then topped with lots of cream. This is, without doubt, the quickest and easiest route to take, as well as the richest and most expensive.

In this recipe, I make a béchamel sauce based on butter, flour and milk, just lifted with some cream and enhanced with a binding of onions and cheese. This dish eats particularly well with most roast meats, and is a superb accompaniment to most roast game.

Method Preheat the oven to 160ºC/325ºF/Gas 3. Melt the measured butter in a saucepan and, once bubbling, add the flour. Cook on a low heat for 2 minutes. While cooking the butter and flour (known as a *roux*), bring the milk to a simmer. Add this a little at a time, stirring it into the *roux* base. Once all of the milk has been added, the sauce can be whisked quickly to ensure a smooth consistency. Simmer the sauce very gently for 15 minutes, then add 100ml (3½fl oz) of the whipping cream and season with salt, pepper and nutmeg. If slightly too thick, add the remaining cream to give a coating consistency.

While the sauce is cooking, peel the artichokes, then cut them into 5mm (¼in) slices. Blanch them in boiling salted water for 5 minutes, drain and allow to cool. Melt the knob of butter in a frying pan. Once bubbling, add the sliced onions and season with salt and pepper. Cook gently for 5–6 minutes, until the onions have softened. Mix the artichokes with the sliced onions and half of the grated cheese, then stir in the creamy sauce. Spoon the mix into a greased ovenproof gratin dish and finish with a sprinkling of the remaining cheese.

Finish the Jerusalem artichokes in the preheated oven for 30–40 minutes, until tender and golden brown. The dish is now ready to serve as a vegetable accompaniment.

Serves 4
- 550g (1¼lb) new potatoes (see below)
- 40g (1½oz) butter
- 1 tablespoon caster sugar

- 16 cooked chestnuts (page 201 – if braising, omit the glazed finish), cut into quarters
- salt and pepper
- 1 heaped tablespoon 1cm (½in) chive sticks

Sweetened potatoes and chestnuts with chives

New potatoes hold two seasons – the first earlies between May and July and the second earlies from August through to March. For this dish, varieties like Charlotte or Estima will fit the bill, first cooked in boiling water, then caramelized with chestnuts in butter and sugar. The flavours suit many different main courses, although eating with most game birds and meats would be the first choice. They also make a very good stand-in for roast potatoes, perhaps even to accompany the Christmas turkey.

Method Cook the potatoes in boiling salted water for approximately 20 minutes, until tender. Drain in a colander.

Melt the butter in a frying pan and add the caster sugar. Cook on a low heat for 1–2 minutes, then add the cooked potatoes and chestnuts. Continue to cook on a medium heat for 5–6 minutes, turning the potatoes and chestnuts from time to time, to ensure an even caramelization.

Season with salt and pepper and sprinkle with the chive sticks. The rich golden potatoes and chestnuts are ready to serve.

● *Once boiled, the new potatoes can be peeled before caramelizing.*

● *This recipe can be doubled (or more) in volume, providing plenty for larger numbers.*

Serves 4–6 as a snack or starter (makes 30–35 fritters)
- 1kg (2¼lb) parsnips, peeled
- salt and pepper
- ½ onion, very finely chopped
- 2 eggs
- 25g (1oz) butter, softened
- 25g (1oz) plain flour

For the blue cheese walnut whip
- 75g (3oz) blue cheese (see below), crumbled and at room temperature
- 150ml (¼ pint) *Mayonnaise* (page 198, or bought)
- juice of 1 lime
- 8–10 walnut halves, chopped into small pieces
- pinch of cayenne pepper
- 100ml (3½fl oz) double cream
- oil, for deep-frying

Parsnip fritters with blue cheese walnut whip

Deep-frying these fritters gives them the nutty caramel amber edges so recognizable when roasting the white roots. Not difficult to make, they are the perfect warm snack for winter social gatherings and the blue cheese and walnut whip is the perfect dip for them. A selection of blue cheeses can be used, but my favourite is the Irish cow's-milk Cashel Blue, made in roughly the same way as Roquefort (a ewe's-milk cheese that whips just as well into this recipe), but with a slightly softer texture and less salty finish. The whip is put together with mayonnaise (for home-made, try the one featured on page 198, but I do admit a quality bought variety works just as well), lime juice, double cream and walnuts.

Method Quarter the parsnips lengthwise and remove the central woody core. Cook in boiling salted water until completely tender, then drain. Place the parsnips back in the saucepan and stir over a low heat, allowing them to dry. Then purée with a potato masher for a coarse finish or blitz until smooth in a food processor.

Rinse the chopped onion in a sieve (this helps remove its raw flavour), dry it well and add to the parsnips along with the eggs and butter. Add the flour, beating it in well. Season with salt and pepper.

While the parsnips are cooking, make the whip. Whisk the cheese into the mayonnaise, breaking it down until reasonably smooth. Add the lime juice and walnuts, and season with a pinch of cayenne pepper. Lightly whip the cream into soft peaks, then gently fold it in to achieve the required whipped consistency. It can now be chilled for a firmer consistency or served at room temperature for the creamiest of finishes.

Preheat the oil for deep-frying to between 160°C/325°F and 180°C/350°F. The parsnip mix can literally just be spooned (using dessert or soup spoons) into the hot fat (oiling a spoon first helps create a non-stick effect). Turn the fritters from time to time, until a deep golden brown. Once they are cooked, remove them from the hot fat, drain on kitchen paper and lightly salt. The fritters and walnut whip are now ready to be enjoyed.

● *The walnuts can be blanched in boiling water for a minute, which will enable their skins to be scraped away. It's a bit of a fiddly job, but will remove the bitter edge that the skins carry.*

● *If chilled, the blue cheese walnut whip can be piped into a bowl to emulate its chocolate predecessor.*

**Serves 6 as a starter
or 4 as a main course**
- 900g (2lb) parsnips, peeled
- salt and pepper
- 2 tablespoons olive or cooking oil
- 2 tablespoons clear honey
- 1–2 tablespoons balsamic
  vinegar

For the risotto
- 50g (2oz) butter
- 1 large onion, finely chopped
- 1 large garlic clove, crushed
  (optional)
- 225g (8oz) Vialone, Arborio or
  other risotto rice

- 1 litre (1¾ pints) hot *Vegetable
  stock* (page 197) or *Instant stock*
  (page 194)
- 225g (8oz) fresh spinach, picked
- 4 tablespoons whipping cream
- 50g (2oz) Parmesan cheese,
  finely grated

Sharp roasted parsnips with creamed spinach and Parmesan cheese risotto

Parsnips are with us, and at their best, throughout the autumn and winter months. The sharp edge is to be found not only on their pointed tips, but also through the extra kick these vegetables are given with a caramelization of honey and balsamic vinegar. The touch of vinegar balances the sweetness of the honey and the natural sweetness of the parsnip. The risotto is flavoured and coloured with a spinach cream purée. Parmesan, a cheese so often added to risottos, works well with both vegetables. Spinach loves this cheese flavour, as does the parsnip. Roasted, this root vegetable adores a finishing of finely grated fresh Parmesan. So all the tastes work for one another here, with a good variety of textures.

This is a vegetarian dish that somehow suits a cold January day perfectly, the warming smoothness of the risotto and crispy bite of the parsnip helping you forget what is happening outside.

Method Preheat the oven to 220°C/425°F/Gas 7. Quarter the parsnips lengthwise and remove the central core from each piece. This woody part of the vegetable can spoil the tender 'meat'.

Blanch the parsnips in rapidly boiling salted water for just 2 minutes, quickly drain in a colander and allow any excess moisture to steam away. Heat the oil in a roasting tray on top of the stove. Fry the parsnips in this over a medium heat, until golden brown on all sides, allowing them to become slightly burnt on the edges. This will help create a slightly bitter flavour to counter the natural sweetness of the vegetable. Roast in the preheated oven for 20 minutes.

After the parsnips have been roasting for 10 minutes, start the risotto. Melt half of the butter in a large saucepan and add the chopped onion and garlic, if using. Cook on a low heat for 6–8 minutes, until the onion is beginning to soften. Add the rice and continue to cook for a further 2 minutes. Pour in a quarter of the hot stock and simmer very gently, stirring until virtually all of the stock has been absorbed. Just a ladleful at a time can now be added each time the stock has been absorbed, while you continue stirring. Repeat this stirring and adding process for approximately 20 minutes, until the rice is creamy and tender, with still the slightest of bites. Not all of the stock may be needed to reach this stage.

While the risotto is cooking, make the spinach cream. Shred the spinach leaves quite finely. Pour 2 tablespoons of water into a large saucepan on top of the stove. Once bubbling, add the spinach, season with salt and pepper and cook for 6–7 minutes. The spinach will now be completely tender. Transfer the spinach and liquor from the pan into a liquidizer and add the cream. Blitz to a smooth purée and keep to one side.

Remove the parsnips from the oven and pour over the honey. Return the parsnips to the oven and continue roasting, turning them from time to time, for a further 10 minutes. Remove the parsnips from the oven and place on top of the stove. If the honey is only lightly caramelized, place on a medium heat, allowing the honey to colour as the vegetables are turned in the pan. Once approaching a rich deep golden brown, carefully add a tablespoon of the vinegar (this may well begin to spit once in the pan); for a sharper bite, add the remaining tablespoon. Turn the parsnips once or twice more before removing from the heat and seasoning with salt and pepper.

To finish the risotto, stir the spinach cream, Parmesan and remaining butter into the rice, then check for seasoning with salt and pepper. The complete dish is now ready to serve – offer both components separately or spoon the risotto into large bowls and top with the sharp roasted parsnips.

● *An alternative finishing method for this dish is just to add the finely shredded raw spinach to the rice, about 6–7 minutes before the end of the risotto's cooking time. The cream can then be omitted or added at the very end.*

● *Thin Parmesan shavings can be sprinkled over the finished dish.*

Serves 4

- 100g (4oz) cooked ham (one 5mm/¼in thick slice should be plenty)
- 450g (1lb) small Brussels sprouts
- salt and pepper
- 1 dessertspoon sesame seeds
- 1 tablespoon sesame oil
- knob of butter

Sesame and ham sprouts

Whenever choosing Brussels sprouts, it is important to buy them as small and tight-leafed as possible. These signs will indicate their freshness, and they will thus need less cooking time. The ones you should steer clear of are the loose-leafed ones, almost like small fully grown cabbages, or those that are yellowing around the edges.

Bacon and sprouts do eat well together, but for a change I'm introducing ham. This adds a more subtle bacony touch, with the roasted sesame seeds enhancing the already nutty flavour of the sprout.

This recipe is easily doubled/trebled in volume for larger numbers at Christmas.

Method Cut the slice of ham into 5mm (¼in) dice and chill until needed. To prepare the sprouts, remove any damaged outside leaves, then halve each sprout. Cook them in a large saucepan of rapidly boiling salted water for a few minutes until tender, but still with the slightest of bites. Drain in a colander.

While the sprouts are cooking, heat a non-stick frying pan and add the sesame seeds. Cook on a medium heat for just a minute or two to roast the seeds to a golden brown. Remove the seeds from the pan. Add the sesame oil to the pan, along with the knob of butter, and warm the ham in the bubbling butter and oil, then add the drained sprouts. Increase the heat and fry for just 1–2 minutes, then season with salt and pepper.

To finish, add the roasted sesame seeds, and spoon the sprouts into a vegetable dish.

● *If the sprouts are particularly small, it is best to leave them whole, rolling them in the oil, butter and seeds once cooked.*

● *The sprouts can be cooked in advance, refreshed in iced water, drained and chilled until required. To reheat, either microwave or plunge them back into boiling water and simmer for a minute before draining.*

● *Chopped hazelnuts or walnuts, with their respective oils, can be used in place of the sesame seeds.*

**Serves 6–8 as a starter
or 4–6 as a main course**
For the pastry
- 100g (4oz) walnut halves
- 175g (6oz) unsalted butter at room temperature, plus extra for greasing
- 1 small egg
- 225g (8oz) plain flour, plus extra for dusting
- salt and pepper

For the filling
- 450g (1lb) broccoli
- 2 large shallots, finely chopped
- 100g (4oz) blue cheese (see below), crumbled
- 3 eggs, plus 1 egg yolk
- 150ml (¼ pint) double cream
- 150ml (¼ pint) milk
- cayenne pepper (optional)

Broccoli, blue cheese and walnut tart

Here the walnuts are to be found in the pastry, while the filling holds the soft creamy blue cheese broccoli. Broccoli is available throughout the year, but without doubt it is in the winter months, particularly January, when this vegetable begins to take on a fuller flavour and colour.

For an extra bite to the filling, chopped shallots are added, creating a cheese and onion flavour. Gorgonzola, Dolcelatte or Stilton can all be used, each providing its own distinctive taste.

Method First make the pastry. Blitz the walnut halves to a ground almond consistency in a small food processor or coffee grinder. In a food processor, mix together the butter and the egg. This mixture may well curdle, but will combine again when other ingredients are added. Add the flour, a pinch of salt and the walnuts and mix to a dough. Wrap the pastry in cling film and chill for a minimum of 30 minutes.

While the pastry is resting, make the filling. Trim the broccoli stalks and divide into small florets, splitting any large ones in half. Blanch the broccoli pieces in boiling salted water for a few minutes until tender, not leaving the pieces too firm. Refresh in iced water and leave to drain. Also rinse the finely chopped shallots under cold water, as this releases their basic raw flavour, leaving a more edible finish, but still with a bite.

On a lightly floured surface roll the pastry large enough to line a greased 25cm (10in) flan ring – any excess pastry can be left hanging over the edge. Place on a greased baking tray. Chill for 20 minutes to allow to

rest. Preheat the oven to 200°C/400°F/Gas 6. Line the rested pastry case with greaseproof paper and baking beans or rice. Cook in the preheated oven for 20 minutes. Remove, allow to cool and then remove the paper and beans. The excess pastry can now be trimmed away, leaving a neat finish.

Reduce the oven temperature to 160°C/325°F/Gas 3. Place the broccoli florets in the case, season with salt and pepper and sprinkle with the chopped shallots and crumbled blue cheese. Whisk together the eggs, egg yolk, double cream and milk and season with salt and pepper or cayenne pepper.

Pour the mixture into the pastry case and cook in the oven for 35–40 minutes, until the flan is just beginning to set. Should the flan begin to colour too quickly, cover it loosely with foil or greaseproof paper.

Once cooked, the flan is best left to rest for 20 minutes, allowing the filling to set to a warm creamy texture.

● *After the pastry case has been baked blind, it can be returned to the oven for 10 minutes, without the baking beans or rice, if you prefer a crisper finish.*

● *A tossed green salad will eat very well with the flan.*

● *Walnut or olive oil can be drizzled over each portion just before serving.*

Serves 4 generously
- 1 very large or 2 medium
  Savoy cabbages
- 25g (1oz) butter
- salt and pepper

English cabbage plate

Most cabbage varieties are with us during autumn and winter, taking pride of place in the three months running from December. This recipe uses the crinkly, crisp Savoy cabbage, which has a fairly tough image, with its outer leaves giving the impression of needing long, slow cooking before softening. In fact, they require very little, the 'tough' leaves becoming tender within minutes.

The title of this recipe describes how the dish is to be presented, pressed between two plates, creating an almost gâteau-like finish. This is a French form of presentation that often carries the name *choux à l'Anglaise*, meaning English cabbage.

The large outer leaves are first blanched, then used to line plates or bowls. The remaining cabbage is shredded, cooked and buttered to sit in between. Once pressed together and reheated, the cabbage plate is ready for presenting and cutting.

Here the recipe is being kept as simple as it sounds. However, numerous extras can accompany the filling. Sliced onions and bacon cooked in butter are my first choice, with diced buttered winter vegetables – carrots, parsnips, turnips and swede – coming a close second. The English cabbage plate will accompany many a dish, in particular a classic Sunday roast.

Method Remove the large outer leaves of the cabbage, rinse well and cut away the central stalks. Enough large leaves will be needed to cover two plates completely. Cut the remaining cabbage into six wedges, trim and discard the central stalks from each. Finely shred the wedges, then rinse in a colander. Blanch the large outside leaves in rapidly boiling salted water for 5–6 minutes, until tender, refresh in iced water and dry on a kitchen cloth. Blanch the shredded cabbage in two or three batches in the boiling water, cooking each batch for just a few minutes, until tender, then refresh and drain. Cooking the cabbage handfuls at a time will speed up the cooking process, as the water maintains its heat – the cabbage will stew if too much is cooked at once.

Line each plate with cling film and brush with a little of the butter. Arrange the large leaves over both plates to cover them completely. Melt the remaining butter, add it to the shredded cabbage and season well with salt and pepper.

Spoon the buttered cabbage on to one of the plates, leaving a 5mm (¼in) border around the edge. Place the other leaf-covered plate on top and squeeze the two together firmly, allowing any excess liquid to drain away. Chill until needed. For extra weight, more plates can be placed on top to press the cabbage down.

To serve, simply microwave for several minutes according to the wattage of the microwave, lifting one of the plates to check the cabbage is heated through. Once ready, remove a plate and layer of cling film, place a suitable presentation plate on top and turn the whole thing over. Remove the other plate and cling film, cut the cabbage into wedges and serve.

● *If a microwave is unavailable, omit the cling film and simply butter ovenproof plates. Once pressed together, bake in an oven, preheated to 190°C/375°F/ Gas 5, for 20–25 minutes before turning out as above.*

Serves 4–6

- 1 Savoy cabbage, trimmed of very large outside leaves
- salt and pepper
- large knob of butter
- 2 onions, finely chopped
- 2 garlic cloves, crushed (optional)
- 450g (1lb) sausagemeat (pork sausages can be skinned and used in place of the sausagemeat)
- 100g (4oz) streaky bacon or pancetta, cut into 5mm (¼in) dice
- 4 thick slices of white bread, crusts removed, broken into crumbs
- 6 sage leaves, chopped
- pinch of ground mace
- dash of Worcestershire sauce (optional)
- 2 eggs
- 4 large carrots, peeled and cut into rough 1cm (½in) dice
- 1.2 litres (2 pints) *Chicken* or *Instant stock* (page 194)
- 1 tablespoon chopped curly parsley (optional)
- cooking oil (optional)

Braised stuffed cabbage with carrots and parsley

Braised stuffed cabbage is a classic French dish but, because of its ingredients, I would like to reintroduce it as a Great British classic. The cabbage, here a typical winter Savoy, has all of its leaves blanched and is then rebuilt, formed into its original cabbage shape around a savoury stuffing. With its intense flavours, this dish will suit all the winter months.

Method Using a sharp knife, cut away each cabbage leaf from the stem, until you reach the small heart. Blanch batches of the leaves in boiling salted water for a minute or two, refreshing them in iced water. Once all are blanched and refreshed, remove them from the iced water and place them on a kitchen cloth to dry.

To make the stuffing, melt the butter in a frying pan and, once bubbling, add the chopped onions and crushed garlic, if using. Cook for 7–8 minutes, until light golden brown and softened. Leave to cool. Place the sausagemeat in a large bowl and add the diced bacon or pancetta, followed by the cooked onions, along with the breadcrumbs and chopped sage. Season with salt, pepper and a good pinch of mace, add a dash of Worcestershire sauce, if using, and mix in the eggs. To check the finished flavour, a small 'burger' of the mixture can be fried in a drop of oil for a few minutes.

To assemble the cabbage, first rinse a tea towel or muslin cloth and squeeze out all the excess water, then lay on a suitable surface. Overlap four or five of the large leaves in a circular fashion on the cloth with the stalks towards the outside and the inside of each facing up. Spread a quarter of the stuffing over and leave a 5cm

(2in) border, then place one or two layers of the next size leaves on top. Season the leaves as you build with a little salt and pepper. Spread another layer of stuffing over, then lay on more leaves. Continue this process until all of the stuffing and leaves have been used. To shape into a sphere, pull together the four corners of the muslin cloth, lift and place in a suitably sized bowl to help maintain the shape. Tie the corners of the cloth together. This can be left as it is or secured with three long pieces of string, each placed at different angles beneath the 'cabbage', pulled together and tied. This will leave an almost star-like shape, with the six wedges formed providing the six portions to be served. Now tie the cloth knot with string to help maintain the cabbage shape.

Scatter the carrots in a large saucepan and sit the cabbage on top, dome-side up. Add the chosen stock and top up with water, if needed, just to cover the cabbage. Bring to a gentle murmuring simmer, cover with a lid and cook for 1½ hours. To check, pierce with a skewer for 10 seconds, making sure it is piping hot once removed. If not, continue to cook for a further 20–30 minutes. The cabbage can now be lifted into a large colander to drain.

Check the cooking liquor for fullness of flavour. If too loose and light in depth, bring to the boil and allow to reduce by a third to a half. Once at this stage, add the chopped parsley, if using, and ladle some carrots and cooking liquor into four or six large bowls. Remove the cabbage from the cloth, cutting away the strings. Cut the stuffed cabbage into six portions and place a wedge in each bowl. *Mashed potatoes* (page 198) eat very well with this dish.

- 4 large floury potatoes, unpeeled (Maris Piper work well, as do Desirée)
- salt and pepper
- 450g (1lb) curly kale
- 2 large onions, sliced
- 50g (2oz) butter
- 12 cooked chestnuts (baked, boiled or braised, see page 201)
- freshly grated nutmeg

Buttered curly kale with broken potatoes, onions and chestnuts

Curly kale is a leafy green vegetable related to the cabbage family, available from late autumn until very early spring. It is during the months of winter that it seems to be at its best, often sold ready-picked, with the stalks removed. This vegetable does have quite an impressive history, having been around for over 2000 years, with various varieties developed by the Romans.

Here the kale is paired with some simple boiled and broken potatoes, fried sliced onions and fresh chestnuts, which are in abundance during autumn and winter, particularly in December. This rustic 'bubble and squeak' style of vegetable dish suits winter so well, offering an alternative accompaniment to roast turkey and trimmings. This side dish also eats very well with most late-autumn game recipes.

Method Place the potatoes in a large saucepan, cover with cold water and add a good pinch of salt. Bring the potatoes to the boil and simmer until slightly overcooked. Depending on the size of the potatoes, this will take 20–30 minutes. Once cooked and soft, drain the water from the pan and cover with a lid to retain the heat.

While the potatoes are cooking, trim the curly kale of its stalks and discard any bruised or yellowing leaves. Each leaf can now be torn into smaller pieces, making them far easier to eat once cooked, before rinsing and leaving to drain in a colander.

Fry the sliced onions for 5–6 minutes in a knob of the measured butter, until golden and tender. Keep to one side. Cut or break the peeled chestnuts into quarters.

To finish, bring a large saucepan of salted water to the boil and add the curly kale leaves. Cook for 3–4 minutes, until tender. Meanwhile, peel the potatoes and break them down into chunky bite-sized pieces with a fork. Melt the remaining butter in a separate pan and add the sliced onions and chestnuts. Once warm, add the potatoes and gently turn them in the pan to coat with the butter. Drain the tender kale in a colander, lightly pressing to remove excess moisture, then spoon into the potatoes. Season with salt, pepper and freshly grated nutmeg to serve.

**Serves 6 as a starter
or 4 as a main course**

- 1 leek
- 225g (8oz) Brussels sprouts
- 1 tablespoon hazelnut oil
- 1 onion, sliced
- 2 large knobs of butter
- black pepper
- 6 eggs
- 50–75g (2–3oz) Parmesan or
  Gruyère cheese, grated (optional)

For the dressing

- 10 hazelnuts, shelled
- 1 teaspoon Dijon mustard
- 1 tablespoon sherry vinegar
- 100ml (3½fl oz) crème fraîche
- 3 tablespoons hazelnut oil
- salt and pepper
- 1 heaped teaspoon finely
  snipped chives (optional)

Leek, sprouts and onion egg cake with hazelnut dressing

Cooked in a similar fashion to a Spanish omelette – cooked potato slices and fried onions set in egg – this winter supper dish takes shape in just the one pan. The leek and sprouts are the two main seasonal items, with hazelnuts adding a nutty finish to this filling omelette. Once golden brown and ready to serve, there's also the nice option of topping the cake with either grated Parmesan or Gruyère and finishing with a bubbling under a hot grill.

Method First make the dressing. Preheat the oven to 200°C/400°F/Gas 6. Roast the hazelnuts in the oven for 6–8 minutes, darkening the skins. Remove from the oven, turning the oven off, place the nuts in a cloth and rub them together to remove the skins. The nuts can now be roughly chopped.

Mix the Dijon mustard with the vinegar and half of the crème fraîche. Slowly whisk in the oil to emulsify. Add the rest of the crème fraîche and season with salt and pepper. The chopped hazelnuts and chives can be added just before serving.

To make the egg cake, split the leek lengthwise, removing the outer leaf layer. Finely shred the two halves, rinsing them in a colander under cold water to remove any grit. Leave to drain. Prepare the sprouts by pulling away and discarding any yellowing outside leaves, trimming the stalk base and halving each sprout. Finely shred them and blanch in boiling salted water for 2 minutes, then drain and allow to cool naturally.

Heat the hazelnut oil in a 20cm (8in) frying pan. Add the sliced onion and cook for 5–6 minutes, until softening and lightly coloured. Season with salt and pepper. Add a knob of butter, along with the leek, and continue to cook for a few minutes more, stirring the onion and leek together. Now add the drained sprouts and season well with salt and freshly milled black pepper. After a few minutes all will be heated through.

Beat together the eggs, season and pour over the vegetables. Cook over a reasonably high heat, until a soft scrambled egg stage is reached. Reduce the heat and leave the cake to cook without stirring for a few minutes, until the base is golden brown. To check, slide a palette knife or spatula down the side and under the omelette. Once completely golden brown, release the cake gently around the edge, then place a large dinner plate on top. The pan can now be turned over, releasing the omelette on to the main course plate. Return the frying pan to the heat and add the remaining knob of butter. Once bubbling, place the cake back in the pan, to cook the other side for 4–5 minutes, then remove from the heat. If glazing with cheese, sprinkle with the Parmesan or Gruyère and bubble under a hot grill.

The egg cake is ready to serve. Finish the dressing with the chopped hazelnuts and snipped chives, and offer it separately.

● *Any leftover egg cake teams up well with cold roast chicken for a light supper dish.*

**Serves 4 as a starter
or light snack**

- 225g (8oz) *Quick puff pastry* (page 203, or bought)
- flour, for dusting
- 50g (2oz) butter, plus 2 large knobs and extra for greasing
- 5 eggs
- 1 large or 2 small leeks
- 1 x 5mm (¼in) thick slice of cooked ham
- 1 tablespoon white wine vinegar
- 6 tablespoons *Vegetable stock* (page 197) or *Chicken* or *Instant stock* (page 194)
- 3 tablespoons crème fraîche
- salt and pepper

Puff pastry scrambled eggs and leeks with ham crème fraîche

Available from autumn to spring, leeks are one of our most versatile vegetables, and certainly one of the finest green varieties on offer during our winter months. The puff pastry is made into individual triangles, baked and then split and filled with the leeks and topped with soft scrambled egg. The dish is finished with the ham crème fraîche, which is similar in consistency to a loose butter sauce.

Method Roll the puff pastry on a floured surface into a rectangle, approximately 20 × 10cm (8 × 4in). Transfer to a greased baking tray and chill for 30 minutes to allow the pastry to relax. Preheat the oven to 220°C/425°F/Gas 7.

Once rested, trim the pastry to a neater rectangle, then cut through the centre to make two squares. Halve the squares diagonally from one corner to another, to create four triangles.

Beat one of the eggs and use to brush the pastries, then bake in the preheated oven for 20–25 minutes, until risen and golden brown. If the pastries still look a little undercooked, continue to bake for a further 5 minutes. Remove the tray from the oven and set the pastries to one side.

Split the leeks in half lengthwise, removing the outer layer. Finely slice the halves, washing off any grit in a colander. Leave the leek slices to drain.

To make the ham crème fraîche, cut the ham into 5mm (¼in) dice and set aside. Heat the white wine vinegar in a saucepan. Once almost all evaporated, add the stock and simmer until reduced by a third. Whisk in

the crème fraîche, followed by the measured butter. Season with salt and pepper.

Cut through the pastries, separating the risen lid from the base. Any uncooked layers inside can be carefully removed and discarded. Keep the pastry tops and bases warm.

Melt a knob of butter in a large saucepan and, once bubbling, add the leeks. Cook on a medium heat, stirring from time to time to ensure an even cooking, for 5–7 minutes, until very tender.

While the leeks are cooking, add the remaining eggs to the one used as the egg wash, beating with a fork to emulsify. In another saucepan, melt the remaining knob of butter and, once bubbling, add the eggs. Season with salt and pepper. As they cook, turn the eggs with a spoon reasonably vigorously, capturing every corner of the pan. When they have reached a very soft, scrambled consistency, remove the pan from the stove. This leaves you with just a minute to 'build' the rest of the dish, while the scrambled egg thickens.

Add the ham to the sauce, warming it through. Place the pastry bases on warm plates and spoon the cooked leeks loosely on top of each. Turn the scrambled eggs just once more, then spoon on top of the leeks and drizzle the ham crème fraîche around and over. Finish by placing the pastry lids on top.

- *The leeks can be quickly blanched in boiling water, cooked until tender, then refreshed in iced water and drained. Season, add a knob of butter, and they are ready to be microwaved once you are ready to serve.*

Serves 4 as a main course
- 3 onions, sliced
- 3 shallots, sliced
- 50g (2oz) raisins
- 3 tablespoons sherry vinegar
- 1 teaspoon demerara sugar
- 3 tablespoons olive oil (walnut or hazelnut oil can also be used)
- 1 scant teaspoon thyme leaves

- sea salt
- black pepper
- flour, for dusting
- 4 x John Dory fillets (each approximately 175g/6oz), skinned
- 2 tablespoons groundnut or cooking oil
- large knob of butter

For the potatoes
- 675g (1½lb) floury potatoes (Maris Piper or King Edward are best), peeled and quartered
- salt and ground white pepper
- 50g (2oz) butter
- 100–150ml (3½fl oz–¼ pint) crème fraîche
- finely grated zest and juice of 2 Seville oranges
- 1 teaspoon caster sugar (optional)

Fillet of John Dory with raisin and thyme onions and bigarade mashed potatoes

John Dory, also known as St Pierre (because of the story that's still told about the John Dory being held by St Peter himself, whose fingers gave it its characteristic black markings), is an all-year-round fish – a bonus for us all, as its texture and flavour are quite exquisite. It is at its absolute prime between the months of January and March, so the last two months of winter suit it best.

To go hand in hand with the fish we have the *bigarade* mashed potatoes. *Bigarade* is French for the bitter orange better known to us as the Seville orange. Arriving in January and gone by mid-February, this famous citrus fruit is the one that suits home-made marmalade better than any other. As it is too bitter to eat raw, cooking is its only passport to the palate. The juices and grated zest are boiled and reduced together, then spooned through the soft potatoes loosened with crème fraîche. The orangey bite of the soft potatoes blends with the flavour of onions, thyme and raisins very well, just as it has so many times before.

Method Boil the potatoes in salted water until tender, approximately 20–25 minutes, before draining off the water. The potatoes can now be mashed, adding the butter a little at a time, along with the preferred quantity of crème fraîche. Season with salt and ground white pepper.

Boil together the orange zest and juice, allowing it to reduce by at least three-quarters. The caster sugar, if using, can now be added to the reduction, balancing the sharp bitter-orange flavour. Stir the juice into the potatoes. These can now be rewarmed just before serving.

While the potatoes are cooking, prepare the onions and shallots. Blanch the onion and shallot slices in boiling water for just 15 seconds, then drain in a colander. This softens both, allowing them to be stewed with the olive oil and thyme, rather than fried.

Place the raisins, sherry vinegar and demerara sugar in a small saucepan and bring to a simmer, then remove from the heat, cover and leave to one side. This opens up the raisins, releasing their quite strong flavour.

Pour the olive oil into a saucepan and add the blanched onions and shallots and the thyme leaves. Cook over a low heat for at least 15–20 minutes, until completely softened. Add the sherry vinegar and raisins and season with sea salt and a good twist of black pepper. Continue to cook for a further 5–10 minutes, until all the flavours have combined.

Lightly flour the filleted presentation side of the John Dory and season with a pinch of salt. Heat the groundnut oil in a large frying pan (two pans may be needed). Once hot, place the fish in the pans, floured-side down. Season the fish again with salt and pepper. Fry for 3 minutes, until golden brown. Add the knob of butter and continue to fry for a further minute, then turn the fish over. Cook for just 1 more minute and turn off the heat. The residual heat of the pan will continue to fry the fish for at least 2–3 more minutes, providing enough time to plate the garnishes.

Present the raisin onions and *bigarade* mashed potatoes side by side on the plates, then place the John Dory fillets on top of the onions. Any remaining butter in the pan can, if wished, be spooned over the fish.

Serves 4 as a starter

- 225–275g (8–10oz) Jerusalem artichokes, peeled (approximately 4 artichokes)
- juice of 1 lemon
- 8–10 walnut halves
- 4 tablespoons walnut oil
- 2 tablespoons groundnut oil
- 2 tablespoons white wine vinegar
- salt and pepper
- flour, for dusting
- 2 x 450–675g (1–1½lb) gurnard, trimmed and filleted
- 2 tablespoons olive oil
- knob of butter
- 1 tablespoon chopped chives
- 2 tablespoons crème fraîche (optional)

Fillet of gurnard with fresh Jerusalem artichoke, walnut and chive salad

So underrated, the gurnard is a meaty fish with a lovely ugly look when seen whole and good firm white flesh once cooked. Mostly found relatively small, it shouldn't be too much of a problem to find 450–675g (1–1½lb) specimens, offering one fillet per portion as a starter. The skin can be removed from the fillets, but if it is bright pink to red, then leave it on for a colourful finish. Many other fish can take the place of the gurnard – plentiful mackerel fall in the same price bracket, but red mullet (probably the ultimate fish to serve with this salad) is so difficult to get hold of during the winter months that, if found, you would need a bank loan to get some in your frying pan.

Jerusalem artichokes are knobbly-looking vegetables, like new potatoes, which hit the shelves around December, taking us through to early spring. Fresh is used in the recipe title, because here they are not to be cooked, just sliced super-thin and dressed with walnuts and chives. There are no other additions, no flashy salad leaves or anything like that (although that's your decision if you want them) – serve it just as it comes, fish and artichoke salad.

Method Peel the artichokes and rinse of any impurities. The artichokes can now be sliced very thinly lengthwise. A mandolin slicer is best for this job, setting the blade almost at its finest point. As the artichokes are sliced, place them in a bowl of water acidulated with the lemon juice (saving a squeeze for the dressing), to prevent discoloration.

The walnut halves for this dish can first be plunged into boiling water, then left to stand for a minute.

Remove them one at a time and scrape off their skins. This is not essential but does result in a less bitter, nutty flavour. Chop the halves, whether peeled or not, into small chunks.

To make the dressing, whisk together the walnut and groundnut oil and the vinegar, adding a squeeze of lemon juice and seasoning with salt and pepper.

Lightly flour the skin (or skinned) side of the fillets and season with salt. Season the fillet side of the fish with salt and pepper. Seasoning with salt only on the presentation side prevents the fish from taking on black spots of pepper during its frying, spoiling the presentation.

Heat the olive oil in a large frying pan and place the fillets in, floured-side down. Fry the fish for 6 minutes over a moderate heat, allowing the skin to take on a golden-brown edge. Add the knob of butter, turn the fillets over and remove the pan from the heat. The bubbling heat of the pan will be sufficient to finish cooking the fish, providing enough time to finish the salad.

Drain the artichoke slices and place in a bowl with the walnuts and chives. Season with salt and pepper. Add half of the dressing and spoon it through the salad. The remaining dressing can be offered separately. Divide between four plates and drizzle each with a little crème fraîche, if using. Present the gurnard fillets next to the salads, trickling them with any of the cooking butter and juices left in the pan.

● *The quantity of dressing is quite generous; any not used can be kept chilled ready to flavour a good mixed salad.*

Serves 4

- 1 x 1.5kg (3¼lb) brill, head removed, fins and tail trimmed and cut into 4 portions
- 450–675g (1–1½lb) purple sprouting broccoli
- 2 tablespoons olive oil
- flour, for dusting
- salt and pepper
- 175–225g (6–8oz) button, cup or chestnut mushrooms, wiped and stalks trimmed
- 25g (1oz) butter
- 4–6 tablespoons crème fraîche
- juice of ½–1 lemon
- 24–28 seedless white grapes, peeled

Baked brill wih grapes, mushrooms and purple sprouting broccoli

It is in the wintry days, particularly during February, that these quite sensational purple broccoli tops begin to show their faces (a good year will present them a month earlier). They should be treated with as much respect as May asparagus; eating the tender colourful stalks with just some *Simple hollandaise sauce* (page 197) is nothing but heavenly, a meal that stands alone.

Here they are the equal main feature with the brill, the grapes and mushrooms becoming the shallow-fried meunière garnish, sizzling in frothy butter, that 'soufflés' with an acidic squeeze of lemon. The only extra is a spoonful or two of warmed crème fraîche to trickle over the purple sprouting broccoli, soothing and smoothing the distinctive broccoli flavour.

Method Preheat the oven to 200°C/400°F/Gas 6. The skin is being left on both sides of the brill portions. The white skin, when fried and roasted, will become crispy, with the dark skin protecting the flesh in contact with the pan as it roasts.

If small trimmed broccoli sprouts can be found, 450g (1lb) will be plenty. If they are large, then simply break the spears from the thicker central stalk. If very fresh and young, the stalks need not be peeled. This is best tested by taking a raw bite: if tender to eat, then leave them unpeeled. Once prepared, the broccoli will take just a few minutes to steam over or boil in salted water.

To cook the fish, heat the olive oil in a roasting pan. Lightly flour the white skin side of the fish and season with a pinch of salt. Season the dark skin with salt and

pepper. Using salt only on the white side prevents the fish from taking on black spots of pepper during cooking, spoiling the finished presentation. Place the fish in the pan, white-side down, and fry over a moderate heat for 6–8 minutes, until a rich golden brown. Turn the fish in the pan, then roast in the preheated oven for a further 8 minutes.

If using cup or chestnut mushrooms, halve or quarter them. Button mushrooms can be left whole. Fry the mushrooms over a fairly high heat in half of the butter. Season with salt and pepper.

While the mushrooms are frying, plunge the prepared broccoli into boiling salted water. Cook for just 3–4 minutes, until tender but still with a bite. Drain in a colander and season with salt and pepper. Warm the crème fraîche (microwaving for a few seconds works well), add a squeeze of lemon juice and season. Add the grapes to the fried mushrooms and warm for just a minute or two.

Spoon the remaining butter into the pan and allow to sizzle to a nut-brown stage. When it is sizzling, present the brill and broccoli on plates and trickle the warmed crème fraîche over the broccoli. To finish, squeeze lemon juice over the mushrooms and grapes, 'souffléing' the butter, and spoon it over the roasted fish. Soft creamy *Mashed potatoes* (page 198) would be a perfect accompaniment for this dish.

Serves 4
- 4 x 175g (6oz) turbot fillet portions, skin left on
- 50g (2oz) butter, plus extra for greasing
- salt and pepper
- squeeze of lemon juice
- 10–12 tarragon leaves, torn into small pieces
- coarse sea salt

For the salsify
- 8–10 salsify sticks
- juice of 1 lemon
- 1 heaped teaspoon finely grated orange zest and juice of 2 oranges
- 1 tablespoon olive oil
- 1 level teaspoon caster or demerara sugar
- knob of butter

Steamed turbot with tarragon and orange caramelized salsify

Turbot tends to be with us almost throughout the year, with a season that begins in mid-spring and goes right the way through to late winter. It is known as 'the king of all flat fish', and has every right to carry that title.

To accompany the turbot we have salsify, which is mostly an imported vegetable during mid-to-late autumn and through the months of winter. Salsify comes in two forms – black and white. Both are similar in shape and size, with long, slightly knobbly roots, and although different in colour, they have more or less identical interiors. Peeling reveals beautiful white roots, which have a distinctive flavour not too dissimilar to that of asparagus. Here the salsify are lightly caramelized with fresh orange juice, creating quite a distinctive finished flavour.

Method First prepare the salsify. Peeling it is made cleaner and easier by wearing rubber gloves and using a swivel peeler. Place the root on a suitable chopping board and peel in long strips. Once each stick has been peeled, rinse under water and then halve it. Place in a saucepan of cold water with the lemon juice. Once all are cleaned, bring the water to a rapid simmer and cook the salsify for 10–12 minutes, until tender; 15 minutes should be the maximum time required. Remove the roots from the pan and leave to drain and cool.

While the salsify are cooling, place the grated orange zest in a small saucepan and cover it with cold water. Bring to a simmer, then drain in a sieve and refresh under cold water. Repeat the same process twice more. This softens the zest and removes the raw bitter flavour. Keep to one side.

Heat the olive oil in a frying pan. Once hot, add the drained salsify and fry until golden brown. Remove from the heat.

At this point, the turbot can be steamed. Place the fillets, flesh-side down, on buttered and seasoned greaseproof paper squares and steam over a pan of rapidly simmering water, covering them with a lid, for 6 minutes.

While the fish are cooking, return the salsify to the heat, adding the sugar. Once this begins to caramelize gently to a richer golden brown, add the orange juice and orange zest. Boil over a high heat to cook to a syrupy consistency. Season with salt and pepper, adding the knob of butter for a smoother and shinier finish.

To make an instant tarragon butter, heat 3 tablespoons of water with a good squeeze of lemon juice. Once boiling, remove the pan from the stove and whisk in the 50g (2oz) of butter, a few knobs at a time. The butter emulsifies with the flavoured water to form a silky liquor to spoon over the fish. Once all the butter has been added, season with salt and pepper and add the tarragon leaves.

To serve, divide the orange salsify between four plates. Remove the turbot fillets from the steamer and carefully pull away the skin, sprinkling each with a little coarse sea salt. The fish can now be presented next to the orange-flavoured salsify, and the tarragon butter spooned over and around the fish.

● *When taking the fish from the greaseproof paper squares, strain any juices through a tea strainer into the tarragon butter sauce for maximum flavour.*

Serves 4 as a main course
- 4 x 175g (6oz) sea bass fillet portions
- 1 tablespoon olive oil
- flour, for dusting
- knob of butter

For the leeks
- 4 medium potatoes, suitable for mashing (Maris Piper or King Edward), peeled and quartered
- salt and pepper
- 3 medium leeks
- 25g (1oz) butter, plus an extra knob
- 100–150ml (3½fl oz–¼ pint) milk, warmed

- 50–100ml (2–3½fl oz) whipping or double cream (optional)
- freshly grated nutmeg
- 100–150ml (3½fl oz–¼ pint) natural yoghurt
- 1 teaspoon chopped dill (optional)

Pan-fried sea bass with two leeks

Sea bass is looked upon as a glittering star among the many superb products of the sea. This delicate but rich fish, with such a distinctive flavour, is expensive to buy, because there is so huge a demand from restaurants and hotels alike. A fish that can take its place is sea bream, which comes in many varieties, with gilt-head, red and black all working well here.

'Two leeks' actually refers to the two parts of the vegetable, which are separated for this dish: the whites creamed with potatoes to form a sort of vichyssoise purée; the greens shredded, softly buttered and finished with a spoonful of yoghurt.

Nothing else is needed, all the ingredients speaking for themselves. The sea bass portions are best cut from a fish at least 1.3kg (3lb) in weight, that has been scaled, filleted and the pin bones removed (page 11). The fish meat is then thick enough not to overcook while the skin is crisping.

Method Place the potato quarters in a large saucepan and cover with cold water. Add a level teaspoon of salt, bring to a rapid simmer and cook for approximately 20 minutes, until tender. Drain well in a colander. Return the potatoes to the pan, stirring over a very low heat to help draw off any remaining moisture.

While the potatoes are cooking, top and tail the leeks and split them in half lengthwise. Rinse and wash well to remove any soil and grit, then cut across to separate the white and green. There is obviously a very pale green point – this can be included with the white. Cut the white into rough 1cm (½in) dice.

Melt half of the measured butter in a saucepan and add the diced leek whites. Cook for a few minutes, adding 1–2 tablespoons of water and covering to create steam that helps to soften the leeks, stirring from time to time, until completely over-cooked. This will take up to 15 minutes. Drain, saving all of the buttery leek juices. To purée, place the cooked leeks in a food processor and blitz until smooth. Add the potatoes, a few at a time, quickly blitzing so as not to be left with a starchy finish. To help soften, pour in some of the warm milk, little by little, until the right consistency is achieved. The double cream can be used to replace some of the milk, or simply added to provide you with the softest of vichyssoise-like purées. Add the remaining measured butter and season with salt, pepper and nutmeg to finish. The potatoes can be mashed quite separately from the leeks, and the milk, cream, butter and seasonings added before the puréed leeks are stirred in. This can now be kept to one side ready to rewarm when needed.

Finely shred the leek greens, ready to cook while the fish is frying. Heat the olive oil in a large frying pan. Lightly flour the skin side of the sea bass and season each side with a pinch of salt. The flesh side can also be seasoned with pepper (seasoning any fish with salt only on the presentation side is to prevent the finished appearance being speckled with black spots of pepper). Place the fish, skin-side down, in the pan, adding the knob of butter. Cook on a moderate heat for 6–7 minutes, until the skin has become richly coloured and crispy. Turn the fish over in the pan and remove the pan from the heat. The residual heat in the pan will continue to cook the fillets without leaving a leathery edge, also providing time for the garnishes to be brought together.

While the fish is frying, melt the extra knob of butter in a saucepan and add the shredded leek greens. Cook for 5–6 minutes, seasoning with salt and pepper. The leeks can now be finished with 100ml (3½fl oz) of the natural yoghurt, stirring in to achieve a softening, but not too loose, effect. The extra 50ml (2fl oz) can be added if needed. Finish with the chopped dill, if using, and check the seasoning.

Spoon the leek greens on to plates and top each with the fried sea bass portions. Spoon the creamy vichyssoise purée beside. The buttery leek juices saved from the whites can be quickly warmed and a little spooned over the purée.

● *Finely chopped fennel seeds (10–12) can be cooked with the leek greens for an aniseed flavour.*

● *A level teaspoon of Dijon mustard can be added to the yoghurt before it is spooned into the leeks.*

● *Extra nutmeg can be grated over the vichyssoise purée just before serving.*

Serves 4 as a main course
- 4 x 175–225g (6–8oz) black bream fillets, scaled and pin bones removed (page 11)
- flour, for dusting
- 2 tablespoons olive oil
- knob of butter

For the potatoes
- 450–675g (1–1½lb) second early new potatoes (see below)
- salt and pepper
- 2 tablespoons olive oil
- 8–10 kumquats
- 8 juniper berries, crushed and finely chopped
- 50g (2oz) butter
- 1 tablespoon chopped parsley
- squeeze of lemon juice

Pan-fried black bream with sautéed juniper and kumquat potatoes

Black bream approaches the end of its popular season during the first month of winter, so it's a question of cooking it before missing it. Red and gilt-head bream hold on for an extra couple of months, and both also work well in this recipe. Black bream is often looked upon as the least impressive of the three but, as with most fish caught and cooked fresh, it easily earns its own place.

I prefer to use second earlies here, which are the second run of new potatoes, available from August to March. Charlotte and Estima both have a pale-yellow skin, with quite a waxy texture, sautéeing nicely. The potatoes also eat well with lamb and game meats. The juniper berries are crushed and chopped very finely to resemble coarse pepper (a coffee grinder does this very well), with their distinctive flavour matching the orangey bite from thinly sliced kumquats.

Method With the point of a sharp knife, score three or four lines in the skin of the black bream. These can now be chilled ready for frying.

Cook the new potatoes in boiling salted water for 20–25 minutes, until tender. Drain in a colander. While the potatoes are still warm, cut them in half lengthwise. Heat the olive oil in a large frying pan or wok and fry the warm potatoes until beginning to take on a little colour.

While the potatoes are colouring, top and tail the kumquats, then slice them into thin rounds, removing any seeds.

Add the chopped juniper berries to the potatoes and continue to sauté to a richer colour. Add the kumquat slices and the butter, allowing it to melt rather than fry. Add the chopped parsley and lemon juice just before serving.

While the potatoes are sautéeing, flour the skin side of the sea bream and season with a pinch of salt. Heat the olive oil in a large frying pan and place the fish in the oil, skin-side down. Should the fillets begin to curl, press them down with a fish slice. After a minute or two they will have relaxed and won't curl. Add the knob of butter and fry the fish for 4 minutes, seasoning the flesh side with salt and pepper, before turning the fish in the pan. Remove the pan from the stove. The residual heat in the pan will continue to cook the fish, providing enough time to finish the potatoes without overcooking the bream.

Spoon the finished sautéed potatoes on to warm plates, drizzling with any remaining butter from the pan. Place the black bream fillets just next to the potatoes and serve.

● *A slice of* English cabbage plate *(page 113) or* Sesame and ham sprouts *(page 110) are good accompaniments. Spinach cooked in sizzling butter is a simple alternative.*

Serves 4

- 4 x 175g (6oz) halibut fillet portions, skinned
- salt and pepper
- 50g (2oz) sesame seeds
- 1 egg, beaten
- 675g (1½lb) Brussels sprouts, outside leaves removed
- 6–8 kumquats (optional)
- 50g (2oz) shallots or small onions, sliced
- 2 teaspoons white wine vinegar
- 150ml (¼ pint) white wine
- 100ml (3½fl oz) orange juice
- 50g (2oz) butter, plus an extra knob
- 2 tablespoons olive oil
- 2 teaspoons picked and torn (or chopped) tarragon leaves

Sesame halibut with Brussels sprout choucroute

Choucroute is the more appetizing French word to describe sauerkraut. Sauerkraut is usually made from shredded white cabbage, pickled in white wine vinegar, with juniper berries and more. The basic idea is adapted here for the much softer member of the brassica family, the Brussels sprout. Marinating a green vegetable in any acidic liquid would result in a total discoloration, making it quite unappealing. Instead, a more mellow acidic reduction is prepared and mixed with the sprouts at the last moment. To enhance the flavour, fresh tarragon is added, along with very thin slices of kumquat and orange juice. These two are designed to complement, working so nicely with the nutty sesame-topped halibut, while at the same time accompanying the softened sprouts. All the ingredients mentioned suit late-autumn to early-winter eating.

Method Season the halibut with salt and pepper, and scatter the sesame seeds on a plate. Dip the filleted presentation side of each fish portion in the beaten egg, then lay in the sesame seeds to coat, patting them on generously. As the fillets are coated, place them, sesame-side up, on a large plate, and chill.

Halve the Brussels sprouts, cutting away the small stalk base. Finely shred the halves and blanch in a pan of rapidly boiling salted water for just 2–3 minutes, until tender. Drain in a colander and allow to cool.

If including the kumquats, each one can be sliced into very thin rings, removing any seeds. Place the shallots or onions and kumquat rings, if using, in a saucepan with the vinegar. Bring to a rapid boil and

reduce until almost dry. Add the white wine and boil to reduce by three-quarters. Add the orange juice, bring back to a simmer and cook for a few minutes more, until reduced by just a third. Whisk the measured butter into the liquor and season with salt and pepper.

To cook the fish, heat the olive oil in a frying pan over a medium heat. Place the halibut fillets in the pan, sesame-side down. Cook for 2–3 minutes until golden brown. Should the seeds begin to colour earlier, then turn the fish at that point to maintain an attractive finish. Once turned, add the extra knob of butter and continue to cook for a further 8–10 minutes (thin fillets of the fish could take just 6 minutes).

For the last 4–5 minutes of the fish cooking time, add the shredded sprouts to the orange choucroute liquor to reheat (they can also be quickly microwaved). Season with salt and pepper and add the tarragon.

To present the dish, divide the sprout *choucroute* between the plates, spooning any liquor over and around. The sesame cod can now be placed on top.

- *One or two lightly crushed juniper berries can be added to the shallots, and left in the finished dish to offer an extra flavour.*

- *Diced or strips of fried bacon can be added to the choucroute.*

- *Almost all flat fish can be used in this recipe – skate, turbot and brill are all favourites – with our round-shaped salmon very close behind.*

Serves 4

- 3 thick slices of white bread, crusts removed
- 50g (2oz) curly parsley, picked and roughly chopped
- 1 teaspoon picked thyme leaves (optional)
- salt and pepper
- 8 walnut halves, chopped
- 2 shallots, very finely chopped

- 3 tablespoons walnut, olive or groundnut oil
- 4 x 175g (6oz) cod fillet portions, skinned
- butter, for greasing

For the parsnip sauce

- 2 parsnips, peeled and quartered lengthwise
- knob of butter
- 200ml (7fl oz) milk
- squeeze of lemon juice

For the carrots (optional)

- 4 medium carrots, peeled
- still mineral water
- knob of butter, plus extra 15g/½oz (optional)
- ½ teaspoon sugar

Walnut-crusted cod with parsnip sauce

Cod has more or less an all-year-round season, really coming to the fore and shining between the months of September and February. The parsnip also runs during the prime cod months, but is usually at its best between November and January.

This quite meaty, succulent fish really suits a breadcrumbed crust, and here the oily nuttiness of walnuts creates an even greater overall taste.

Method Cut the crusted bread slices into cubes, then place in a food processor, blitzing until beginning to crumble. Alternatively you could buy fresh white breadcrumbs. Add the parsley and thyme, and continue to blitz until the crumbs are reasonably fine and a rich green colour. Season with salt and pepper, and add the chopped walnuts. To break down their texture a stage further, quickly blitz again, crushing the walnuts into the mix. Add the shallots, and pour in the oil as the crumbs turn, simply to moisten their loose texture.

Season the cod fillets with salt and pepper, then cover the flat skinned side of each fillet with the crumbs. Place the topped cod fillets on a greased baking tray. These can now be chilled until needed.

To make the sauce, cut away the central core of each of the parsnip quarters. Cut each piece of parsnip into 1cm (½in) thick pieces. Melt the knob of butter in a saucepan and, once bubbling, add the parsnip pieces. Cover and cook over a low heat for 6–8 minutes, stirring from time to time and not allowing the parsnips to colour,

until just beginning to soften. At this point add the milk and bring to a simmer. Cook gently for 15 minutes, until the pieces are completely cooked through. Season with salt and pepper. Liquidize the parsnips to a silky-smooth puréed sauce. A squeeze of lemon juice can now be added to enliven the finished flavour. Keep to one side ready to reheat.

If serving the carrots, cut each into quarters lengthwise. These can now be cut into 1cm (½in) thick pieces. Place them in a saucepan, pour enough still mineral water on top just to cover and add the knob of butter and the sugar. Bring to a simmer and cook for approximately 10 minutes, until tender. Increase the heat and continue until the carrots are overcooked, allowing the water to reduce by at least two-thirds to three-quarters, developing a loose syrup consistency. Just before serving, the extra 15g (½oz) of butter can be added, if using, stirring it into the pan to emulsify. Season with salt and pepper.

Preheat a grill to hot. Place the cod fillets under the grill, not too close to the heat, for a few minutes, allowing the crumbed topping to reach a slightly golden edge. Transfer to an oven heated to 200°C/400°F/Gas 6, cooking for approximately 8–10 minutes. The cod will now be cooked through, but still maintaining a moist finish.

To serve, present the cod fillets and parsnip sauce on plates, offering the overcooked sweet carrots separately, if serving. The dish is now ready; offer any extra parsnip sauce separately.

**Serves 6 as a starter
or 4 as a main course**

- 350g (12oz) potatoes (preferably Maris Piper), peeled and quartered
- salt and pepper
- 1 tablespoon finely chopped shallot or onion
- 3 tablespoons olive oil, plus extra for greasing

- 375g (12oz) natural smoked haddock fillet, pin bones removed (page 11)
- 150ml (¼ pint) white wine
- squeeze of lemon juice
- 450–675g (1–1½lb) curly kale
- 2 large knobs of butter, plus extra for brushing
- flour, for dusting
- 4 or 6 poached eggs (page 202)

For the sauce
- 1 heaped tablespoon very finely grated horseradish (or 1 heaped teaspoon of horseradish cream)
- 200ml (7fl oz) crème fraîche
- 2 tablespoons snipped chives
- knob of butter

Smoked haddock cakes with poached eggs and curly kale

The crinkly leaves of winter curly kale offer a great strength of flavour, holding their own well when partnered with such a smoky fish. The horseradish crème fraîche sauce adds extra warmth, along with a piquant bite to complement the golden smoked haddock cakes. This dish is perfect for a cold winter's day.

Method Cook the potatoes in boiling salted water for approximately 20 minutes, until totally tender. Drain in a colander for a few minutes.

While the potatoes are cooking, sprinkle the chopped shallot or onion in a small greased roasting tray or frying pan and top with the smoked haddock. Season with a twist of pepper, then pour over the white wine, followed by 150ml (¼ pint) of water and a squeeze of lemon juice. Bring to a gentle simmer, cover with a lid and cook for just 2 minutes. Remove from the heat, keeping the lid on, and allow to cool.

Once the fish has cooled, remove it from the liquid and pull the skin from the flesh and discard. Break the haddock into flakes. Strain the shallot or onion pieces from the cooking liquor over a bowl, squeezing to release all their juices, before adding the shallot or onion to the haddock. Set the bowl of cooking liquor to one side.

Mash the warm potatoes, seasoning with salt and pepper. Beat half of the smoked haddock mix into the potatoes until quite smooth, then gently fold in the remainder. Cover the fish cake mix with cling film and chill for several hours. This allows the mix to rest, becoming far more compact and not as likely to break up during frying.

The curly kale can be prepared and cooked in advance or at the last minute. To do so, remove the stalks from the kale and wash the leaves, then tear them into bite-sized pieces. Plunge the leaves in lots of boiling salted water for 3–4 minutes, until tender. Drain in a colander, then plunge into iced water, if cooking in advance. Once cold, drain again, squeezing out all excess moisture, then season with salt and pepper, adding a knob of butter and covering with cling film, ready to microwave. If cooking at the last minute, drain, squeeze gently, season, butter and serve.

To make the sauce, boil the reserved fish cooking liquor with the grated horseradish or horseradish cream, allowing it to reduce by two-thirds, and keep to one side.

Preheat the oven to 180°C/350°F/Gas 4. To make the fish cakes, divide the haddock mix into four (six if serving as a starter) and roll into balls. Press these into round cakes and lightly dust and coat with flour. Heat the 3 tablespoons of olive oil in a frying pan. Place the fish cakes in the pan and fry over a medium heat until golden brown. Turn over carefully with a fish slice and colour the other sides. Transfer to a baking tray and finish in the preheated oven for 10–12 minutes.

To serve, reheat or cook the curly kale as mentioned above, also warming the poached eggs in simmering water for 1 minute. Rewarm the sauce, whisking in the crème fraîche, chopped chives and the knob of butter. Divide the kale between the plates, top with a smoked haddock cake, followed by a poached egg, and spoon the sauce over.

Serves 4 as a starter

- 2 medium–large raw beetroots (approximately 225g/8oz)
- 2 apples
- knob of butter, plus extra for brushing and greasing
- 4 mackerel fillets, preferably from 2 x 350g (12oz) fish, pin bones removed (page 11)
- 50–75g (2–3oz) blue cheese (see below), crumbled

For the dressing (optional)

- 1 small raw beetroot
- 1–2 tablespoons red wine vinegar (preferably a strong Cabernet Sauvignon)
- salt and pepper
- 4 tablespoons olive oil

Grilled blue cheese mackerel with soft beetroot and apple

Mackerel, blue cheese, beetroot and apples are all so available throughout the autumn and winter. I enjoy putting this dish together in the last of our winter months, February. It's the time when being able to find all of these ingredients in our own soils and waters is coming to an end, so this makes it quite a special occasion.

Most blue cheeses will fit the bill here, but there are a couple that work particularly well, so do give them a try if they are available. Beenleigh Blue, a crumbly sheep's-milk cheese, releases a slight spiciness as it melts across the mackerel. Harbourne Blue is a goat's-milk, semi-soft cheese that also has an aromatic and distinctive edge.

Apples still around in February include Royal Gala, Ellison's Orange Red, Laxton's Superb, Crispin, Cox's, Red Pippin, Red Falstaff, Newton Wonder and more – so we're spoilt for choice. I've included in the recipe a beetroot dressing, which is not essential but adds another essence to the finished dish.

Method In a saucepan, cover the two beetroots with cold water, bringing to the boil and cooking until tender. This can take up to 1 hour or more. To check, rather than piercing them, as this releases their juices and flavour, push the skin away from the flesh beneath with the thumb. This will tell you when they are ready. Remove from the pan and allow to cool slightly until comfortable to handle.

While the beetroots are cooking, peel the apples and cut each into eight wedges, removing the central core and pips. Roughly chop the wedges.

Melt the knob of butter in a saucepan and add the apples and 1 tablespoon of water. Cover with a lid and cook on a low heat, stirring from time to time, until completely softened, then leave to cool.

If serving the dressing, it's best made well in advance. Peel the raw beetroot and finely grate into a small bowl. Add 1 tablespoon of the vinegar and season with salt and pepper. Stir in the oil and leave to infuse until the dressing is needed.

Peel and roughly dice the cooked beetroots. Place in a food processor or liquidizer and blitz to a purée, adding the apples as the beetroot breaks down. This combines the two flavours, with the apple loosening the beetroot. Season with salt and pepper. If not silky-smooth, the purée can be pushed through a sieve. This can be served warm, but also eats very well cold.

Preheat a grill to hot. Place the mackerel fillets on a greased and seasoned baking tray, skin-side up, and brush each with butter. The fish can now be cooked under the grill for 5–6 minutes, until becoming crispy. Crumble the blue cheese over each fillet, return to the grill and warm until the cheese begins to melt.

To serve, strain the dressing, if using, through a sieve, pressing out all the juices from the beetroot. The grated waste can be discarded. Taste the dressing for piquancy. For a sharper bite, add the remaining tablespoon (or just a few drops) of the red wine vinegar.

To finish, spoon the soft beetroot and apple purée on to the plates and place the grilled mackerel fillets on top. If serving with the dressing, drizzle it over and around the fish.

- 12 scallops
- drizzle of olive oil
- knob of butter
- coarse sea salt
- 2 tablespoons brandy (optional)
- 1cm (½in) chive sticks (approximately 2 sticks per scallop, optional)

For the shallot purée
- 2 tablespoons olive oil
- knob of butter
- 325g (12oz) shallots, peeled and thinly sliced
- 4 tablespoons double cream
- salt and pepper (use ground white for the shallot purée)

For the tangerines
- 24 fresh tangerine segments, plus the juice of 6 tangerines
- oil, for greasing
- butter, for brushing

Scallops with puréed shallots and black-peppered tangerines

Scallops are without doubt one of the culinary luxuries of the world. To eat these heavenly little beasts raw or cooked brings pleasure to the palate, and you can always find room for more. Although they are available throughout the year, winter is their prime time.

When buying scallops, it's only really worth taking them home in the shell, ready to open and eat as soon as possible after opening. It is only with this freshness that their full succulent sweetness will be appreciated. Scallops sold opened and cleaned have often been soaked in water to plump up their size and get a better price. Unfortunately, the soaked scallop is washed of its flavours, and can become a quite tasteless muscle.

Attached to the scallop is the brightly coloured coral. These I find are best for sauce-making, or perhaps eating fried in salads. They're not to be used in this recipe, but do freeze well, or can be blitzed to a purée with an equal quantity of butter, for dropping a knob or two into a fish sauce to act as a thickening agent.

The scallops themselves can be eaten just fried for a minute or two on each side in butter, then finished with a squeeze of lemon juice. Pleasure enough can be found within such a simple recipe. There are many ingredients that can be introduced to help the scallops along, a few of which have been chosen here. In this recipe, the shallots are cooked until completely tender, then puréed with cream. To balance, the sweet flavour of tangerines (also in season during the winter months), with a peppery bite, a sort of *à l'orange* and *au poivre* combination, finishes the overall experience.

Method To make the shallot purée, warm the olive oil and the knob of butter in a saucepan. Once bubbling, add the sliced shallots, cover and cook over a gentle heat for 15 minutes, without allowing to colour, stirring from time to time. To guarantee the shallots do not stick and colour in the pan, 3–4 tablespoons of water can be added once the shallots begin to soften. Add the cream and continue to cook for a further 5 minutes, then remove from the heat, season with salt and pepper, and liquidize to a smooth purée. The shallot cream is now ready. This stage can be made several hours in advance, chilled until needed, then simply reheated gently when required.

To prepare the tangerines, gently peel away the thin outer skin that surrounds each segment with the point of a small knife. This is a little time-consuming, but does produce a far more tender finish. Place the peeled segments on a lightly oiled baking tray, brushing each with melted butter and topping with a twist of black pepper. These are now ready to warm when needed.

To clean the scallops, begin to prise the shells open with a knife, scraping and loosening the scallop from the flat shell. The scallop can now also be detached from the lower shell, by cutting beneath the white muscle with a knife. The surrounding membrane can now be pulled away and discarded (unless used to flavour a stock or sauce). The coral can now also be separated from the 'meat' (use as mentioned in the introduction). Rinse the scallops briefly and dry on kitchen paper or a cloth. The scallops are now ready to cook.

To cook the scallops, heat a drizzle of olive oil in a large frying pan. Once hot, place the scallops in the pan, adding the knob of butter. Cook for 1–1½ minutes, depending on the size of the scallops. Once coloured with deep tinges on their border, turn them over and continue to cook for a further 1–1½ minutes. This will leave the scallops at a medium-rare stage. For particularly large scallops, 2 minutes on each side will be the maximum cooking time needed to reach this stage. Season each with a few granules of coarse sea salt. Transfer the scallops from the pan to a plate and keep to one side. Preheat a grill to hot.

Pour away excess fat from the scallop pan and return it to the heat. Add the brandy, if using, to lift all residue from the pan, possibly flambéeing. Once the pan is almost dry, add the tangerine juice and boil quickly, allowing it to reduce by at least half, to a syrupy consistency. Strain the syrup through a fine sieve or tea strainer into a small bowl.

While the tangerine juice is boiling, warm the peppered segments under the grill.

Lay 3 tablespoons of the warm shallot purée on each plate (offering any remaining separately). Place a scallop on top of each, then place two warm peppered tangerine segments on top of each scallop. The syrup can now be drizzled over, finishing with two chive sticks, if using, per scallop.

● *Any shallot purée not used can be kept and added to mashed potatoes for an oniony bite.*

- 6 small-to-medium potatoes, peeled
- 1 large onion, finely chopped
- 25g (1oz) butter, plus an extra knob for the onion
- 1kg (2¼lb) leeks, thinly sliced and rinsed
- salt and ground white pepper
- 600–750g (1lb 6oz–1¾lb) salmon fillet, skinned and cut into 8 equal portions
- 1 teaspoon 1cm (½in) chive sticks (optional)
- 2–3 teaspoons lime juice (optional)
- 2 tablespoons olive, walnut or hazelnut oil (optional)

Buttered salmon with a leek velouté soup and steamed potatoes

Leeks are one of our most luxurious home-grown autumn and winter green vegetables. Not only do they offer a rich depth of flavour, but they also provide us with a range of green tones to add colour to our plates. It is during the winter months that this vegetable is at its best, so with that in mind I thought I would pair this soup with softly cooked salmon, the two very natural flavours working well together, particularly as a starter on that big day in late December.

As you can see, the leeks are almost left to work on their own, with just a little kick from the onions. The potatoes can be omitted from the recipe, but do offer another texture, also reflecting the leek and potato soup combination, but served in a slightly different form. The potatoes can be shaped as you like, just large or small dice, or perhaps even formed into balls or small barrels. The extras are purely optional, the chives lending an additional bite and the dressing of lime juice and oil a glossy sharp finish.

Method As mentioned in the introduction, the potatoes can be shaped as wished, cutting them into dice or scooping them into balls. Another method is to 'turn' them into barrel shapes. To do so, quarter the potatoes lengthwise, then cut a little away from top to bottom with a small knife to establish a curved barrel shape. The potatoes can be steamed from raw or parboiled for 5–6 minutes, until tender, then removed from the water and allowed to cool. They can now be reheated when needed, either by steaming, boiling or microwaving. The

quantity of potatoes listed will provide enough for 3 pieces per portion as a garnish.

In a large saucepan, cook the chopped onion in the knob of butter for 6–7 minutes, until softening without colouring. Add 900ml (1½ pints) of water and bring to the boil. Once at boiling point, season with salt, then add the leeks. Cook on a high heat, bringing back to the boil for a few minutes, until the leeks are tender. Remove the pan from the heat and liquidize the soup to a purée in batches, then push through a sieve. It's important when straining the soup to push well to get all of the liquor and texture through. You will now be left with a very naturally flavoured leek soup. Season with salt and ground white pepper.

To cook the salmon, melt the measured butter in a saucepan over a low-to-medium heat. Once gently bubbling, place the salmon in, skinned-side down. Season with salt and pepper, and cook gently for just 4–5 minutes, then turn the fillets over in the pan and remove from the heat. The residual heat of the pan will finish the cooking of the fish, if you leave it to stand for just a further 2–3 minutes.

The salmon fillets can now be presented in soup plates, with the leek velouté soup ladled around. The steamed potatoes can be arranged around the salmon or presented on top of the fillets. If adding the optional garnishes, sprinkle the chive sticks on top of the potatoes, then whisk the lime juice and oil together, and season with salt and pepper. This can now be drizzled over and around the salmon.

Serves 4 as a starter
- 2 medium–large kohlrabi, peeled
- 1–2 tablespoons olive oil
- flour, for dusting
- 4 x 100g (4oz) salmon fillets, skinned and pin bones removed (page 11)
- knob of butter
- 1 tablespoon chopped chives

For the *rémoulade* sauce
- 100ml (3½fl oz) *Mayonnaise* (page 198, or bought)
- 1 teaspoon Dijon mustard
- 1 teaspoon chopped capers
- 1 teaspoon chopped gherkins
- 2 tinned anchovy fillets, chopped
- 3 tablespoons double cream
- salt and pepper

Kohlrabi rémoulade *with warm salmon fillets*

Kohlrabi, a member of the cabbage family, is found in colours ranging from white to pale green and even purple. This vegetable is best eaten when it is at its most tender, basically when about the size of a medium-to-large turnip; any bigger and the texture seems to toughen, almost becoming spongy. The smaller types of this vegetable are delicious grated and eaten raw. The flavour of the kohlrabi can range from that of cabbage, moving on to that of celeriac with a sort of radish bite. As with many other vegetables, braising, boiling, sautéeing or steaming all suit it well.

Rémoulade is a mayonnaise, a bit like tartare sauce, enhanced with mustard, capers, gherkins and anchovies. Normally the flavouring ingredients are just chopped and left in the sauce. Here I liquidize them into the mayonnaise base, before straining. The *rémoulade* will now contain all of the flavours, but with the kohlrabi, helped along with chives, to create texture. The salmon is gently fried in a knob of butter and enjoyed with this smooth tartare-like dressing.

Method First make the *rémoulade* sauce. Blend together the mayonnaise, mustard, capers, gherkins and anchovy fillets until smooth. Add the double cream and season with a twist of pepper, adding more salt if necessary (taking into account the anchovies' salt content).

Coarsely grate the kohlrabi and dry on kitchen paper. Season with salt and pepper, then stir in enough *rémoulade* sauce to bind.

Heat the olive oil in a frying pan. Lightly flour the presentation side of the salmon fillets and place them in the oil, floured-side down. Cook on a gentle heat for 6–7 minutes, only allowing the fish to become a pale golden brown. Season the fish with salt and pepper and add the knob of butter to the pan just before turning the fish over. Once turned, remove the pan from the heat, also lightly seasoning the presentation side with a pinch of salt only. Left in the pan for a further 2–3 minutes, the fish will continue to cook in the residual heat, maintaining a moist pink finish.

Add the chopped chives to the kohlrabi and divide it between the plates. Present the salmon on top of, or beside, the kohlrabi, ready to serve.

- *A trickle of olive oil flavoured with a squeeze of lemon or lime juice can be drizzled over the salmon before serving.*

- *Small dice of smoked salmon (50–75g/2–3oz would be plenty) can also be added to the kohlrabi, offering an extra smoky edge to the finished dish.*

Serves 4
- 2 x oven-ready hen pheasants, each halved and trimmed as below
- 1 tablespoon groundnut oil
- knob of butter
- 4 large shallots or 2 small onions, sliced
- generous sprig of thyme
- 3 tablespoons calvados (brandy can also be used, optional)
- 2 teaspoons brown sugar
- 2 teaspoons clear honey
- 300ml/½ pint beer
- 100–150ml (3½fl oz–¼ pint) double cream
- squeeze of lemon juice

For the vegetables
- 3–4 large potatoes, suitable for mashing and boiling (Desirée, King Edward or Maris Piper all work well), peeled and quartered
- salt and pepper
- 2 leeks
- 100g (4oz) piece of streaky bacon, cut into 1cm (½in) dice (this can be obtained pre-cut, or diced pancetta can also be used)
- 15g (½oz) butter
- 8–10 ready-to-eat prunes, halved

Beer-braised pheasants with leeks, potatoes, prunes and bacon

Pheasant begin their season in early October, leading through to the beginning of February. There are not many to be found during October, however, and they only really show their plump faces in November, eating at their best at this time, leading through to December and January too. Today they can quite easily be found oven-ready, with little or no preparation needed at all. You can choose either cock or hen pheasants – the cock is quite a large bird, carrying enough meat for three or four portions, while the hen is smaller and perfect for two portions, with a much more delicate taste.

In this recipe, half hen pheasants are cooked, so when ordering from your butcher, ask for the birds to be halved, and any excess backbone carcass trimmed away. This will leave the legs attached to the breast, which is still sitting on the bone. Braising usually requires several hours' cooking. The pheasants here, though, are only braised in the beer for 15–20 minutes, long enough to preserve a moist tender touch in the breasts, while the beer takes on the gamey flavour.

Leeks are very much an early-winter vegetable. Although they have a longer life span, they are probably at their best during December and January. Together with the potatoes, prunes and bacon, the leeks help form a bowl of mixed flavours to be presented as one.

Method First prepare the vegetables. Place the potatoes in a saucepan, top with cold water and add a generous pinch of salt. Bring to the boil and cook until completely tender, approximately 20 minutes.

While the potatoes are cooking, start cooking the pheasants. Preheat the oven to 220°C/425°F/Gas 7. Season the birds with salt and pepper. Heat the groundnut oil and butter in a roasting tray. Once bubbling, place the birds in, flesh-side down, and fry over a moderate heat for a good 5–10 minutes, until golden brown. Turn the halves over in the tray and cook for a further 2 minutes. Remove the pheasants from the tray and keep to one side. Return the roasting tray to the heat, add the shallots or onions and the thyme, and fry for a few minutes, until they are softening. Add the calvados, if using, and allow it to boil and reduce until almost dry. Add the sugar and honey, stir them in well, top with the beer and bring to a simmer. Return the pheasants to the tray, flesh-side up and, once simmering, place in the oven and roast for 15–20 minutes.

While the birds roast, prepare the leeks. Trim the base stalk and untidy tops from each, removing the outer layer, and wash well. Cut each across into 1cm (½in) thick slices and place to one side.

The potatoes will have reached their tender stage while the birds are roasting. Simply drain, return to the warm pan, cover with a lid and keep warm to one side.

Dry-fry the bacon pieces in a wok or frying pan over a moderate heat. This helps release their own fat, in which they will begin to fry until golden brown. For a very crunchy finish, continue to cook until dark and crispy, drain and keep warm to one side.

Remove the pheasants from the oven and their cooking liquor and leave to rest in a warm place. Return the pan to the hob, bring the liquid to the boil and allow it to reduce by half. Remove the sprig of thyme from the liquor. Add 100ml (3½fl oz) of the double cream and simmer for a few minutes, until the sauce is thickening slightly. For a creamier finish add the remaining cream. Season with salt and pepper, skimming away any impurities. Finish with a squeeze of lemon juice.

While the sauce is simmering, cook the leeks. Melt the butter in a saucepan. Once bubbling, add 3 tablespoons of water and drop in the leeks. Stir, cover with a lid and cook for 1 minute. Stir again, covering once more, and repeat this process for 4–5 minutes, until the leeks are tender. At this point, add the prunes and continue to cook with a lid on for a further minute. This will create steam, helping to soften the prunes and finish the leeks. Season with salt and pepper.

Cut the potatoes roughly while still in the saucepan, using a small knife, or break them with a fork into rough chunks. Season with salt and pepper.

The pheasants can be left as halves, with the meat on the bone. If so, they can be quickly rewarmed in the preheated oven for 2 minutes before plating. To take off the bone, cut the legs away from the breasts. The breasts can now also be cut from the bone with a sharp knife, naturally following the breast bone. These can now be placed into the oven, with the legs skin-side up, and warmed for just a minute or two. In a warm serving bowl, mix the potatoes, leeks, prunes and bacon, then spoon over any buttery liquor from the leeks. Divide the pheasant halves or portions between the plates. Spoon the sauce over the pheasants and the dish is ready to serve.

Serves 4 as a starter
- 2 large wood pigeons, prepared as below
- 2 Cox's Orange Pippin apples
- knob of butter, plus extra for greasing
- juice of 1 lime
- caster sugar, for sprinkling
- ½ small or ¼ medium red cabbage (approximately 175g/6oz)
- 1 tablespoon groundnut oil
- 2 shallots, very thinly sliced

For the dressing
- 2 tablespoons red wine
- ½ teaspoon caster sugar
- 1 level teaspoon Dijon mustard
- 2 tablespoons red wine vinegar
- 1 level tablespoon bought ready-made mayonnaise
- 4 tablespoons groundnut oil
- 4 tablespoons walnut oil (or groundnut or olive oil)
- salt and pepper

Pippin's pigeon red cabbage salad

The pigeons here are, in fact, wood pigeons, which are available throughout the year. In this recipe, the breasts are to be cooked on the bone, with the legs and central backbone cut away: these are not used in this recipe, but should be frozen, ready to turn into a game stock or sauce at a later date. The quantities listed provide four small starters, offering just one breast a portion. The recipe will, however, double very comfortably.

The 'Pippin' in the title represents the Cox's Orange Pippin apple, which is with us throughout the autumn and winter. Red cabbage is usually braised, with the addition of apple, onion and red wine. The apple this time is with the pigeon, while red wine and shallots become the dressing, bound with the raw cabbage itself.

Method Remove the wishbone from the pigeons by scraping with a small knife to reveal the bone. Cut either side against the wishbone, then twist to release. Chill the birds until ready to cook.

Preheat a grill to hot. Peel the apples, quarter each and cut away the core from the pieces. Cut each quarter into five or six slices and place them on a greased baking tray. Brush the apple slices with the lime juice (any leftover juice can be added to the dressing), then sprinkle very lightly with the caster sugar. Place the apples under the preheated grill and cook until approaching a golden brown and tender. Remove and leave to cool.

Halve the red cabbage again. Turn each piece on its side and cut away the core, then finely shred the cabbage, preferably with a mandolin slicer for the finest of results.

To make the dressing, warm the red wine with the caster sugar. Once the sugar has dissolved, remove from the heat and pour the wine into a bowl. Add the Dijon mustard, red wine vinegar and mayonnaise, and mix all together. Slowly whisk the oils into the mix, as you would when making mayonnaise. This will help emulsify all of the ingredients. Season with salt and pepper, and the dressing is ready.

Preheat the oven to 220°C/425°F/Gas 7. To cook the pigeons, heat the groundnut oil in a small roasting tray. Season the birds with salt and pepper, then place them on one side in the tray. Fry for a minute or two until golden brown, turn and continue to fry until the other sides are also golden brown. Arrange the pigeons breast-side up, and roast in the preheated oven for 6–8 minutes. At this stage, the pigeons will be very moist and pink. Leave to rest for 8 minutes, then remove the skin from the breasts and release the breasts from the bone.

Preheat a grill to hot. Lay the four breasts on a baking tray, skinned-side up. Cover them from top to bottom with apple slices, overlapping the slices. The softened apples will follow the natural curve of the breasts, giving a neat, natural finish. Quickly warm under the grill.

Finish the red cabbage and sliced shallots with the red wine dressing, spooning over just enough to bind. Any remaining apple slices can also be added to the salad. Divide the red cabbage between the plates and top each with a Pippin's pigeon. Extra dressing can be drizzled around each portion.

- *Watercress or rocket leaves can be drizzled with walnut oil and served with the salad.*

Serves 4

- 2 mallards, legs removed
- 2 tablespoons groundnut oil
- salt and pepper
- 1 tablespoon plain flour
- 2 shallots or 1 onion, roughly chopped
- 3 juniper berries, lightly crushed
- 1 strip of orange peel
- 1 bay leaf
- sprig of thyme

- 1 bottle of red wine
- 4 pears, preferably Comice
- squeeze of lemon juice
- 1 tablespoon plain flour
- 300ml (½ pint) *Chicken Stock* (page 194) or *Game stock* (page 195) or tinned game consommé
- 2 tablespoons cooking oil
- 2 knobs of butter

For the onions

- 1 tablespoon groundnut oil
- large knob of butter
- 675g (1½lb) onions, preferably sweet white, peeled and sliced
- 1 garlic clove, crushed (optional)
- 10 juniper berries, very finely chopped
- 2 tablespoons red wine vinegar
- 1 level teaspoon demerara sugar

Roasted and braised wild duck with red wine juniper onions and buttered pears

Wild duck is in season from early September to the end of January and includes the mallard, the largest of the wild duck family, as well as widgeon and teal. You may have to pre-order from your butcher to guarantee finding these birds. Here, I use mallard with the legs removed and braised, while the breasts are roasted on the bone. I have found this to be the most successful way of cooking mallard. The legs are then completely well done, soft and succulent, while the breasts are kept pink and tender. This is not essential – you can simply roast a whole duck or even just duck breasts, and serve the tasty garnishes on the side.

The onions – sweet white onions, if available, will enrich the finished flavour – are softened and stewed in red wine with crushed juniper berries, giving a spicy edge and aroma. The chosen pears are Comice, which are at their best during the winter months and suit meats, game in particular, more than most other types of fruit. One pear per portion may appear to be a little over-generous, but it is only a 2.5cm (1in) central slice (to include the stalk) per portion. The trimmings are then braised with the legs, giving the finished sauce a slightly fruity edge.

Method Preheat the oven to 180°C/350°F/Gas 4. With the legs removed, the duck breasts are still attached to the bone – this will help maintain their shape and prevent the breasts from shrinking during cooking. The backbone of the carcass can also be cut away, then rinsed and chopped to add to the legs while braising for extra flavour.

Heat 1 tablespoon of the groundnut oil in a suitable braising pot. Season the duck legs with salt and pepper and generously dust them with the plain flour, saving any excess. Fry the duck legs in the oil, along with the chopped backbone, until well coloured. Remove the legs, pour away most of the excess fat and return the pot to the stove. Add the chopped shallots or onion, crushed juniper berries, orange peel, bay leaf and thyme, and continue to fry over a moderate heat for a further 6–8 minutes. Add the duck legs and pour over two-thirds of the red wine. Increase the heat to a rapid simmer and allow the wine to reduce by half.

While the wine is reducing, prepare the pears. You need a 2.5cm (1in) thick central slice, cutting either side of the stalk with the skin left on to give a natural pear-shaped slice. Place the slices in a saucepan, cover with water and add the lemon juice to prevent them from discolouring. Bring to a simmer and cook for just 2 minutes, then leave to cool, before drying the slices on a kitchen cloth.

Cut each of the pear 'trimmings' in half and add them to the pot containing the reduced red wine and the duck legs. Add the stock or consommé, bring back to a simmer and skim away any impurities. Cover with a lid and braise in the preheated oven for 1¼ hours.

The moment the legs are in the oven, start preparing the onions. Heat the groundnut oil and the large knob of butter in a large saucepan. Once bubbling, add the sliced onions and garlic, if using, with half of the crushed juniper berries. Cover with a lid and cook over a very low heat, stirring from time to time, for 15 minutes. It's

important to cook over a low heat to prevent the onions from colouring. Remove the lid and add the red wine vinegar. Increase the heat and allow the vinegar to reduce until almost dry. Add the sugar along with the remaining red wine. Continue to braise the onions for approximately 15 minutes, stirring from time to time, until they are taking on the rich red wine flavour. At this point the wine should be almost completely reduced. If not, increase the heat and reduce until dry. Season with salt and pepper and add the remaining crushed juniper. This now offers a fresh spiciness to the onions. Cover with a lid and keep to one side.

About 10 minutes before the duck legs are due to be ready, start cooking the duck breasts. Season them with salt and pepper. Heat the cooking oil in a roasting tray. Place the birds in, breast-side down, and fry on one side for a few minutes until golden, then turn on to the other breast and repeat the frying and colouring. Turn the birds breast-side up before removing the cooked legs from the oven and increasing the oven temperature to 200°C/400°F/Gas 6. Place the breasts in the oven and roast, basting from time to time, for 15 minutes, for a good medium-rare finish; an extra 5 minutes will be needed for medium and 25–30 minutes for well done. Once cooked to your preferred taste, remove the birds from the oven and leave to rest for 10 minutes.

While the breasts are roasting, remove the duck legs from their cooking liquor and keep warm to one side. Remove and discard the carcass pieces, then place the pan on top of the stove and bring the liquor to a simmer. Skim off any impurities, then allow it to reduce a little if needed to increase the flavour. It is important to taste while reducing. If the liquor is too thin, mix the reserved flour with a knob of butter, and whisk this into the sauce a bit at a time over a gentle simmer, until a sauce-like consistency is obtained. The pure cooking liquor may well provide this, offering a very rich and strong flavour. Only a few tablespoons per portion will be needed. Season with salt and pepper and strain through a sieve, squeezing all of the juices from the pear pieces. The legs can now be placed back in the sauce.

To finish the pear slices, heat the remaining groundnut oil in a frying pan with the other knob of butter. Once the butter is foaming, place the pears in the pan and fry over a fairly low heat, until just golden brown. Turn the pears over and continue to fry for a few minutes, basting as they cook, until golden brown.

To assemble the dish, warm the legs through in the sauce. Remove the breasts from the bone and trim into a neat shape (the skin can be left on or removed, as you wish). Spoon a pile of juniper onions on each plate, then place a pear slice beside it, its stalk pointing towards the top of the plate. Place a leg on top of each pear and spoon a little of the sauce over and around the onions before topping them with the duck breasts.

● *A tablespoon or two of the finished sauce can be quickly boiled and reduced to a sticky, treacly consistency. When brushed over the cooked legs, this gives a very shiny, glazed finish.*

- 1 x 3.5–4.5kg (8–10lb) turkey
- 50g (2oz) butter
- salt and pepper
- cooking oil

For the pâté

- 75g (3oz) raisins
- 100ml (3½fl oz) sweet sherry
- 16–18 rashers of unsmoked streaky bacon (20–24 if only very thin)
- small knob of butter, plus extra for greasing
- 350g (12oz) rindless pork belly, chopped into rough small dice
- 175g (6oz) streaky or back bacon, chopped into rough small dice
- 100g (4oz) pork fat, chopped into rough small dice
- 175g (6oz) chicken livers, chopped into rough small dice
- 1 onion, finely chopped
- 5 tablespoons whisky
- 1 teaspoon ground mixed spice
- ½ teaspoon dried herbes de Provence
- 2 tablespoons freshly chopped parsley
- 1 egg
- 4 slices of thick white bread, crusts removed and crumbed (approximately 100g/4oz)

Crown of roast turkey served with its own bacon and sherry raisin pâté

To make a 'crown' of turkey, the legs and backbone are removed, leaving only the breasts on the bone. This reduces the cooking time of the bird quite considerably and also enables you to take full advantage of the leg meat, as we will here with the pâté recipe. It is only the thigh meat that is needed to flavour the pâté mix. The drumsticks can be chopped and used in the stock or you can roast them with the crown, adding them just 1 hour before completion of the cooking time, and offering these two favourite cuts to the highest bidder!

We all know that turkey has a 12-month season, but it's during winter that it appears in almost every household, so this recipe is perfect for this chapter. It's ideal for both Christmas and Easter festivities, but suits Christmas particularly well, presenting the bird with its royal crown touch, and with all the preparation having been completed in advance, ready for the special day. The pâté mix can be made up to 48 hours in advance, giving it time to mature and develop, all the flavours mingling and enlivening each other. This country pâté recipe replaces the almost compulsory chestnut stuffing that turkey has been served with for so long. It has a more meaty finish, with a depth of flavour that works well with the classic garnishes of chipolatas and bacon, while also offering the sweet sherry touch of raisins.

Please don't be put off by the length of the ingredients' list. I'm sure you'll notice that many are storecupboard regulars at this time of year.

Method The legs can simply be removed from the bird by cutting between the breast and leg itself. Once reaching the thigh joint connecting the leg to the carcass, pull the leg away from the bird at an angle of 180°. Continue to cut the leg away, following the meat connected to the bone. The leg will now come free. Repeat the same process with the remaining leg.

Separate the thigh from the drumstick by simply cutting between the joint. The drumsticks can now be kept for roasting or chopped for making stock (see above). Remove the skin from the thigh and cut the meat away from the bone. Chop 350g (12oz) of it into rough small dice. Any remaining trimmings can be kept for the stock.

Now cut away the backbone. Stand the bird upright with the backbone facing you. Cut either side of the bone, following it to the neck end and releasing. The breasts are now left sitting on the breastbone, still with wings attached. The wings can be left on the bird as they are, the wing tips folded beneath the bird.

To help enrich the flavour of the turkey, gently release the skin from the breasts. Beginning from the neck end, 25g (1oz) of the butter can be pushed between the skin and meat. This will melt during the roasting, enriching the finished flavour. The remaining butter can now be brushed over the breasts ready for roasting. Chill the turkey and wrap in cling film once the butter has set. Store in the fridge until needed.

Before making the pâté, place the raisins in the sherry, leaving to soak for 1–2 hours. Once soaked, drain the raisins, collecting the sherry in a small saucepan, and keep to one side. Lay four of the bacon rashers between two sheets of cling film and roll with a rolling pin. This will extend the length of the rashers and thin

For the stock

- 1–2 tablespoons cooking oil
- 1 onion, chopped
- 2 celery sticks, chopped
- 1 carrot, chopped
- 2 x 400g/14oz tins of consommé or 1.25 litres (2 pints) *Instant stock* (page 194)
- 1 tablespoon butter (optional)
- 1 tablespoon flour (optional)

the texture. Repeat the same process with the remaining rashers. As the pâté is to be presented as a savoury gateau, butter a 20 × 6cm (8 × 2½in) loose-bottomed cake tin and line it with the streaky bacon rashers, placing an end of each rasher in the central point of the tin base. These will encase the pâté and add flavour to the finished dish, as well as ensuring a moist result. Press the bacon into the tin firmly, leaving any excess hanging over the edge. Continue this process, very slightly overlapping each rasher, until the tin is completely lined. Refrigerate.

Pass the 350g (12oz) of chopped turkey thigh meat, the pork belly, chopped bacon and pork fat through the coarse blade of a mincer once. Add the chicken livers and repeat the mincing process. Place in the bowl of an electric mixer and refrigerate. Add the chopped onion to the reserved sherry and bring to a simmer. Cook over a moderate heat for 6–7 minutes, until the onion is tender, and allow the sherry to reduce to an almost-dry finish. Leave to cool. Add the sherry, onion, raisins, whisky, mixed spice, herbes de Provence, chopped parsley, egg and breadcrumbs to the minced meat, and season well with salt and ground white pepper. With a beater attachment, place the bowl on the machine and beat moderately for a few minutes (or by hand) until completely mixed in.

To check for seasoning, make a mini-burger and fry in a small knob of butter for a few minutes on each side. This can now be tasted and more salt and pepper added to the mix, if needed.

Spoon and press the pâté stuffing into the lined cake

tin, then fold the overhanging bacon over the top. Cover the pâté with a disc of buttered greaseproof paper and place a suitable plate on top to press lightly. Seal the lid with foil. This can now be refrigerated for up to 48 hours (see above), maturing in flavour with time.

To make the stock, heat the cooking oil in a large frying pan. Add the chopped turkey bones and trimmings and fry until well coloured. Transfer to a saucepan (previously draining in a colander if too fatty), then add the chopped vegetables to the frying pan. Fry over a moderate heat for 8–10 minutes, until beginning to soften and taking on a golden edge, lifting any turkey flavours left in the pan. Add the vegetables to the turkey bones, top with the consommé and 300ml (½ pint) of water, or the 1.25 litres (2 pints) stock. Bring to a gentle simmer and cook for 30 minutes.

Strain the stock through a fine sieve or muslin cloth and skim off any fat for a clean finish. This element of the complete dish can also be made up to 48 hours in advance, ready for reheating on the day. Should a thicker consistency be preferred, mix together the flour and butter and whisk a little at a time into the simmering stock. Once added, continue to simmer for a few minutes. The finished colour of the gravy, particularly if thickened, will be a pale *café au lait* colour but with a rich turkey flavour.

For the crown roast, preheat the oven to 220°C/425°F/Gas 7. Spoon a tablespoon of cooking oil into a roasting tray and place in the buttered turkey crown and the drumsticks, if using. Put the pâté on a baking tray and place with the turkey crown in the preheated oven. The cooking time for both is the same, between 1½ hours and 1 hour 40 minutes. During this time the turkey can be basted with its melted butter and juices every 20–30 minutes. To test if the pâté is cooked, pierce it with a trussing needle, skewer or small knife and leave this in the pâté for 10–15 seconds. Carefully check the warmth of the needle against your lip – the pâté should be very hot to be cooked through. If using a temperature probe, the reading must reach that of 70–72°C (see below). The same testing process can also be used to check the turkey.

Remove the turkey, drumsticks and pâté from the oven and leave to rest for 10–15 minutes before carving. During the cooking of the pâté, some bacon and other juices will have been released into the baking tray. These can be carefully added to the loose gravy just a little at a time, taking into account the strength of the salty bacon flavour.

Turn out the pâté from the tin. To give the flat presentation side a richer golden-brown finish, preheat a hot grill. Place the pâté cake under the grill, cooking until well coloured.

The turkey is now ready to carve; offer the slices with a wedge of the pâté and some warmed turkey gravy. Here are a few suggestions for perfect seasonal accompaniments to be found within the book: *Cranberry sauce* (page 198), *Sweetened potatoes and chestnuts with chives* (page 105), *Sesame and ham sprouts* (page 110), *Roast parsnips, apples and prunes* (page 160). A generous bunch of watercress can also be used to garnish the roast.

● *The temperature probe instructions may suggest cooking poultry to 90°C. This can, of course, be adhered to. However, I have always found 70–72°C to be more than sufficient, offering a well-cooked and moist finish.*

● *Should potatoes or vegetables be roasted with the turkey and pâté, an extra 20–30 minutes' cooking time may be needed.*

● *When using chicken livers for any recipe, it is best to buy them 24–48 hours in advance. During this time the livers can be soaked in milk and chilled before use. This will help remove the blood and any excess bitterness. This is not essential, but does produce a more refined finish.*

● *If a mincer is unavailable, a food processor can be used to bind the pâté ingredients together. It is important, however, that the various meats and chicken livers are first cut into rough small dice. This will help the processor bind and break down their texture quickly, without overworking and puréeing them.*

● *For a deeper gravy colour, an instant gravy thickener can be used in place of the butter and flour listed in the recipe.*

● *A tablespoon of redcurrant or cranberry jelly can be whisked into the finished gravy for a sweeter flavour.*

Serves 8 generously

- 1 x 2.25kg (5lb) turkey breast, skin removed
- cooking oil
- salt and pepper
- 500g (approximately 1lb) *Quick puff pastry* (page 203, or bought)
- 16–20 rindless rashers of streaky bacon
- flour, for dusting
- 1 egg, beaten
- *Cranberry sauce* (page 198), to serve

For the stuffing

- 2 onions, finely chopped
- knob of butter
- 225g (8oz) pork sausages, skinned
- 2 eggs
- 150g (5oz) dried cranberries, roughly chopped
- 150g (5oz) unsweetened chestnut purée
- 100g (4oz) fresh white breadcrumbs

For the sauce

- 25g (1oz) butter, plus an extra knob
- 50g (2oz) shallots or onions, sliced
- 1 tablespoon clear honey
- 1 tablespoon red wine vinegar
- 400ml (14fl oz) red wine (approximately ½ bottle)
- 300ml (½ pint) *Instant stock* (page 194) or tinned consommé
- 1 heaped teaspoon plain flour

Roast turkey and cranberry Wellington

Turkey took over from goose as our first choice for the Christmas roast bird and, although available all year round, has become very much a seasonal favourite, hence its inclusion in this book. In our British tradition, we normally roast the bird and accompany it with a chestnut and pork stuffing, chipolata sausages and bacon, with cranberry sauce on the side – a great combination of flavours all working so well together. It is with these tastes in mind that this recipe was born.

The term 'Wellington' is usually associated with beef fillet baked within a pastry case, enhanced by the addition of pâté and mushrooms. Here the turkey – the breast only – is wrapped in a stuffing made from its own meat and some pork sausage, and flavoured with chestnut purée and dried cranberries, most of which find their way to us from North America at this time of year. As the turkey bakes and cooks, the fruits soften and begin to sweeten the stuffing. The turkey is also encased in rashers of bacon and puff pastry. Thus many of the extras usually offered separately are wrapped together, working as a team to provide the right results. This recipe will provide eight generous portions from just one large 2.25kg (5lb) turkey breast. A loose red wine gravy is also included to accompany the Wellington, and *Cranberry sauce* (page 198) can be served on the side.

Method The natural shape of the turkey breast does not really suit the rolled and wrapped Wellington. So, first trim off the wider meat at the thicker neck end to establish a more cylindrical shape. The trimmings from a breast of this size should be about 350g (12oz), which is enough to make the stuffing. Once trimmed, tie the breast in sections, leaving a 2.5cm (1in) gap between each one, to secure its cylindrical shape. Heat 2–3 tablespoons of cooking oil in a large frying pan or roasting tray. Season the turkey with salt and pepper, then fry, turning, until golden brown all over. Remove from the pan and leave to cool. The breast can now be chilled to firm and set before the string is removed.

To make the stuffing, cook the chopped onions in a knob of butter for several minutes until softened. Remove from the heat and allow to cool. Roughly chop the turkey trimmings, then blitz in a food processor until smooth. Add the skinned sausages and continue to blitz for a further 30–40 seconds until mixed in. Season with salt and pepper and add the eggs, blitzing them into the meat for a further minute, until the texture has thickened. Remove the stuffing from the processor and put into a large bowl. Mix in the cooked onions with the remaining stuffing ingredients. The stuffing can now also be chilled while the pastry and bacon are prepared.

The streaky bacon first needs to be rolled out thinly to extend the length of the rashers and help them wrap around the turkey and stuffing. The easiest method to follow is to lay four or five rashers between two sheets of cling film and simply press with a rolling pin as if rolling pastry. Peel away the top layer of cling film, remove the rashers and place them on a tray. Repeat the same process until all are rolled, then chill until needed.

Roll the puff pastry on a floured surface into a rectangle approximately 46 × 35cm (18 × 14in).

Lay the bacon rashers on top of the pastry, leaving a 3–4cm (1¼–1½ in) border around the edge and slightly overlapping each rasher as they are laid. Covering the pastry should use 14 or 15 of the rashers. Spread three-quarters of the stuffing over the bacon, first mixing well to loosen if chilled and set, reserving a quarter to finish the covering. Remove the string from the turkey and lay it, presentation-side down, on top of the stuffing. Spread the remaining stuffing along the top of the turkey. Lift four or five of the bacon rashers and stuffing at a time over the turkey breast and press against it. This is a simple operation and the stuffing holds well. Continue until all the rashers from both sides have been lifted. The remaining rashers can now be laid lengthwise along the top to cover the extra stuffing. Fold one long side of the puff pastry over. Brush the other with beaten egg along the edge before lifting and sealing in all of the ingredients. Now brush both ends with egg before folding both on top. Turn the Wellington over and place on a large greased baking tray (alternatively the tray can be covered with greased parchment paper or non-stick sheets) and chill until needed.

Preheat the oven to 200°C/400°F/Gas 6. Place the Wellington in the oven and bake for 1¼–1½ hours. After the first 45 minutes of baking, brush the Wellington with egg to help colour the pastry. For the most golden of finishes, brush again with the egg about 15–20 minutes before it is due to come out of the oven.

Remove from the oven and leave to rest for 15–20 minutes, then lift carefully with two large fish slices, transferring it to a carving board.

While the Wellington is baking, make the sauce. Melt the knob of butter in a saucepan and, once bubbling, add the sliced shallots or onions. Cook on a medium-to-high heat until well coloured and taking on a rich deep colour. Add the honey and continue to cook for a few minutes more, until bubbling well and approaching a caramelized stage. At this point, add the red wine vinegar and red wine, bring to the boil and reduce by half. Add the chosen stock and bring back to a simmer. While the stock is warming, mix the flour with the measured butter. Spoon and whisk well into the sauce until completely mixed in. The flour serves as the thickening agent, but this small quantity doesn't make it over-starchy or too thick. Bring the sauce back to the boil, then reduce to a gentle simmer and cook for a few minutes. Strain the sauce through a fine sieve and season, if needed, reheating before serving. The turkey Wellington is now ready to carve and serve, offering the sauce separately.

For accompanying potatoes and vegetables, I suggest *Noisette potatoes* (page 199) and *Buttered Brussels sprouts* (page 199).

● *Should other items such as roast potatoes or roast parsnips be cooked in the same oven with the Wellington, extra cooking time will be needed, as these items draw the heat from the Wellington. An extra 20–30 minutes will cover the lost heat.*

● *For a looser or extra sauce, simply add extra* Instant stock *(page 194), or consommé.*

Serves 4

- 2 medium carrots
- 1 medium swede
- 2 large turnips
- 2–3 celery sticks
- 2 parsnips
- 4 chicken legs
- ½ small onion, very finely chopped
- 1 bay leaf
- salt and pepper
- 25–50g (1–2oz) butter (optional)
- squeeze of lemon juice (optional)
- 1 tablespoon picked and torn flatleaf parsley

Steamed chicken leg jardinière

Jardinière is a French culinary term for a dish garnished with a selection of vegetables. The other feature with a *jardinière* dish is the way the vegetables are cut. This doesn't have to be followed, but it does help with the presentation. Each item is cut into batons approximately 5cm × 5mm × 5mm (2 × ¼ × ¼in). These are scattered around the plate, in this case ready to hold and surround the steamed legs. There is no chicken stock used in this recipe, as the steaming water from cooking the chicken and vegetables is used to finish the dish, giving a very natural flavour.

One of the advantages of this dish is that it will hold its own through both the autumn and winter seasons. The vegetables can be as varied as you wish, but I prefer to use the root vegetables – carrots, turnips, swedes, parsnips and celery.

Most of these, bar the celery, are still in season up to the last month of winter – you could always use imported celery instead. February could be a good month to try this dish, making sure we enjoy the last run of these greats.

Method Cut the carrots, swede, turnips and celery into batons as described above. Cut the parsnips into 5cm (2in) pieces. These can now also be cut into rough batons, discarding the woody central core of each parsnip.

It is best to remove any backbone that may still be attached to the base of the chicken thighs. The thighbone itself can also be removed, if you wish. To do so, cut along the thighbone on the opposite side to the skin. Once revealed, gently cut either side of the bone, then scrape the meat away towards the drumstick. At this point, the drumstick and exposed thighbone can be folded against themselves to break the connection. The only remaining bone is that within the drumstick. The boning process of the thigh is not essential, but can make eating a little easier.

Sprinkle the chopped onion and bay leaf in a saucepan large enough to accommodate a suitable steamer to hold the four chicken legs. Cover with 1.25 litres (2 pints) of water and bring to a rapid simmer. Season the legs with salt and pepper and sit them in the steamer, skin-side up. Place over the simmering water and cover with a lid. The total cooking time needed for the chicken legs is 25 minutes. After 15 minutes, add the carrots, swede and celery to the steaming water. Bring to a simmer again before returning the chicken legs to steam. Continue to steam for a further 5 minutes, then add the turnips and parsnips to the steaming water. Once simmering again, the legs can be replaced to finish their cooking time with a further 5 minutes.

At this point the vegetables will also be tender. Remove the chicken legs and keep them warm within the steamer. Strain the vegetables from the pan, discarding the bay leaf, saving the liquor in a saucepan. Arrange the vegetables on large warmed plates or bowls. Remove the skin from the chicken and place the legs on top of the vegetables.

Whisk the butter into the simmering cooking liquor and add a squeeze of lemon juice, if using. The liquor can be left absolutely natural, if preferred. Finish the liquor with the torn parsley, then pour it over the chicken and vegetables. The dish is ready to serve.

- 1.75kg (4lb) free-range chicken
- 4 parsnips
- 2–3 tablespoons groundnut or cooking oil
- 2 knobs of butter
- 150–200ml (¼ pint–7fl oz) *Chicken* or *Instant stock* (page 194) or tinned chicken consommé or water
- 4–8 rindless rashers of streaky bacon

For the garlic and parsley butter (optional)
- 25–50g (1–2oz) butter
- 1 large garlic clove, crushed
- 1 tablespoon chopped parsley
- salt and pepper

For the red cabbage
- knob of butter
- 1 small or ½ large red cabbage, finely shredded
- 2 onions, sliced

- peeled rind of ½ orange
- 1 bay leaf
- 6 juniper berries
- ⅛ teaspoon ground cinnamon
- ⅛ teaspoon freshly grated nutmeg
- 2 cloves
- 4 tablespoons red wine vinegar or cider vinegar
- 2 tablespoons demerara sugar
- 300ml (½ pint) apple juice

Parsnip pot-roast chicken with spicy red cabbage and bacon

The very thought of this wintry-sounding dish warms you through, let alone all of the lovely winter tastes it contains. Parsnips are at the height of their season during the winter, as is the red cabbage which, as with all cabbage running from autumn to summer, responds to the chill with crisper leaves and a sort of fresher taste.

This recipe will happily work with all poultry and game birds, so the chicken is by no means essential. Guinea fowl is a great choice, with pheasant – which so often needs a helping hand to maintain its moistness – following on. An optional extra which can be added is a garlic and parsley butter left to melt into the bird itself. It's really not essential, but does give an extra edge to the overall flavour of the dish.

Method Preheat the oven to 200°C/400°F/Gas 6. To make the optional garlic and parsley butter, mix together the butter, crushed garlic and chopped parsley, seasoning with salt and pepper. This will now be placed between the chicken skin and breast, melting within the bird as it roasts. To do so, release the skin carefully from the chicken breasts, starting at the neck end. This is very easy, but it is important to do it gently so as not to split the skin. Spoon the butter mix underneath the skin and over the breast, dividing between the two sides. Pull the skin over and press gently to spread the butter across the breasts. Pull the excess skin underneath the bird and secure with one or two cocktail sticks. To maintain a good chicken shape, tie the legs together. Set to one side.

Peel each of the parsnips and quarter, cutting away the woody central core. Heat 1–2 tablespoons of the groundnut or cooking oil in a large frying pan. Place the parsnips in the pan and fry reasonably quickly until golden brown on all sides. Season with salt and pepper. The parsnips can now be transferred into a suitably sized pot in which to cook the chicken.

Season the chicken with salt and pepper. After wiping the frying pan clean, heat the remaining tablespoon of groundnut oil and fry the bird on both breasts and legs, to colour to a rich golden brown. Place the chicken on top of the parsnips and brush with a knob of butter. Cover with a lid and place in the oven for 1 hour. After 20 minutes, remove the lid and baste the chicken with the juices. Add a third of the stock, consommé or water, replace the lid and continue to pot-roast for a further 20 minutes. As the chicken is cooking, the parsnips will be softening, becoming overcooked with a creamy texture as they absorb the juices. For the final 20 minutes of cooking, remove the lid and add another third of the stock, if required, basting regularly.

While the chicken is in the oven, the red cabbage can be cooked. Melt the knob of butter in a large saucepan and add the shredded cabbage, onions, orange rind, bay leaf and spices. Cook for 6–7 minutes, until beginning to soften, then add the red wine vinegar or cider vinegar. Continue to cook until the vinegar has almost completely evaporated. Add the demerara sugar and apple juice, cover with a lid and gently simmer until completely tender. This can take up to 40 minutes or more, depending how finely the cabbage has been shredded. Once tender, remove the lid and increase the heat to allow any excess apple cooking liquor to boil and reduce, just leaving enough to maintain a moist finish. Season with salt and pepper, discarding the orange rind.

To crisp the bacon, lay the rashers on a baking tray and cover with another. Place in the preheated oven for 20 minutes while the chicken is pot-roasting. If the bacon is not yet at a crispy stage after this time, pour away excess fat from the tray and return to the oven for a further 10–15 minutes. Remove the rashers from the oven and tray and leave to cool. The bacon will now be very crispy, ready to reheat quickly in the oven when needed. It's not essential to cover the rashers with the

second tray, but this does keep them completely flat and helps them crisp. They can, of course, be baked and left to curl, or grilled.

Remove the chicken from the pot and keep warm to one side, along with the soft parsnips. Boil any juices, adding the remaining stock. Cook for a minute or two, checking for seasoning. This is not a sauce, purely a cooking liquor with which to moisten the carved bird. A large knob of butter can be whisked in to emulsify the flavours and consistency slightly.

To serve, remove the chicken breasts and legs, offering either a thigh or drumstick with a half a breast per portion. Arrange the softened parsnips and cabbage on plates, along with the chicken pieces and warmed crispy bacon. Spoon the cooking liquor juices over the chicken and serve.

● *Extra chopped parsley can be added to the liquor before serving, along with a tablespoon or two of crème fraîche or double/whipping cream. This creates a more sauce-like consistency.*

Serves 4

- 6–8 tangerines
- 450–675g (1–1½lb) greens (curly kale, spinach, cabbage or Brussels sprouts)
- salt and pepper
- 15g (½oz) butter, plus a large knob for the greens
- 4 x 175–200g (6–7oz) lamb steak escalopes, prepared as below
- 1 tablespoon groundnut oil
- 1 shallot, finely chopped
- 2 teaspoons green peppercorns, lightly crushed
- 4 tablespoons brandy or Grand Marnier
- 200ml (7fl oz) whipping cream
- 1 tablespoon picked and torn flatleaf parsley (optional)

Seared escalopes of lamb with tangerines and greens

Escalope is a French culinary term meaning a thin slice, with which we are now all familiar. These escalopes are to be taken from lamb leg steaks. The steaks, each 175–200g (6–7oz), need to be without bone. This can quite easily be cut away, before batting the steak to a thinned-out slice with a meat tenderizer. If a tenderizer hammer is unavailable, simply place the meat between two sheets of cling film and beat it flat with a rolling pin. This will spread and tenderize the meat. To guarantee the escalope does not curl during its cooking, snip with scissors around the border of fine sinew, making four or five cuts.

The tangerines and greens make a lovely winter combination, the fruits imported and plentiful, and many different home-grown greens to choose from. Curly kale, spinach, cabbage or Brussels sprouts can all be used, each just gently softened before they are rolled in a knob of butter and seasoned.

The sauce to accompany the lamb will basically be *au poivre vert*, with green peppercorns. The peppercorns and tangerines are brought together in the pan once the lamb escalopes are cooked, with a quick brandy or Grand Marnier flambé, and a splash of cream.

Method Halve and juice four of the tangerines, peeling and segmenting the remainder. Each segment can now be carefully peeled of its fine skin to reveal the fruit itself. The peeled segments can be left whole or halved into smaller chunky pieces and kept to one side.

To prepare the greens, if using curly kale or spinach, tear away the tough stalks, breaking the leaves into bite-sized pieces. Cabbage can be quartered, removing any damaged and tough outside leaves, along with the central core. It can then be finely shredded or torn into bite-sized pieces. Brussels sprouts are best peeled of their outer leaves and halved, with the root cut away, then finely shredded.

Any of these greens can be cooked in advance by blanching in boiling salted water until tender. Kale and cabbage will take 4–5 minutes, the spinach and shredded sprouts needing just half that time. Once cooked, refresh in iced water and drain, squeezing out excess water. Melt the large knob of butter, mixing it with the greens, and season with salt and pepper. These can now be arranged in a vegetable dish, covered with cling film, ready to microwave just before serving. To cook the greens while frying the lamb, melt the butter in a large saucepan with 4–5 tablespoons of water. Once bubbling, add the greens, cover with a lid and cook, stirring from time to time, for more or less the same time as above. Season and drain once tender and ready to serve.

To cook the lamb, first season the escalopes with salt and pepper. Heat two large frying pans (once beaten, the lamb steaks become quite large) and add the groundnut oil and measured butter. Once hot and sizzling, place the lamb in the pans and sear for just 2 minutes, then turn over and continue to fry for a further 2 minutes. At this point the lamb will still be pink to serve. For well-done, at least double the cooking time. Remove the lamb from the pans and keep warm to one side.

Pour away excess fat from the pans and divide the shallot and green peppercorns between them. Add 2 tablespoons of brandy or Grand Marnier to each. Over a fairly high heat this will flambé very quickly and reduce until almost dry. Divide the tangerine juice between the two pans. Once simmering, one pan can be poured into the other. Allow the juice to reduce by two-thirds, then add the cream. Simmer to a loose coating consistency and season with salt and pepper. The peeled tangerine segments can now be quickly warmed in the sauce. Finish the sauce with the torn parsley leaves, if using. The making of the sauce takes literally minutes, with all reducing very quickly. There may be impurities from the pan in the sauce, which are not so good to look at but full of lamb flavour. If you prefer a cleaner finish, the sauce can be made in a small saucepan totally separate from the lamb pans.

To present, divide the greens between four plates with the lamb escalopes (any juices from the meat can be added to the sauce), spooning the *au poivre* sauce over.

Serves 4–6
- 1 leg of lamb on the bone (approximately 1.5–1.75kg/3¼–4lb)
- 4 garlic cloves, peeled and cut into slivers
- 2 onions, sliced
- 8 juniper berries, crushed
- 12 black peppercorns, finely crushed
- 3 cloves
- 1 teaspoon crushed coriander seeds
- 5cm (2in) piece of cinnamon stick
- large sprigs of thyme
- large sprigs of rosemary
- 3 bay leaves
- strips of peeled rind from 1 orange, plus the juice
- 1 bottle of red wine
- 2 tablespoons cooking oil
- salt and pepper
- 2 tablespoons demerara sugar

For the cabbage
- 1 large Savoy cabbage
- 4 rindless rashers of smoked streaky bacon
- 3–4 Cumberland sausages (taken from a standard 450g/1lb pack)
- 1 tablespoon butter
- 2 carrots, sliced
- 2 onions, sliced
- 4 juniper berries
- 1 bay leaf
- freshly grated nutmeg
- sprigs of thyme and rosemary, tied together
- 450ml (¾ pint) *Chicken* or *Instant stock* (page 194) or water

Parson's 'venison' with Cumberland braised cabbage

Parson's 'venison' is not actually venison at all. Venison used to have a reputation as a rich man's food, not readily available to the more humble folk like the local parson. As a substitute, lamb would take its place, marinated for days in lots of red wine and spices. Over the days, the marinade would imbue the lamb with a deeper and richer, almost gamey, flavour. The lamb certainly does not lose its own distinctive character; instead it offers variety, the flavour changing from the skin down to the centre. For this dish really to work, you need to plan a minimum of 4 days ahead, but preferably 5 or 6.

The cabbage, with so much of it around at this time of year, is to be braised in stock with carrots, onions, bacon and Cumberland sausage – hence its name. The 'real' Cumberland sausage has been missing from our larders for over 40 years now, or so the story goes. It is said that, in 1960, the last sow from a special breed of pig used for the Cumberland left us, with other replicas following after. The flavour of Cumberland sausage is given by a variety of herbs mixed with the pork, and enhanced by a spiced seasoning mix of cayenne pepper, nutmeg, salt and white pepper. Classically the sausage was sold by length, twisted to form the characteristic Catherine-wheel roll, rather than by weight. Today the sausages are also sold in ordinary 450g (1lb) packs, shaped and sized like a standard sausage.

Method To prepare for the 4–6 day marinating, make small incisions into the leg of lamb with the point of a small knife, then fill each with a slice of garlic. Place the lamb into a suitably sized bowl or deep tray. Scatter with the onions, juniper berries, peppercorns, cloves, coriander seeds, cinnamon stick, sprigs of thyme and rosemary, bay leaves and orange rind, then pour over the red wine and orange juice. Cover well with cling film and chill for 4–6 days (see above). To ensure even marinating, turn the meat in the wine twice a day. When ready to cook, preheat the oven to 200°C/400°F/Gas 6.

Remove the lamb from the marinade and pat dry with kitchen paper. Heat the cooking oil in a roasting tray and, once hot, season the leg with salt and pepper and place it into the roasting tray, presentation-side down. Fry, turning until completely golden brown all over. Pour away any excess fat from the pan. Turn the lamb presentation-side up and strain a quarter of the marinade into the tray. Roast in the preheated oven, allowing approximately 15 minutes per 450g (1lb) for a medium-rare finish, 20 minutes for medium and 30 minutes for well done. After the first 20 minutes of cooking, turn the joint in the tray and add another quarter of strained marinade. Continue to roast for a further 20 minutes, then turn once more and continue to roast, adding more marinade if the meat starts to look dry, until the required cooking time is complete.

Once the lamb has been placed in the oven, prepare the cabbage. Remove any damaged outside leaves, and then cut it into six wedges. The central core from each can now be cut away. Break the leaves into a few layers, leaving the small central heart as it is. Blanch them in batches in a large saucepan of boiling salted water for just 1 minute, then refresh in iced water and drain well in a colander.

Cut the rashers of bacon into 2.5cm (1in) pieces and split each of the sausages in half lengthwise. Melt half of the butter in a frying pan. Once sizzling, add the sausages, cut-side down, and fry quickly to seal and colour, then turn over and repeat on the other side. Remove the sausages from the pan.

Mix together the cabbage, bacon, carrots, onions, juniper berries and bay leaf, season with salt and pepper, and add a pinch of freshly grated nutmeg. Place half in an ovenproof braising pot, top with the sausages, herb sprigs and remaining cabbage mix, then top with the remaining butter. Bring the stock or water to the boil and pour it over. Cover with a lid and bake in the oven with the leg of lamb for 45 minutes. Remove from the oven and keep warm to one side. The cabbage will have lost some of its rich green colour as it has been cooked for such a long time. It will, however, have taken on lots of flavour and be very tender to eat.

When the lamb is cooked, remove it from the oven and the tray and allow to rest in a warm place for a good 15 minutes. Strain the remaining marinade into the roasting tray, and bring to the boil on top of the stove, skimming away any rising fat. Sprinkle in the demerara sugar and continue to simmer and reduce. When beginning to approach a syrupy consistency, return the lamb to the tray and baste and turn the leg for it to take on the rich red wine spicy flavour. As the wine syrup continues to reduce, the lamb becomes glazed, taking on an even more gamey flavour and appearance.

To serve, spoon the Cumberland cabbage with its flavoursome liquor between plates or bowls, then carve the lamb to finish. There is no sauce or gravy to accompany this dish, with the cooking liquor from the Cumberland cabbage serving as the moist finish.

● *Unsmoked bacon can also be used in the cabbage recipe, replacing the smoked streaky bacon.*

Serves 8–12 as a main course

- 1 x 3.5–4.5kg (8–10lb) leg of pork
- 2 tablespoons lard or cooking oil
- salt and pepper
- 4–6 onions, halved and skins left on (optional), plus 1 extra onion, finely chopped
- 8 apples
- 600ml (1 pint) *Chicken* or *Instant stock* (page 194)
- 20 ready-to-eat prunes, halved
- 300ml (½ pint) white wine
- 1.75kg (4lb) parsnips, peeled and quartered lengthwise
- 4–6 tablespoons olive oil
- 1 bay leaf
- 150ml (¼ pint) double cream (optional)
- squeeze of lemon juice (optional)
- 50g (2oz) butter
- 1–2 tablespoons chopped sage leaves
- 1–2 tablespoons clear honey (optional)

Roast leg of pork with sage roast parsnips, apples and prunes

A whole leg of pork is the sort of thing you cook for a big event day, a family and friends day. Christmas Day is the most obvious, particularly as it happens to fall during the season of home-grown parsnips and apples. Whole legs are about 3.5–4.5kg (8–10lb) in weight, so more than enough for 8 people, more like 10 or even 12. Apples and prunes are mixed with parsnips while they roast, with more of these two fruits soaking and cooking in chicken stock. The extra flavours are there to strengthen the juices, thickening the liquor to finish the sauce. The *Classic roast potatoes* on page 199 can be doubled to serve with this dish, giving you plenty to share between 10 or 12 people.

An optional extra is to roast the pork on halved onions, leaving their skins on to protect them and prevent them from breaking during the long cooking process. The onions are by no means essential, but do roast well; serve them spooned from their skins to accompany the pork. If roasting without them, a wire rack can be used to prevent the meat from sticking to the base of the pan.

Method Preheat the oven to 200°/400°F/Gas 6. To achieve a good crisp crackling, the leg must be scored in lines just deep enough to break through the skin. Brush with the lard or cooking oil and sprinkle liberally with the salt. Place the onion halves, skin-side up, if using, or a wire rack, in a large roasting tray. Place the leg of pork on top of the onions or rack and roast in the preheated oven for 30 minutes without basting. Turn the oven temperature down to 180°C/350°F/Gas 4 and continue to roast, again without basting, for a further 3½–4 hours. If becoming too deep in colour, loosely cover with foil. To check the meat is cooked, pierce the thick end of the joint with a skewer. When clear moist juices are released, the pork is ready. Remove it from the oven and keep warm to one side (along with the onions, if using), allowing it to relax for a good 20–30 minutes before serving.

While the pork is roasting, the parsnips can be cooked and the sauce prepared. For the sauce, peel and core two of the apples and roughly chop into relatively small pieces. Add these to the stock, along with seven or eight of the halved prunes. Bring to a simmer and reduce by two-thirds. Remove from the heat and keep to one side to allow the flavours to infuse. Boil the white wine in a separate pan until reduced by three-quarters, then add it to the apple and prune stock.

Cut the central core from the parsnips. Heat 3–4 tablespoons of the olive oil in a large roasting tray, add the parsnips and fry over a moderate heat until a rich golden brown on all sides. This can be done well in advance, ready to finish roasting in the pan for

30 minutes. The parsnips can be cooked while the pork is resting; if so, increase the oven temperature back to 200°C/400°F/Gas 6.

Prepare the remaining six apples. Peel, quarter and cut away their cores and seeds. Fry them in batches in the remaining olive oil, allowing them to colour to a golden brown, ready for adding to the parsnips when needed.

Season the parsnips with salt and pepper and place them in the oven. After the first 15 minutes, add the apples and continue to roast for a further 10 minutes before adding the remaining prune halves. These will now have just 5 minutes to soften and warm through. Should the apples feel too firm, continue to roast with the parsnips, which can now be overcooked for a further 5–10 minutes to give a soft fluffy filling.

While the parsnips are roasting, remove the pork and onions from the tray and pour away the fat. Scoop the onions from their skins and warm through in the oven. Season with salt and pepper.

Warm the tray on top of the stove and add the finely chopped onion and bay leaf. Cook for a few minutes, until beginning to soften, then add the flavoured (prune, apple and white wine) stock. Bring to a gentle simmer and cook for 5 minutes, lifting all of the flavours from the pan. Liquidize to a purée and strain through a sieve for a smooth finish. The liquor can now be checked for seasoning and served as it is or simmered for a few minutes with the addition of the double cream. Check the seasoning again. Add a squeeze of lemon juice to lift the flavour, if necessary.

To finish the parsnips, remove the tray from the oven and place it on top of the stove over a very low heat. Add the butter and chopped sage, then trickle over the clear honey, if using. Spoon the parsnips into a large hot vegetable dish, to be presented on the table.

Remove the crackling from the pork and carve the meat, presenting each portion with a piece of crackling. The dish is ready to serve.

● Mashed potatoes *(page 198) are also a lovely accompaniment for roast pork – double or treble the recipe for mash lovers. Other vegetable accompaniments that work well with the roast pork are* English cabbage plate *(page 113),* Sesame and ham sprouts *(page 110) and* Sweetened potatoes and chestnuts with chives *(page 105).*

Serves 6

- 1 x 6–8-bone 'French trimmed' loin of pork
- salt and pepper, plus coarse sea salt for sprinkling
- cooking oil, for brushing
- 1 tablespoon clear honey

- 1 teaspoon picked thyme, saving the stalks (optional)
- juice of ½ lemon
- 300ml (½ pint) *Chicken* or *Instant stock* (page 194) or tinned consommé or water
- 25g (1oz) butter

For the parsnip cream

- 1.3kg (3lb) parsnips
- milk, to cover (approximately 450–600ml/¾–1 pint)
- knob of butter
- 1 tablespoon Dijon or wholegrain mustard

Salted roast pork ribs with mustard parsnip cream

Parsnips can be found from late summer through to the following spring. They are, however, a root vegetable that prefers very cold ground, even enjoying a touch of frost, so December probably finds them at their best.

The mustard flavouring of the purée should be either French Dijon or wholegrain (English mustard can be too strong for this sweet vegetable). The Dijon almost works as an enhancer, with very little needed to lift the basic parsnip flavour. For a more robust bite, as we have here, a touch extra is required. The wholegrain mustard provides more of a tartness, carrying a soft warmth behind it. Both work well with parsnips, so the choice is yours.

The pork ribs are roasted as a French trimmed loin, with coarse sea salt to help flavour the crispy crackling, which will be balanced by the moist tenderness of the meat. 'French trimmed' is purely a loin left on the bone. This basically means the number of bones, all exposed and cleaned, indicates the quantity of portions. It is important to ask your butcher to remove the chine bone. This is the central bone that runs down the back of the joint, connecting the two loins together. Once this is removed you are able to cut cleanly between each rib, using the chine bone as a trivet on which to roast the pork.

To make a loose gravy, honey, lemon and thyme will help lift the residue from the pan, loosened with some stock or water. This is quite a simple dish that will eat well with honest *Classic roast potatoes* (page 199), or offer its services as an alternative Christmas lunch.

Method Preheat the oven to 230°C/450°F/Gas 8. Score the skin of the pork with a sharp knife in a line between each bone. Season the underside and meat ends of the pork with salt and pepper. Brush the skin with cooking oil, then sprinkle with table and coarse sea salt. Place the joint in a roasting tray, sitting on its arched bones, skin-side up. To prevent the meat from becoming dry in contact with the roasting tray, the removed chine bone can be placed in the tray and any exposed meat sat on top of it. Place in the oven and roast for 15 minutes at this high temperature to begin the crisping of the skin. Reduce the oven temperature to 200°C/400°F/Gas 6 and continue roasting, basting from time to time, for a further 50–60 minutes. During this time, the skin will have crisped to a salted crackling finish. Remove the joint from the pan and keep warm to one side, allowing to rest for a good 15 minutes.

Pour away any excess fat from the roasting tray and place it on a medium heat. As the residue begins to bubble and crackle, add the honey and thyme stalks, if using. The honey will melt instantly and begin to sizzle within a minute or two. When it begins to caramelize, add the lemon juice, which will begin to spit, lifting all of the flavours. Add the stock, consommé or water and bring to a simmer. Cook gently for a few minutes, seasoning with salt and pepper. Stir in the butter, then strain through a fine sieve. Add the fresh thyme leaves just before serving, if using.

While the pork is roasting, make the parsnip cream. Peel the parsnips, splitting each lengthwise into quarters and cutting away the core. Cut the strips into

rough dice. Place the diced parsnips in a saucepan and add enough milk almost to cover. Season with salt and pepper and bring to a gentle simmer. Place a lid on top and cook for 15–20 minutes, until the parsnips are completely tender. Using a slotted spoon, place some of the cooked dice into a liquidizer and blitz to a smooth purée, adding some of the milk if needed. As the parsnips begin to cream, more parsnips can be added. This may have to be done in two batches. If slightly grainy, then push through a sieve. Once all of the purée has been made, keep to one side, ready to rewarm when needed. When reheating, the knob of butter and mustard can be added and the seasoning rechecked.

To carve the pork, simply separate the portions by carving between each rib. An alternative is first to cut away the crackling. This can now be broken into pieces ready to serve with the carved pork. Present the pork on plates with a spoonful of the parsnip cream and a drizzle or two of the thyme-flavoured gravy.

● *An extra 10–15 minutes can be added to the pork roasting time, ensuring completely well-done meat.*

● *A teaspoon of flour can be added to the 25g (1oz) of butter before stirring it into the stock. This will immediately thicken the liquor; cook for a few minutes to finish the gravy.*

● *The mustard quantity can be increased or omitted from the parsnips, along with the honey or lemon or thyme (or all three) from the gravy.*

Serves 4

- 8 × 100g (4oz) lean pieces of chuck or braising steak
- salt and pepper
- 2 tablespoons plain flour
- 2 tablespoons groundnut oil
- large knob of butter
- 2 large carrots, quartered
- 2 medium onions, quartered
- 3 tablespoons red wine vinegar
- 1 bottle of red wine
- 8 pared strips of peel from 1 Seville orange, plus finely grated zest of 2 more and juice of all 3
- sprigs of thyme
- sprigs of rosemary
- 3 bay leaves
- 3–4 black peppercorns
- 2 teaspoons demerara sugar
- 600ml (1 pint) *Beef stock* (page 195) or tinned consommé or water

Braised Seville orange beef with horseradish dumplings

Seville oranges have a very short season, first arriving in the UK in January and gone by mid-February. Known in France as *bigarade* (bitter orange), the Seville is not an orange to buy for general eating; instead it is one that comes into its own when cooked. To increase its already pretty intense flavour, the rind can be pared in curls from the fruit, then dried in the oven on its lowest setting for 45–60 minutes (this can even sometimes take up to 2 hours). As the peel dries, its bitter flavour becomes stronger and richer. The dried peel can now be kept in an airtight jar, ready to add to stews and casseroles throughout the year, or for the making of classic sauces to go with duck.

The beef to be used here is braising or chuck steak. This has an open texture that absorbs the juices, leaving the meat moist as well as very tender after a long stewing. The beef can just be diced, but here it's kept as 100g (4oz) pieces, like mini beef joints, so that the meat is not lost amongst the carrots and onions cooking with them.

The horseradish dumplings are steamed rather than poached in the sauce. This keeps the flavours quite separate during cooking, only to meet while being eaten and enjoyed.

Method Preheat the oven to 160°C/325°F/Gas 3. Season each piece of beef with salt and pepper, then roll them in the flour, saving any excess flour. Melt the groundnut oil in a large frying pan and add the beef. Fry for 6–8 minutes, until coloured on all sides.

While the beef is frying, heat a braising pan on top of the stove and melt the large knob of butter in it. Add the carrots and onions, and cook on a gentle heat until golden brown. Remove the vegetables from the pan and add the red wine vinegar. Boil until almost dry. Add the red wine, along with four strips of the orange peel (the rest can be dried as described in the introduction for later use), the thyme, rosemary, bay leaves, peppercorns and demerara sugar, and bring to the boil. Reduce by two-thirds, then add the stock, consommé or water. Add the pieces of beef along with the carrots and onions, and any remaining flour. Bring to a simmer, cover with a lid and cook in the preheated oven for 2½–3 hours, until very tender. During this cooking time, the sauce can be skimmed of impurities from time to time, to produce a cleaner finish.

To make the dumplings, place the self-raising flour, white breadcrumbs, butter, grated horseradish (or horseradish cream or purée) and salt and pepper in a food processor. Blitz to a crumbly consistency, then stir in the chopped herbs and orange zest. Add the egg white to bind; if slightly too dry, a little milk or the egg yolk can be added for a looser, richer finish. Once it is forming into a ball, dust your hands with flour, then separate the mix into eight small dumplings. These can now be cooked once the stew is almost ready, steaming

- 75g (3oz) self-raising flour, plus extra for dusting
- 75g (3oz) fresh white breadcrumbs
- 75g (3oz) butter, diced
- 2 heaped tablespoons fresh grated horseradish (or 50g/2oz horseradish cream or purée)
- 1 tablespoon chopped parsley
- pinch of chopped thyme
- pinch of chopped rosemary
- 1 teaspoon finely grated Seville orange zest
- 1 egg white, or 1 whole egg (optional)
- milk, to loosen (optional)

them on buttered greaseproof paper for approximately 15–20 minutes over rapidly simmering water, until risen and firm.

To finish the stew, remove the meat, onions and carrots from the pan, cover and keep warm to one side. Strain the sauce through a fine sieve, then bring it to the boil, skimming off any impurities. Reduce, if necessary, to a loose sauce consistency. Boil the orange juice in a separate pan and reduce by three-quarters, then add it to the sauce. Season with salt and pepper. Return the meat and vegetables to the saucepan and bring to a gentle simmer.

The stew is now ready to serve, dividing the meat, vegetables and sauce between plates and topping with the dumplings. Strips of dried zest can also be used as an optional garnish if available (see above). This dish eats very well with *Orange caramelized salsify* (page 124).

● *If you wish to cook the dumplings in the beef pot, leave the meat and vegetables in the sauce, adding the reduced orange juice, then place the dumplings on top. Cover with a lid and gently simmer for 15–20 minutes. The complete dish is now ready to serve straight from the pot.*

● *The horseradish can be omitted from the dumplings, replacing it with 2–3 teaspoons of Dijon or wholegrain mustard, or leave them just flavoured with the orange and herbs.*

● *For a glossy finish, brush the dumplings with melted butter before serving.*

● *For a thicker sauce, stir in a little arrowroot or cornflour loosened with red wine or water.*

● *The more often the sauce is skimmed of any impurities during the braising of the beef, the cleaner and neater the finished result will be.*

Serves 4

- 900g (2lb) Jerusalem artichokes
- 1 lemon
- drop of cooking oil (optional)
- 1 x 900g (2lb) loin of veal, net weight without bone
- salt and pepper
- 3 tablespoons olive oil
- 400ml (14fl oz) *Chicken* or *Instant stock* (page 194)
- 100ml (3½fl oz) double cream (optional)
- 25g (1oz) butter (optional), plus an extra knob for the artichokes
- 2 tablespoons finely chopped shallots, rinsed
- 1 tablespoon roughly chopped curly parsley

Roast loin of veal with Jerusalem artichokes Lyonnaise

The knobbly Jerusalem artichokes are at their best from winter into spring. When buying them, it is always best to choose the smoothest as this makes for easier peeling and less wastage. Jerusalems do purée and roast very well, and are also delicious sautéed, as here.

The Lyonnaise concept has been borrowed from the French potato repertoire, where it consists of sauté potatoes with fried onions and chopped parsley. Here the onions are replaced with raw chopped shallots.

Veal is the meat from young calves. The imported Dutch variety is mostly milk-fed, giving a pale pink colour to the meat. There is also grass-fed, which is what you'll normally find here with our home-reared veal (organic is also available), carrying a richer darker colour but never quite reaching red. The loin cut of veal is the equivalent to that of the beef sirloin. It is a very tender piece of meat that, when off the bone, needs no more than 15–20 minutes' roasting.

Method Preheat the oven to 200°C/400°F/Gas 6. Peel the artichokes using a small paring knife, placing them in a bowl of water acidulated with the juice from half of the lemon. This will maintain the white colour of their flesh.

If it is possible to obtain the veal bone as well as the meat, ask your butcher for it to be chopped into relatively small pieces. To help add flavour to the sauce, these pieces of bone can now be fried in a drop of cooking oil to a golden brown and added to the veal once ready to place in the oven. Season the veal loin with salt and pepper. Heat 2 tablespoons of the olive oil in a roasting tray and place the veal in, fat-side down.

Fry on a medium heat, turning, until a deep golden brown on all sides. Leave the joint fat-side up in the tray, place in the preheated oven and roast for 15–20 minutes for a rare-to-medium-rare stage. Add another 6–7 minutes to take on to each further stage.

Remove the joint from the oven and roasting tray and leave to rest for 10 minutes. Pour away any fat, then heat the juices in the pan on top of the stove. Once hot, add the stock and bring to a simmer (if using the veal bones, it is here they will help flavour the stock), until the liquor has reduced by half. If using the cream, add it at this point and return to a simmer, then cook for just a few minutes and add the butter, if using. Whatever the choice, the thin cooking liquor will have taken on a good veal flavour, the cream and butter offering a softer finish. Squeeze the remaining lemon half into the liquor and strain the sauce through a fine sieve.

While the veal is roasting, pat the artichokes dry and slice into 5mm (¼in) thick slices. Heat the remaining olive oil in a frying pan and add a handful or two of the artichoke slices. Fry over a medium heat to a golden brown, turning the chokes from time to time. Season with salt and pepper and transfer to an ovenproof dish to keep warm in the oven while the rest are fried. Once all are done, return them to the frying pan and add the knob of butter, chopped shallots and parsley. Season with salt and pepper.

Once rested, carve the veal, offering two or three slices per portion, accompanied by the Jerusalem artichokes and lemon cooking liquor.

Serves 6
- 8 sticks of forced rhubarb
- 50g (2oz) caster sugar
- butter, for greasing
- icing sugar, for dusting

For the batter
- 100ml (3½fl oz) milk
- 150ml (¼ pint) whipping cream
- 100g (4oz) caster sugar
- 3 eggs
- 25g (1oz) plain flour
- pinch of salt
- 2–3 tablespoons Amaretto or Kirsch (optional)

Champagne rhubarb clafoutis

The word champagne in the recipe title merely refers to the actual variety of rhubarb. During the late autumn and winter months, it's forced champagne rhubarb that is available to us.

Clafoutis is a French speciality, originating in the Limousin region of central France. Classically it consists of cherries embedded in a soft creamy batter, but plenty of other fruits, such as peaches, plums and apricots, have all been introduced at some stage. Here the sweet rhubarb works very well. This style of pudding is normally served in individual *sur la plat* dishes. Here I'm simply using one large 20–23cm (8–9in) flan or earthenware dish.

Method Preheat the oven to 190°C/375°F/Gas 5. To make the batter, blitz all of the ingredients in a food processor, adding the Amaretto or Kirsch, if using (or whisk them), to a smooth consistency. Leave the batter to relax while cooking the rhubarb.

Top and tail the rhubarb sticks, then cut each into 2cm (¾in) pieces. Scatter these on a baking tray and sprinkle with the caster sugar and 4 tablespoons of water. Place the tray in the oven and bake for 6–8 minutes, until the rhubarb is just becoming tender. If too firm, continue for a further few minutes. Once the rhubarb is just approaching tender, remove it from the oven and carefully spoon it into a large colander. Leave to drain and cool, saving all of the juices.

Butter the flan dish and spoon in the rhubarb pieces. It is not essential to use all of the fruit; any excess can be made into a syrup to serve with the finished dessert. Stir the batter, then pour it over the rhubarb sticks.

Bake the pudding in the preheated oven for approximately 25–30 minutes. The pudding will have risen, more predominantly around the edges rather than in the centre, which will have just set. If the batter still appears to be too soft, simply continue to bake for a few extra minutes. About 40 minutes should really be the maximum.

Remove from the oven and leave to rest for 10 minutes, before serving very warm. During this time the batter will have collapsed from its soufflé look; this is exactly how this dessert is served, with the main concentration on the flavour. Dust lightly with icing sugar just before serving.

During the cooking of the pudding, any remaining pieces of rhubarb can be placed in a small saucepan with all of the saved juices and a few more tablespoons of water. Bring to a gentle simmer and cook for a few minutes until the rhubarb is very tender. This can now be squeezed through a sieve for a loose syrup, or just liquidized to a thicker sauce consistency. Should either need to be slightly sweeter, just add icing sugar to taste.

When serving the *clafoutis*, you can brush it with the syrup before dusting with icing sugar or offer the syrup separately.

● *The rhubarb syrup can be stirred into clotted cream. This loosens the cream, offering a very rich, creamy rhubarb sauce.*

- 675g (1½lb) forced rhubarb, plus
  1 or 2 extra sticks for the crisps
- 175g (6oz) caster sugar, plus
  extra for dusting
- juice of 3 tangerines
- 1 vanilla pod (optional)
- 300ml (½ pint) double cream

Rhubarb fool with its own crisps

Joining us in late autumn and going through to mid-spring, this gentle forced fruit (actually a vegetable) should be taken full advantage of, whether it is in desserts or with savoury dishes. This fool is quite quick and easy to make, the rhubarb helped along in the pan with the juice of some tangerines, providing an orangey syrup with which to enhance the finished dish. The crisps need some planning, but don't feel you have to make them; they're purely an extra, replacing the usual shortbread biscuits offered with a fool. You do need to plan ahead, though – at least a full half-day (12 hours).

Method Preheat the oven to its lowest possible temperature. To make the crisps, cut the extra rhubarb sticks (choosing the pinkest) into 10cm (4in) pieces, then slice them lengthwise into very thin strips. For consistency, it is best to use a mandolin slicer. Lay the strips on a baking tray lined with greaseproof paper and sprinkle each lightly with caster sugar. Place the tray in the warm oven and leave for up to 12 hours, possibly longer. During this time the moisture will be dried from the rhubarb strips, leaving them crisp. If the heat is increased, the rhubarb begins to bake rather than dry, becoming discoloured and spoilt. Once the strips are crisp, leave to cool.

To make the fool, first top and tail the rhubarb, peeling any that appears to be stringy. Chop it into 1cm (½in) pieces and place in a large saucepan with the caster sugar and the tangerine juice. Cover with a lid and cook over a low heat on top of the stove for 15–20 minutes, stirring from time to time. The pieces will now be at a

pulp stage, softened through and tender. Strain through a sieve, collecting the syrup. Once drained and cooled, the pulp can be used as it is, producing a chunkier and more rustic finish to the fool. For a smoother touch, blitz the purée in a food processor.

Boil the reserved syrup, allowing it to reduce by two-thirds, then leave it to cool.

Whip the double cream to a loose soft-peak stage. If using, split the vanilla pod lengthwise, scraping out the seeds with the point of a small knife. Add the seeds to the whipped cream, along with the rhubarb purée and half of the syrup. Spoon everything together and the fool is ready to be served in glass bowls or dishes, topped with a drizzling of the remaining syrup and the rhubarb crisps.

- *For an extra-orangey edge, the zest from the tangerines can be finely grated and added to the rhubarb while it is cooking.*

- *For a thicker fool, half of the cream can be replaced with 'fresh' bought (or tinned) custard.*

Serves 6–8
- 175g (6oz) butter at room temperature, diced, plus extra for greasing
- 175g (6oz) caster sugar
- 175g (6oz) ground almonds
- 2 eggs

For the quince
- 200g (7oz) caster sugar
- 3 strips of lemon peel
- 1kg (2¼lb) quince (4 small or 2–3 medium-to-large)

Quince-topped almond bake

In December there are still a few quince around, some joining us from Greece, maybe even one or two of our own. So this is a perfect early-winter dessert. With the *Baked cider, cinnamon and honey quince* (page 79), the quince are simply halved and then baked, to bring out the full depth of their flavour and fragrant scent. In this recipe they are cut into chunks and cooked in a sweet lemon-flavoured syrup, before they are spooned over a rich almond bake. The bake consists of almonds, butter and sugar, creating a frangipane texture. Omitting the flour – a small quantity is usually added to a frangipane mix – leaves the bake with a more moist finish, the oils from the almonds lending their buttery edge.

Method Preheat the oven to 190°C/375°F/Gas 5. Place the butter, sugar, ground almonds and eggs in a food processor and blitz to a smooth, creamy finish. Butter a 23cm (9in) pudding dish (4–5cm/1½–2in deep), then spread in the almond mix. Bake in the preheated oven for 35–45 minutes, until firm to the touch. Remove from the oven and keep to one side.

While the sponge base is cooking, prepare the quince. Pour the sugar into a large saucepan with 300ml (½ pint) of water and the lemon peel. Bring to the boil and simmer for 5 minutes. Peel the quince, cut it into quarters and remove the cores. Cut the flesh into small dice and add it to the syrup. Bring to a simmer, stirring from time to time, then cover with a circle of greaseproof paper and gently cook for 25–30 minutes, until the fruit is tender. Remove from the heat and discard the lemon peel.

Spoon the warm quince on top of the almond bake, allowing just a little of the syrup to seep into the sponge. Any excess syrup can be offered separately, or chilled for later use with other fruits.

The bake is now ready to serve just warm or cold, perhaps offering whipped or pouring cream (or crème fraîche) to accompany.

● *A vanilla mascarpone cream is a luxury extra to offer with the bake. Split a vanilla pod and scrape it into 100g (4oz) of mascarpone. Whisk 150ml (¼ pint) of whipping cream with 2 heaped tablespoons of icing sugar to soft peaks, then fold it into the vanilla-flavoured mascarpone. The cream is now ready to serve; for a firmer finish chill for 30 minutes.*

Serves 6–10
- 225g (8oz) chocolate chip cookies
- 100g (4oz) cooked chestnuts (page 201), chopped
- 50g (2oz) butter, melted
- 200g (7oz) tin of sweetened chestnut purée
- 225g (8oz) mascarpone
- 25g (1oz) caster sugar
- 300ml (½ pint) double cream

For the kumquats
- 350g (12oz) kumquats
- 300ml (½ pint) orange juice
- 225g (8oz) caster sugar

For the chocolate topping
- 225g (8oz) bitter dark chocolate, chopped
- 250ml (9fl oz) whipping cream
- 50g (2oz) butter, softened

Chestnut mascarpone cheesecake with chocolate and warm syruped kumquats

Cheesecake is a good dessert to offer, particularly during the busy Christmas period, or on other special occasion days. It has probably become so popular because it is something that can be made in advance and has quite a good shelf-life. It also has a long but mixed history, with very similar recipes dating back to the Romans in the second century BC. Other recipes found their way into the records during the thirteenth and seventeenth centuries, and today almost all cookbooks contain a version. This one is very much in the English mode – cold and creamy. Usually digestive biscuits are used as the base, but I'm exchanging these for chocolate chip cookies, lightly crushed and mixed with freshly cooked chopped chestnuts (these are optional – hazelnut chocolate chip cookies work just as well).

Kumquats are small, oval, orange-coloured fruits. Once thought to be part of the citrus family, in fact they stand quite proud as a species all on their own. Kumquats at their ripest can be eaten whole. I'm not sure we have a citrus fruit that offers such an eating experience. Here they are to be cooked until very tender, served warm to help melt the chestnut and chocolate cheesecake.

Method To make the base, place the cookies in a plastic bag or between sheets of cling film and crush them with a rolling pin. Mix the crumbled biscuits in a bowl with the chopped chestnuts. Add the melted butter and stir it amongst the crumbs. Spoon and press the mix into the base of a 23cm (9in) loose-bottomed cake tin and chill to set.

To make the cheesecake cream, beat the chestnut purée in a bowl until smooth. Add the mascarpone and sugar and continue to beat until totally combined. Lightly whip the double cream to soft-peak stage, then fold the cream into the chestnut mascarpone mix. Spoon the mix on top of the chestnut biscuit base and spread for a smooth finish. This will now need to be chilled for several hours to set completely.

While the cheesecake is setting, prepare and cook the kumquats. Halve each kumquat across, not lengthwise, gently removing any seeds. Place the orange juice and sugar in a saucepan with 150ml (¼ pint) of water and bring to the boil, then reduce the temperature to a simmer and cook for 5 minutes. Add the kumquats to the orange syrup, bringing the liquor back to a very gentle simmer. If very young and ripe, the fruits may only take 30 minutes to become tender. They can, however, take up to 1–1½ hours (2 hours maximum), before they are tender to the bite. Whatever the cooking time, the results will be the same – very tender and sweet with a slight bitter bite. Once cooked, leave to cool slightly to a warm serving temperature. If stored in airtight preserving jars, the syruped fruits will have a fairly long shelf-life, particularly if refrigerated.

To make the chocolate topping, melt the chocolate with the cream in a bowl over simmering water, making sure the bowl is not in contact with the water, as this overheats the chocolate, leaving a grainy consistency. Once the chocolate has melted, remove the bowl from the saucepan and add the softened butter.

Remove the cheesecake from the fridge and release around the edge of the cake tin with a small warmed knife. Remove the cake from the surrounding tin. To reset the edge quickly, place the cake in the freezer for 5–10 minutes.

The chocolate topping can now be poured and spread across and around the sides of the cake. This can now be left to set just at room temperature or chilled until needed. If chilling, it is best to remove the cheesecake from the fridge 20 minutes before serving, to help the chocolate return to a softer finish.

For an extra-glossy finish, a gas gun (page 11) can be quickly and lightly flashed over the chocolate. Rather than melt completely, it just softens, leaving the shiniest of finishes.

The cheesecake is now ready to serve, with spoonfuls of the warm kumquats.

Serves 4
- butter, for spreading and greasing
- 10 dates (preferably Medjool), halved and pitted
- 1 teaspoon caster sugar
- 3 tablespoons brandy
- 2 tablespoons mincemeat
- 8 slices of extra-thick white bread

For the custard
- 250ml (9fl oz) milk
- 250ml (9fl oz) whipping cream
- 1 vanilla pod, split (optional)
- 2 eggs
- 50g (2oz) caster sugar
- caster or icing sugar, for dusting (optional)

Date and brandy puddings

Dates show their wrinkly faces between the months of July and February. Most are imported from either the Middle East or California – the fat, sticky, fudge-like Medjool date is, for me, by far the best. Here the dates are soaked in brandy, then lightly bound with a spoonful or two of mincemeat. The mincemeat establishes the dessert as a winter choice, with the latter days of the season being the perfect excuse to use the last of the dates and that half-empty jar of mincemeat still sitting in the cupboard from Christmas.

Method Butter four 300ml (½ pint) soufflé pots (the next size up from the standard ramekins). Split each piece of date in half lengthwise once more, then cut into rough dice. Mix the diced dates with the caster sugar and brandy. For maximum flavour these can be covered and left to stand for several hours, before continuing with the recipe.

Once the dates have soaked, add the mincemeat. Butter the slices of bread. Using a pastry cutter, cut discs from the slices of buttered bread to fit the soufflé pots. Place a slice into each mould, buttered-side up, then divide the date mix between each. Top with the remaining slices of bread, buttered-side down.

To make the custard, pour the milk and cream into a saucepan, along with the split vanilla pod, if using. Bring to the boil, then remove from the heat and leave to infuse. Whisk together the eggs and caster sugar until soft and creamy, the sugar having dissolved. Pour the heated milk and cream into the sweetened eggs, whisking to a custard. The vanilla pod can now be removed and the custard ladled over each pudding; press gently, to help the bread slices absorb the warm vanilla cream. It may be necessary to pour half of the mixture in, leave the puddings to absorb it for 5–10 minutes and then repeat with the remaining mixture. These are now best left to stand for 30 minutes, pressing them from time to time.

Preheat the oven to 160°C/325°F/Gas 3. When hot, place the soufflé dishes in a roasting tray, fill with boiling water to two-thirds of the way up the sides of the dishes, and cover the tray with foil. Bake in the preheated oven for 25–30 minutes, until only just beginning to set. Remove the foil and bake for a further 10 minutes, to give a thick custard consistency towards the centre. Remove the dishes from the tray and leave to one side to relax for 10–15 minutes. This pudding will eat at its best just warm.

To serve, the puddings can simply be dusted with icing sugar, or sprinkle them with caster sugar and glaze under a preheated hot grill, or with a gas gun (page 11), to give a crème brûlée-style finish.

**Serves 4 as a starter
or 2 as a main course**
- 6 ripe figs
- knob of softened butter
- sprinkling of soft light brown sugar
- 100ml (3½fl oz) port
- 3 tablespoons crème fraîche
- 1 tablespoon cider vinegar
- 3 tablespoons olive oil
- salt and pepper
- 12–16 thin slices of Parma ham
- 2 handfuls of mixed salad leaves (rocket, curly endive, radicchio, oak leaf, watercress, etc., see below)
- 100g (4oz) Stilton cheese, crumbled and at room temperature
- 1 tablespoon 1cm (½in) chive sticks

Roast fig and Stilton salad with Parma ham and a port vinaigrette

Figs, although a wonderful dessert fruit, lend themselves equally well to savoury dishes. This winter and autumn recipe is ideal for lunch or supper, especially when served with crusty bread. Having said that, it also makes a perfect starter for the Christmas meal.

Christmas and Stilton have been together since one can remember, with the port sitting comfortably on the sideboard waiting to be opened. In this recipe, the port visits the kitchen, trying to please the palate in another way.

Whenever purchasing Parma ham, it is always best to take the cut from the middle of the ham. Here it will be at its most plump and tender, without an over-fatty edge. Also try to get the thinnest of slices. Three to four slices of ham per person will be plenty for a starter portion, particularly if following it with roast turkey and all the trimmings. For the salad leaves, bags of pre-washed mixed leaves can be found in most supermarkets. As a starter, one bag for four people will be plenty.

Method Preheat the oven to 220°C/425°F/Gas 7. Trim the tips off the fig stalks, and then halve each fig. Place the figs, cut-side up, in a lightly buttered roasting tray. Brush each fig with butter and lightly sprinkle a little sugar over each.

Place in the preheated oven and roast for 10–12 minutes, until softening. Remove the figs from the tray and keep warm by turning off the oven and returning the figs to it on a separate plate.

Place the roasting tray over a medium heat on the stove and add the port. Boil to reduce by three-quarters, until slightly syrupy. Remove from the heat.

In a bowl, whisk together the crème fraîche, cider vinegar and olive oil. Strain the reduced port into the dressing through a tea strainer or sieve and whisk it in well. Season with salt and pepper.

Place the slices of ham on large plates. Season the salad leaves with just a little pepper, then add the crumbled Stilton and chives. The salad and warm figs can now be arranged in a rustic fashion towards the top or centre of the plate, and drizzled with the port dressing. Any juices released from the figs while keeping warm can also be spooned over the salad.

- *Roquefort cheese will also work very well with this recipe.*

Serves 4

- 2 apples (preferably Cox's Orange Pippin), peeled and cored
- 300ml (½ pint) dry cider
- 4 thick slices of black pudding (each 1–2cm/½–¾in thick)
- butter, for brushing
- 4 thick slices of goat's cheese log (each 50–60g/2–2¼oz)

For the dressing

- 2 teaspoons wholegrain mustard
- pinch of caster sugar
- 6 tablespoons single cream
- salt and pepper
- squeeze of lime juice (optional)
- 1 teaspoon snipped flatleaf parsley
- 1 teaspoon snipped chives

Grilled goat's cheese on cider apples and black pudding with a cider and mustard cream

Cheese has a double value. It can be eaten as a course on its own, but is also the perfect enhancer for savoury dishes. Here I've created a combination of the two goat's cheese with apples and, for an extra bite, some spicy black pudding. This dish will eat well as a simple lunch or supper dish or as an alternative to a dessert.

Goat's cheese can have quite a dry and crumbly texture, which works well broken into salads or creamed into dressings. This recipe, however, grills the cheese, softening its finish. The slices are melted on top of thickly cut apples that have been poached in cider, then placed on black pudding. The dressing utilizes the cider cooking liquor, increasing the finished flavour. Most apples can be used, but for this dish I prefer home-grown Cox's.

Method Halve the apples to provide four thick apple rings. Place these in a saucepan and cover with the cider. Bring to a simmer and cook for 2 minutes. Remove the pan from the heat, leaving the apples in the cider to continue cooking, without losing their texture.

To make the dressing, drain two-thirds of the cider into another pan and simmer and reduce by three-quarters. Whisk 3 tablespoons of the reduced cider into the mustard along with the caster sugar and single cream. Season with salt and pepper and a squeeze of lime juice, if using. If the cider flavour has become masked by the strength of the mustard, simply add a few more drops of the reduction to increase its flavour. The herbs are best added to the dressing just before serving. If added too early, the acidic bite of the cider

and lime juice will discolour their rich green colour and diminish their flavour.

Preheat a grill to hot. Brush the black pudding slices with butter and cook under the grill for 2–3 minutes, then turn the slices and repeat the cooking time. Meanwhile, warm the apple rings in the remaining cider. Place the slices of grilled black pudding on a baking sheet and top with the apples, followed by the slices of goat's cheese.

Place the stacked savouries under the hot grill until the cheese is golden brown and beginning to melt. The dish is now ready to serve; mix the herbs into the dressing and spoon it over. The three different textures of cheese, apple and black pudding eat so well together, each offering their individual flavour and complementing one another.

● *A tossed salad of leaves and fresh herbs (chives, parsley, tarragon, chervil) can be served with this dish, as a simple garnish or side salad. A quick mix of 4 tablespoons of olive or hazelnut oil, whisked with 1–2 tablespoons of reduced cider and 1 teaspoon of lime juice, provides a dressing for the leaves.*

Serves 6

- 200g (7oz) self-raising flour, plus extra for dusting
- pinch of salt
- 1 level teaspoon ground mixed spice
- 1 level teaspoon baking powder
- 150g (5oz) butter, at room temperature, plus an extra knob for the pears and more for greasing
- 150g (5oz) caster sugar
- finely grated zest and juice of 2 limes
- 2 eggs
- 6 Comice pears
- 1 heaped teaspoon icing or caster sugar
- *Chocolate sauce* (page 204), to serve

Spicy Comice pudding with hot chocolate sauce

The Comice pear has the reputation of being one of the finest of all pears. Joining us at the beginning of autumn and going through to mid-spring, this much smoother and less grainy fruit works perfectly here with the other flavours involved. The flesh is sweet, with an almost buttery consistency, containing just a little acidity and some natural spiciness. It's the spice that's to be enhanced and lifted here with the addition of mixed spice. This slightly warms the finished flavour, making sure the pudding itself is not lost beneath the chocolate sauce. This recipe is for six portions, using 150ml (¼ pint) moulds (preferably plastic); for one large pudding a 1 litre (1¾ pint) basin will be needed.

Method Sift together the flour, salt, mixed spice and baking powder into a large bowl. Add the measured butter, the caster sugar, grated lime zest and the eggs, then whisk to a smooth creamy consistency (an electric hand mixer will make life a lot easier).

Peel and quarter three of the pears, cutting away the core and seeds. The quarters can now be chopped into small rough dice (approximately 5mm/¼in). Place them in a bowl with the lime juice to prevent discoloration. Strain the pears from the juice (keeping the juice for later use), then stir them into the pudding mix.

Lightly butter the pudding basins and dust with flour, then divide the mix between them, smoothing the tops and covering the basins with buttered foil. Cook in a large or stacked steamer over boiling water for 50 minutes, until firm to the touch. If the puddings still feel slightly undercooked, continue to cook for a

further 10 minutes. A large pudding will take at least 2–2½ hours. Once cooked, remove the puddings from the steamer, and allow to stand for 10 minutes to relax.

About 10 minutes before the puddings are due to be ready, the extra pears can be prepared and cooked. Peel and quarter the pears, removing the core and seeds. Chop each into rough dice and place them in a bowl with the reserved lime juice. Melt the knob of butter in a saucepan. Once bubbling, strain the pears from the juice and add them to the butter with the teaspoon of icing or caster sugar and 2 tablespoons of water. Cook on a medium heat for a few minutes, until tender.

To serve, loosen the puddings and turn out on to warm plates or bowls. Top each with the cooked Comice pears, and drizzle with some of the syrup, offering the chocolate sauce separately.

● *When cooking the diced pears, Poire William, the pear liqueur, can be used in place of the water for a much stronger finish (sweet pear cider or perry can also be used).*

Serves 8

- butter, for greasing
- 150ml (¼ pint) sunflower oil
- 100g (4oz) soft brown sugar
- 2 eggs
- 75g (3oz) golden syrup
- 175g (6oz) self-raising flour, sifted, plus extra for dusting
- 1 level teaspoon ground cinnamon
- ½ teaspoon ground cloves
- ½ teaspoon ground ginger
- ½ teaspoon bicarbonate of soda
- 200g (8oz) carrots, finely grated

For the syrup

- 16 hazelnuts, shelled
- 150g (5oz) orange marmalade
- 3–4 tablespoons Grand Marnier

For the mascarpone cream

- 150ml (¼ pint) mascarpone
- 150ml (¼ pint) double cream
- 2 teaspoons icing sugar
- 1 teaspoon freshly grated nutmeg

Warm carrot cake with hazelnut marmalade syrup and nutmeg mascarpone cream

This carrot cake is quite spicy and rich, with added syrup and oil to keep it moist, also extending its shelf-life. To soften the total eating experience, I've included a recipe for a mascarpone cream and a hazelnut and orange syrup to finish.

Method Preheat the oven to 200°C/400°F/Gas 6. To prepare the hazelnuts for the syrup, place them on a baking tray and cook for 8 minutes in the preheated oven. These can now be rubbed in a cloth while still hot to remove all of the skins. If the hazelnuts are still a little opaque, return them to the oven for just a minute or two, to give them a roasted edge. Leave the nuts to cool before chopping roughly. Reduce the oven temperature to 180°C/350°F/Gas 4.

Butter and flour a 15cm (6in) cake tin or eight size-1 (150ml/¼ pint) ramekins. To make the carrot cake, whisk together the oil, sugar, eggs and golden syrup until well combined. Beat in the flour, spices and bicarbonate of soda, then add the finely grated carrots. Transfer the mix to the buttered and floured tin, and bake in the preheated oven for 50–55 minutes, or divide between the ramekins and bake for 20–25 minutes. To test if it is done, place a skewer into the centre of the cake; if it comes out clean, the cake is cooked. Leave to rest in the tin or moulds for 10 minutes before turning out.

While the cake is baking, make the syrup and mascarpone cream. Place the marmalade and 3 tablespoons of the Grand Marnier in a small saucepan with 100ml (3½fl oz) of water and bring to a simmer. Cook on a low heat until the marmalade has completely

dissolved. Add the remaining Grand Marnier, if preferred. Strain through a sieve.

To make the mascarpone cream, place the mascarpone, double cream, icing sugar and nutmeg in a bowl and whisk together to a lightly whipped cream stage.

To serve, place wedges cut from the warm carrot cake (or whole small individual cakes) on to warmed plates. Add the chopped roast hazelnuts to the warm syrup and spoon it over and around the cake. The nutmeg mascarpone cream can be offered separately or spooned on top of each portion, beginning to melt as it warms.

● *The carrot cake also eats well cold, simply accompanied by the nutmeg cream. If serving cold, the roasted and chopped hazelnuts can be added to the cream along with 50–75g (2–3oz) of raisins.*

● *If you have any cake left over, it reheats very well in the microwave.*

- 3 tablespoons lukewarm milk
- 2 teaspoons dried yeast or a 7g packet of dried, rapid-action yeast
- 225g (8oz) plain flour, sifted, plus extra for dusting
- 1 tablespoon caster sugar
- pinch of salt
- 3 eggs, lightly beaten
- 75g (3oz) butter, softened, plus extra for greasing

For the syrup
- 325g (11oz) caster sugar
- 250ml (9fl oz) rum (or more)

For the pineapple sauce
- 1 small pineapple (approximately 350–450g (12oz–1lb), peeled, cored and chopped into small pieces
- 200ml (7fl oz) coconut milk
- 2 teaspoons cornflour
- icing sugar, to sweeten (if needed)

For the pineapple (makes 8 portions)
- 1 small–medium pineapple
- 15g (½oz) butter or 2 tablespoons vegetable oil
- 3 tablespoons caster sugar

Rum baba buns with caramelized pineapple and pineapple sauce

Pineapples are available throughout the year, but it's the winter pineapple that reaches prize-winning form. When selecting pineapples, use the nose rather than the fingers. The rich fruitiness finds its way through the skin, whispering that it is ready to be enjoyed. Rum and pineapple make many a cocktail, the pina colada being the most famous. The pina colada is also characterized by the addition of coconut cream. Similarly, coconut milk is included in this fruity sauce.

Rum babas are usually cooked in dariole moulds, giving them a domed flowerpot look. I just roll the dough into balls and bake them like buns. Individual tartlet cases (about 7.5cm/3in) or large Yorkshire pudding trays can be used to help maintain the base shape. It is often a good idea to make the buns 24–48 hours in advance. This is not essential, but does allow the buns to firm and dry, ready to absorb the warm rum syrup and resoften in it. If baked, cooled and soaked within just a few hours, the texture can sometimes finish a bit stodgy.

Method To make the babas, pour the lukewarm milk into a bowl. Sprinkle over the yeast and leave for a few minutes to dissolve. Sift the flour, sugar and salt together into a mixing bowl. Add the yeast mixture to the flour mix and stir in. Then add the eggs and work for a few minutes until a smooth dough is reached. This stage can be achieved with an electric mixer. Dot the dough with nuggets of the softened butter, cover the bowl with a damp cloth and leave to rise in a warm place for 45 minutes.

If using tartlet cases or moulds, butter them well and refrigerate to set, then repeat the process with a second coating of butter. If just using a baking tray, butter it only once. Preheat the oven to 200°C/400°F/Gas 6.

At the end of the rising time, the butter will have started to work its way into the dough. Knead the dough back to a smooth consistency. It will now have a quite firm elastic texture. Divide it into 8–10 pieces with a spoon. With well-floured hands, roll these into 8–10 balls and place them on the prepared baking tray or in the moulds. Leave uncovered in a warm place, to rise for 15–20 minutes.

Bake the baba buns in the preheated oven for 10–15 minutes, until golden brown. Remove from the oven and, if moulds were used, leave to stand for 10 minutes before turning out. As mentioned in the introduction, these are best made in advance, and stored in an airtight container once cooled.

To make the syrup, boil the ingredients together with 450ml (¾ pint) water, then simmer for a few minutes. Keep to one side and reheat when needed.

To make the pineapple sauce, place the chopped pineapple in a food processor and blitz it to a purée. Place the purée in a small saucepan with the coconut milk and cornflour. Whisk all together, bringing the sauce to the boil. Remove from the heat and strain through a fine sieve for a smooth finish. If necessary, sweeten with icing sugar to taste. This can be served just warm or cold.

Before cooking the pineapples, it is best to soak the babas in the hot syrup for at least 20–30 minutes, allowing plenty of time for the syrup to be absorbed, swelling and softening the buns. These can now be turned from time to time, ensuring an even soaking. Just before serving, the buns can be split in half horizontally to ensure the syrup has soaked to the centre.

Prepare the pineapple by topping and tailing, then cut away the skin. Split the pineapple into quarters lengthwise, then cut each in half again to provide eight shorter pieces. Heat the butter or oil in a large frying pan over a moderate heat. Once bubbling, place in the pineapple pieces and cook for 5–6 minutes on each side. Add the caster sugar, sprinkling it over the fruit. Slightly increase the heat and the sugar will begin to caramelize. As it does so, turn the pineapple to spread the flavour. Add 2 tablespoons of water to lift the caramel from the base of the pan, creating a syrup. Continue to cook for just another minute or two, basting the wedges with the caramel.

To present the dish, place the warm soaked rum babas on plates, along with a caramelized pineapple wedge. Any remaining caramel can be drizzled over the fruit, and extra rum syrup offered separately. Spoon the pineapple sauce on to the plates and the pudding is ready.

● *Extra-thick cream makes a lovely accompaniment.*

● *If using fresh yeast, 15g (½oz) will be needed.*

Serves 4
- 4 tangerines
- about 300ml (½ pint) orange juice (fresh or from a carton)
- 150ml (¼ pint) cranberry juice
- 225g (8oz) fresh cranberries
- 100g (4oz) granulated sugar
- 150ml (¼ pint) ruby port
- 1 sachet of powdered gelatine (approx 11g)

For the biscuits (makes 12–16)
- 100g (4oz) butter
- 75g (3oz) icing sugar
- 100g (4oz) plain flour, sifted

Cranberry, orange and port jelly with tangerine biscuit fingers

Christmas pudding is a great British tradition that no Christmas meal should be without. This recipe, although certainly not trying to compete with it, does offer a cold, lighter alternative. It is during this month, December, that cranberries and tangerines are in such abundance. Although today both are imported, cranberries were and still are, although not commercially, grown wild within our own soil. This fruit, which now comes to us predominantly from the USA, is enhanced by cranberry and orange juice (the two often meet in cranberry sauce recipes), finishing with the inclusion of rich ruby port. The tangerine biscuits to accompany are very simple, sweet, buttery, crumbly affairs lifted by a touch of bitter-orangey tangerine (satsumas or clementines can also be used).

Method Finely grate the zest from the tangerines and reserve for the biscuits. Halve and juice the fruits. Pour the juice into a measuring jug and top up with orange juice to 300ml (½ pint). Strain this juice through a sieve into a saucepan and add the cranberry juice, cranberries, sugar and port. Bring to the boil, then reduce to a very gentle simmer for 12 minutes. Remove from the heat and whisk in the powdered gelatine. Leave to stand for 10 minutes, stirring occasionally, until the gelatine has completely dissolved. Strain the jelly juice through a fine sieve or muslin cloth, squeezing all the juices from the cranberries. Divide between four glasses, each approximately 125–150ml (4–5fl oz). Once they have cooled, chill for a few hours to allow the jelly to set.

While the jellies are setting, make the biscuits. Preheat the oven to 180°C/350°F/Gas 4. Place all of the ingredients, including the reserved tangerine zest, into a food processor or food mixer, using the beater attachment, and blitz to a soft pipeable consistency. Spoon into a piping bag fitted with a 1cm (½in) plain or star nozzle.

Cover one or two baking trays with parchment paper (or use non-stick trays), then pipe 7.5cm (3in) strips, leaving a 4cm (1½in) gap between each to allow the biscuits to spread. Bake in the preheated oven for 15–20 minutes, until the biscuits are a light golden brown. Remove from the oven and leave for 5–6 minutes to cool and firm up, then transfer to a cooling rack. Once the biscuits are cold, carefully remove them with a palette knife – they will be very crumbly and tender – and place them in a suitable airtight container.

When serving, it's best to remove the jellies from the fridge 10–15 minutes in advance, to allow a slight softening. These are now ready to present with the tangerine biscuit fingers.

● *A little single cream can be poured on top of each jelly, offering a classic jelly and cream combination.*

For the curd
- zest and juice of 8 tangerines (or satsumas)
- 150g (5oz) caster sugar
- 150g (5oz) butter, chopped
- 4 egg yolks

For the ice-cream
- 150ml (¼ pint) crème fraîche
- 150ml (¼ pint) natural yoghurt
- 2–3 tablespoons Grand Marnier

For the syrup
- zest and juice of 6 tangerines (or satsumas)
- 100g (4oz) caster sugar
- 2–3 tablespoons Grand Marnier
- ½ teaspoon arrowroot or cornflour
- 1 teaspoon orange juice or water
- 50g (2oz) candied orange peel, cut into 5mm (¼in) dice (pre-chopped can be used)

Fresh tangerine curd ice-cream with marshmallow meringues and tangerine Grand Marnier syrup

The tangerine, a member of the citrus family, joins us during our winter months and has become a standard on our Christmas shopping lists. There are so many of these small varieties of orange, which all seem to be so closely related, but with different names, and all or any of them can be used in this recipe.

This dessert is very light and refreshing, and many of its features can be made in advance or for completely different dishes. The tangerine curd will keep in a sterilized jar in the fridge for up to 3 weeks. The only other ingredients needed to make the ice-cream are crème fraîche, natural yoghurt and a splash of Grand Marnier to lift them.

The meringues are pretty basic, just a combination of egg whites and caster sugar whisked together, with a little added cornflour and lemon juice to create the gooey marshmallow centres surrounded by the crisp touch. The tangerine curd requires four egg yolks – this will automatically provide you with four egg whites with which to make the meringues.

The syrup will keep for several weeks, so can be made well in advance. One other extra I've included in the recipe is candied orange peel. As we all know, this can be bought ready-made, which will work just fine. If possible, however, I suggest purchasing the whole pieces of candied orange peel, rather than ready-chopped, leaving you in complete control when dicing.

Method First make the curd. Place the tangerine zest and juice in a saucepan and bring to the boil. Cook until reduced by half, then mix in the caster sugar and chopped butter. Once the butter has melted, whisk in the egg yolks. Cook over a low heat, stirring continuously for 3–4 minutes, until thickened. This stage can also be achieved by placing all the above ingredients in a bowl set over a saucepan of simmering water and cooking for 20–25 minutes, stirring from time to time. This will prevent the egg from possibly scrambling, leaving a safe, smooth finish. Once thickened, transfer to a clean bowl and cover with cling film or greaseproof paper, or pour into a sterilized jar (page 11). Leave to cool.

To make the ice-cream, whisk the crème fraîche and yoghurt into the curd, then flavour with the Grand Marnier. Churn the mixture in an ice-cream machine for 20 minutes and then put in the freezer. Alternatively, just freeze the mixture for several hours without churning. If this method is followed, remove the ice-cream from the freezer 20–30 minutes before serving to allow its consistency to soften.

To make the syrup, mix the tangerine zest and juice with the caster sugar in a saucepan, and simmer rapidly until reduced by a third, then add the Grand Marnier. Mix the arrowroot or cornflour with the orange juice or water and whisk into the simmering syrup. Once returned to a gentle simmer, cook for just 2 minutes, then remove from the stove. While still warm, the candied orange peel can be added. Leave to cool. Alternatively, reheat the syrup just before serving, adding the peel while the syrup is warming.

For the meringues
- 4 egg whites
- 225g (8oz) caster sugar
- 2 teaspoons cornflour
- 2 teaspoons lemon juice
- oil, for greasing

For the garnishes (optional)
- 4 tangerines (or satsumas), segmented
- icing sugar, for dusting

To make the meringues, preheat the oven to 140°C/275°F/Gas 1. Whisk the egg whites to soft peaks, then add two thirds of the caster sugar. Continue to whisk until approaching stiff peaks. Now add the remaining sugar, continuing to whisk. The meringue will now have reached a good thick creamy consistency. Add the cornflour and lemon juice, whisking for a further minute. Keep the meringues very naturally shaped, just spooning individual portions on to very lightly oiled parchment paper on a baking tray. Alternatively, spoon the meringue into a piping bag fitted with a 1cm (½in) plain tube and pipe large domes on to the paper. Whichever method you choose, it is important to leave ample space between the meringues to allow them to swell and rise.

Bake in the preheated oven for 45–50 minutes, 1 hour maximum. During this time they will have taken on a very light colour, forming a crisp shell around the pillow-like marshmallow centre. For a touch more colour, the meringues can be cooked at a slightly higher temperature – 150°C/300°F/Gas 2. If so, they will take just 40–45 minutes.

Assemble the dish. If dome-shaped meringues have been made, it is best to crack the tops gently, then place five or six tangerine segments on top, if using. The ice-cream can now be scooped or scrolled using a warm tablespoon, and placed on top of the meringue. The syrup with candied fruit can now be drizzled over to finish. The alternative is simply to sit the ice-cream and meringue side by side, garnishing with the segments and syrup. Whichever way you choose, the dish can be finished with a light dusting of icing sugar and, if it's for Christmas, perhaps a leaf or small sprig of holly.

● *The recipe for tangerine curd can be replaced with bought orange curd.*

● *Tinned mandarin segments can be used for the garnish instead of segmenting your own.*

● *For a cleaner finish, the fresh tangerine segments can be peeled of their outer skin, revealing the rich orange fruit.*

Serves 6
- finely grated zest and juice of 12 clementines
- 225g (8oz) white breadcrumbs
- 150g (5oz) caster sugar
- 50g (2oz) plain flour, plus extra for dusting
- 175g (6oz) dried suet
- 3 eggs, beaten

For the passion fruit syrup
- 10 passion fruits
- 75g (3oz) caster sugar

Clementine dumplings with passion fruit syrup

The recipe for these dumplings is as 'olde English' as you'll find. There's a sort of 'boil in the bag' style about them, but this bag happens to be a square of muslin cloth tied around each dumpling before they are cooked in a large pot of boiling water. So there's nothing fancy about their appearance; they just have lots of flavour. The original recipes usually used lemons, but with all the tangerines, satsumas and clementines on offer and in abundance during our winter months, using them seemed the right seasonal thing to do. Passion fruit are more or less available all year round, but it's during the months of December and February that you'll find them at their best. So all winter months will suit this recipe.

Method Place the clementine zest and juice in a small saucepan and bring to a rapid simmer. Continue to cook until reduced by three-quarters and at a thick syrupy consistency. Leave to cool.

In a large bowl, mix together the breadcrumbs, sugar, flour and suet. Stir in the clementine syrup and the eggs, and mix thoroughly until well combined.

Cut six squares of muslin about 20cm (8in) in size. Rinse each muslin square in water, then squeeze well and place on a worktop. Dust each with flour, then divide the mix between each square. Pull up the corners of the cloths and tie together with string. Place the dumplings in a large saucepan of boiling water, cover and simmer for 1 hour.

To make the passion fruit syrup, halve the fruits, scoop out the pulp from each into a small saucepan and add the sugar and 150ml (¼ pint) of water. Bring to the boil and simmer for 1 minute, then remove from the heat. The syrup is now ready to serve, just warm.

Remove the cooked dumplings from the water and take each from their muslin bag. Present in warm bowls, spooning the passion fruit syrup over them. Lightly whipped or pouring cream can be offered for a nice finishing touch.

● *An extra half of passion fruit can be added to garnish each dish. Half clementines can also be used, sprinkling each with demerara sugar before caramelizing to a crème brûlée-style finish under a preheated grill (or using a gas gun, page 11).*

● *The passion fruit syrup can be lightly thickened with a little arrowroot stirred with water, simmering for a further minute once whisked in.*

● *For a slightly sweeter finish to the syrup, add a teaspoon or two of icing sugar.*

Serves 4
- 4 grapefruit (pink grapefruit can also be used)
- 50g (2oz) caster sugar
- icing sugar, for dusting

For the sabayon
- 3 egg yolks
- 4 tablespoons Grand Marnier or Cointreau
- ¼ teaspoon cornflour

For the apple cream
- 3 Cox's Orange Pippin apples
- squeeze of lemon juice
- 25g (1oz) caster sugar
- 100g (4oz) mascarpone (or full-fat soft cream cheese)
- 100ml (3½fl oz) double cream
- icing sugar (if needed)

Sabayon-glazed grapefruit with Cox's apple cream

Grapefruit are available throughout the year, hitting their peak in the winter and spring months. Regarded as a breakfast fruit, they have also over the years found their way into cold salads and quite a few desserts. The fruit themselves don't really benefit from cooking, with no extra flavour to be found and sometimes more lost. In this dish, they are just warmed and finished with grapefruit juice that has been sweetened, boiled and reduced to intensify its flavour, and a light fluffy sabayon enriched with a drop of Grand Marnier.

Apples and grapefruit suit one another very well. The Cox's Orange Pippin has a season between the months of September and February, offering a quite distinctive spicy, honey, nutty and almost pear-like flavour. The creamy flesh of the apple cooks to a purée very well, blending with the mascarpone cream. The *Tuile biscuits* on page 206 are very nice to serve with this dish, topped with pistachio nuts to offer a nutty crunch. The biscuits can also be shaped into small baskets, as described in the recipe, ready to hold a ball or scroll of the cream.

Method First make the apple cream. Peel and quarter the apples, removing the cores and seeds from each. Roughly chop the apples into small dice, then squeeze lemon juice over them to prevent discoloration. Place the chopped apples in a saucepan with 2 tablespoons of water, cover and cook over a medium heat for several minutes, until the apples begin to soften. Remove the lid and add the caster sugar. Continue to simmer, slightly increasing the heat, until the apples are completely cooked through, breaking and almost dry in the pan. Once they are at this stage, remove from the heat and liquidize until smooth. Leave to cool.

Beat the mascarpone (or cream cheese) until smooth, then stir in the cold apple purée. Lightly whip the double cream to soft peaks, then fold it into the apple mascarpone. Check for sweetness; if a sweeter finish is preferred, add icing sugar to taste. This can now be chilled until needed.

To prepare the grapefruit, cut the tops and bottoms from each, revealing the fruit. Cut the remaining peel and pith away in strips, using a sharp knife, then segment the fruit. As the segments are being cut from the fruit, save all the juice. Also squeeze any remaining in the central membrane once all the segments have been removed and lay the segments on a clean kitchen cloth. Pour the saved grapefruit juice into a saucepan and add the caster sugar. Bring it to the boil and allow to reduce by about half, to a thick syrupy consistency.

This will have intensified the grapefruit flavour, also sweetening as it does so. Divide the segments between four small shallow bowls, arranging them in a circular fashion or in a simple rustic style.

To make the sabayon, place the grapefruit syrup, egg yolks, Grand Marnier or Cointreau and the cornflour in a bowl. Whisk, preferably with an electric hand whisk, over a bowl of simmering water, until thick and creamy and at least trebled – if not quadrupled – in volume. This process will take 8–10 minutes.

Dust a little icing sugar through a small sieve or tea strainer over each portion of grapefruit. Spoon the sabayon on top and glaze under a preheated grill or with a gas gun (page 11). Once golden brown, the glazed fruits are ready to serve. Spoon the Cox's apple cream into scrolls or balls and sit these on top or offer it separately.

● *The sabayon can be made an hour or two in advance. If you wish to do this, once it is at the thick frothy stage, remove it from the heat and continue to whisk until cold. This can now be quickly rewhisked before spooning over and glazing.*

Serves 4
- 16–20 lychees (8–10 halves per portion)
- 2 eggs, plus 1 egg yolk
- 100g (4oz) caster sugar
- juice and finely grated zest of 2 lemons
- 50g (2oz) cold butter, diced

For the shortbreads
- 75g (3oz) icing sugar, sifted
- 1 egg yolk
- 100g (4oz) butter, softened
- 150g (5oz) plain flour, sifted

Lychee lemon whip with shortbreads

This is obviously not a home-grown dessert, but it is too good to be ignored. There are so many imported fruits to choose from that have become a large part of our weekly shopping lists. In December colourfully skinned lychees are in abundance. They are very attractive in and out of their skins, and the perfumed juicy fragrance that's released when you bite into the flesh is really quite something. They are without doubt at their best just eaten raw, a very simple *petit four* to offer friends.

On Chinese menus, lychees are often served as an accompaniment to savoury dishes, such as duck. The lychee also works well in wintry fruit salads. Here it's topped with a lemon whip, flashed under the grill to glaze.

The shortbreads are left in a rustic form, then baked to a crispy crumbly texture to accompany the dessert.

Method The shortbreads can be made in advance. To do so, mix the icing sugar, egg yolk and butter together in a bowl. Add the flour and rub it into the butter to create a crumb texture. Knead the mix by hand into a dough, wrap in cling film and chill to rest for 1–2 hours. The dough can be made in a food processor or electric mixer. It is important, however, not to over-mix, as this will leave you with a tougher elastic texture.

Preheat the oven to 180°C/350°F/Gas 4. Remove the rested dough from the fridge and break and press it into 12–16 rustic shapes directly on to a non-stick baking tray, leaving a space between each to allow for spreading. Bake the biscuits in the preheated oven for 10–12 minutes (15 minutes maximum), until just a pale

golden colour. Remove them from the oven and transfer to a wire rack to cool.

Peel the skin from the lychees by simply cutting around, and remove the central stone to halve each fruit. The halves can now be divided between four shallow bowls, glasses or 150ml (¼ pint) ramekins.

Place the eggs, egg yolk and sugar in a bowl. Heat 5cm (2in) of water in a small saucepan and bring to a simmer. Place the bowl on top of the pan (it is important that the water is not in contact with the base of the bowl) and whisk vigorously. An electric hand whisk is best used here; make sure the electric lead is not in contact with the heat. Once a foaming consistency is reached, add the lemon juice and zest. Continue to whisk until a very thick sabayon is achieved that leaves a thick trail when the whisk is lifted from the bowl. By hand, this will take up to 10–15 minutes, probably just 6–8 if using the electric whisk.

Preheat a grill to hot. Remove the saucepan and bowl from the heat, still together, and continue to whisk while adding the diced butter. This will take some of the warmth from the sabayon, at the same time enriching its finished flavour. Spoon the lemon whip over the lychees and place them under the preheated grill until a rich golden brown. The warm lychee lemon whips are now ready to serve with the shortbreads.

● *The shortbread biscuits can be sprinkled with caster sugar before or after baking, leaving them with a sweeter touch.*

basics

Stocks

Instant stock

Using a whole stock cube to make stock can result in a totally artificial and overpowering flavour. Simply using a pinch of stock cube offers a balanced cooking liquor, enhancing the natural flavours of the ingredients it's supporting.

This recipe can be used to replace any stock, whether it be for a soup, sauce or stew. I would stress, however, that a fresh home-made stock cannot be beaten. The best stock cubes to use here, whether chicken, beef, lamb, fish or vegetable, are those with a thicker paste-like texture, rather than the crumbly blocks.

A richer alternative to instant stock is tinned consommé. Beef is the most common to be found, which will work well with all stock-based recipes. Chicken and game varieties are also available.

Makes 300ml (½ pint)
- 300ml (½ pint) water (natural mineral water can be used if preferred)
- ⅛th stock cube

Method If using the stock immediately, boil the water in a saucepan and whisk in the stock cube piece. Simmer for a minute or two. This tends to clarify the liquor, leaving a clearer stock. Strain through a muslin cloth or fine tea strainer for the cleanest of finishes. For roast gravies and cream sauces, just add the water when required, stirring in the broken cube piece.

Chicken stock

Chicken stock is one of the most important bases in the professional and domestic kitchen. There are two methods for making this recipe, each offering a different finish: the one given here is for a clear white stock, used in most soups and cream sauces; the alternative is a dark chicken stock, which is preferred when making stews, casseroles, sautés and fricassees. If you wish to make the dark variety, the chicken wings and carcasses should first be cut relatively small, then fried or roasted to a rich deep golden brown. While the chicken is colouring, the vegetables are also coloured in the stock pan, by frying in a knob of butter. Add the remaining ingredients and continue as below. The golden touch will offer a different taste to the end result.

Chicken wings and carcasses are listed in the ingredients. Chicken wings would be my first choice, as these obviously contain a quantity of meat to give the stock more flavour.

An alternative method of making a good white stock is to use a whole boiling fowl, cooked with all of the vegetables. After 2–3 hours of boiling/poaching, the chicken has flavoured the water, with the added bonus of the bird itself being ready to eat.

This recipe produces a large quantity, but it can be halved to make approximately 1.25 litres (2 pints) of finished stock. However, bearing in mind the cooking time required, making one large pot provides enough finished stock to freeze, saving a lot of time with future recipes.

Makes 2.25 litres (4 pints)
- 2 onions, chopped
- 2 celery sticks, chopped
- 2 leeks, chopped
- 25g (1oz) butter
- 1 garlic clove, crushed
- 1 bay leaf
- sprig of thyme
- few black peppercorns
- 1.75kg (4lb) chicken wings or carcasses, chopped

Method In a large stock pot (minimum 6 litre/10 pint capacity), lightly soften the vegetables in the butter, without allowing them to colour. Add the garlic, bay leaf, thyme, peppercorns and chopped wings or carcasses. Cover with 3.4 litres (6 pints) of cold water and bring to a simmer. Allow the stock to simmer for 2 hours, skimming from time to time to remove impurities, then strain through a fine sieve.

The stock is now ready to use, or allow it to cool and chill until needed. The stock can also be frozen in quantities, and will keep frozen for 3 months.

Veal or beef stock or jus

This brown stock takes a long time to achieve, particularly if you go on to make the *jus* after the stock, but it's very satisfying and any left over can be frozen. The stock is best started in the morning so that it can cook throughout the day. Good, ready-made stocks and *jus* gravies can also be bought in supermarkets.

Makes approximately 4.5 litres (8 pints) stock or 600ml–1.25 litres (1–2 pints) *jus*/gravy
- 3 onions, halved
- 2.25kg (5lb) veal or beef bones
- 225g (8oz) veal or beef trimmings (from the butcher)
- 225g (8oz) carrots, coarsely chopped
- 3 celery sticks, coarsely chopped
- 1 leek, chopped
- 3–4 tomatoes, chopped
- 1 garlic clove, chopped
- 1 bay leaf
- sprig of thyme
- salt

Method Preheat the oven to 150°C/300°F/Gas 2. Lay the onion halves flat in a roasting tray with 2–3 tablespoons of water. Place in the oven and allow to caramelize slowly for 1–2 hours, until totally softened and coloured.

Pop the onions into a large stockpot and leave on one side. Increase the oven temperature to 200°C/400°F/Gas 6. Place all the bones and trimmings in the tray and roast for about 30 minutes, until well coloured. Roast the carrots and celery in a separate roasting tray for about 20 minutes, until lightly coloured. Add the bones, trimmings, carrots and celery to the onions in the pot, along with the leek, tomatoes, garlic, bay leaf and thyme. Fill the pot with cold water – you'll need about 6 litres (10 pints). Bring the stock to a simmer, season with a pinch of salt and skim off any impurities. Allow to cook for 6–8 hours for maximum flavour.

When the stock is ready, drain and discard the bones, trimmings and vegetables. The remaining liquid is your veal or beef stock, which can be cooled and frozen.

To make a veal or beef *jus*, bring the strained stock to the boil and reduce to 600ml–1.25 litres (1–2 pints), skimming off impurities as it reduces. The stock should be thick and of a sauce-like consistency. Make sure you taste at intervals during the reduction. If the sauce tastes strong enough but is too thin, it can be simply thickened with a little loosened cornflour to create the right consistency.

Game stock

For this stock, I'm using whole frozen wood pigeons. This stock also includes red wine, giving a good all-round flavour, but Armagnac, Cognac, Madeira and port can be used instead. Using chicken stock gives you a thin game stock, while veal *jus* gives an actual game sauce.

Makes 1.25 litres (2 pints)
- 1 tablespoon cooking oil
- 3 frozen wood pigeons, defrosted and chopped into small pieces
- 1 large onion or 2 shallots, roughly chopped
- 1 large carrot, roughly chopped
- 2 celery sticks, roughly chopped
- 4–5 mushrooms, quartered
- 1 bottle of red wine
- 1 garlic clove, chopped
- sprig of thyme
- 5 juniper berries, crushed
- few black peppercorns
- 2–3 tomatoes, chopped
- 1.25 litres (2 pints) *Chicken stock* (page 194), *Veal or beef stock* (see left) or tinned consommé

Method Heat the oil in a large frying pan. Add the chopped pigeons and cook on a medium heat until well coloured. This will take about 20 minutes on top of the stove. Transfer the pigeons to a saucepan.

Add the onion or shallots, carrot, celery and mushrooms to the frying pan and cook until beginning to soften and colour, but do not let them get too dark as this will create too bitter a finish. Increase the heat and add a third of the red wine, allowing it to boil and lift the flavours from the base of the pan. Transfer to the saucepan with the pigeons and add the garlic, thyme, juniper berries, black peppercorns and tomatoes. Cook until the tomatoes have softened in the red wine. Add the rest of the wine, bring to a rapid simmer and reduce by three-quarters. Add the chosen stock or consommé. Return to a simmer and cook for 1–1½ hours. Strain through a fine sieve and the stock is ready.

● *To make a game* jus, *follow the above method, replacing the stock with 600–900ml (1–1½ pints) Veal or beef jus (page 195) and 300ml (½ pint) water. Simmer for 1 hour before straining through a fine sieve. The* jus *is now ready to use as a game sauce.*

Fish stock

To make a good fish stock, the bones of white fish – turbot and sole in particular – should always be used. These give a good flavour and a clear jelly-like finish and do not have an oily texture. This stock is perfect for poaching and for making fish soups and sauces.

The quantities given here can be doubled, providing a larger quantity to freeze, which will then last for up to 3 months.

Makes about 900ml–1.25 litres (1½–2 pints)

● 1 small onion, sliced
● ½ leek, sliced
● 1 celery stick, sliced
● large knob of butter
● few parsley stalks (if available)
● 1 bay leaf
● 6 black peppercorns
● 450g (1lb) fish bones, preferably turbot or sole, washed
● 150ml (¼ pint) white wine

Method Sweat the sliced vegetables in the butter until softened, without allowing them to colour. Add the parsley, bay leaf and peppercorns. Chop the fish bones, removing any signs of blood left on them. Add to the vegetables and continue to cook for a few minutes. Add the wine and reduce until almost dry. Add 1.25 litres (2 pints) of water and bring to a simmer. Allow to simmer for 20 minutes, then strain through a fine sieve. For the clearest of finishes, strain again through a muslin cloth. The stock now left makes approximately 1.25 litres (2 pints). If tasting a little weak, reduce by a quarter to 900ml (1½ pints) before use. The reduction will increase the overall depth of flavour. The stock is now ready to use, be stored in the fridge for a few days, or frozen.

Sauces

Vegetable stock

This is a basic recipe, but it can be adapted in any number of ways: simply add or substitute other vegetables or herb flavours for a subtle difference. Never use root vegetables, however, as they will make the stock cloudy.

Makes about 1.25 litres (2 pints)
- 225g (8oz) carrots (optional)
- 2 onions
- 4 celery sticks
- 2 leeks, white parts only
- 1 bulb of Florence fennel
- 1–2 courgettes
- 1 tablespoon vegetable oil
- 1 bay leaf
- sprig of thyme
- 1 teaspoon coriander seeds
- 1 teaspoon pink peppercorns
- ½ lemon, sliced
- pinch of salt

Method Cut all the vegetables into rough 1cm (½in) dice. Warm the oil in a pan, then add the diced vegetables, herbs, coriander seeds, peppercorns and lemon slices. Cook, without colouring, for 8–10 minutes, allowing the vegetables to soften slightly. Add 1.5 litres (2½ pints) of water with a good pinch of salt and bring to a simmer, then cook without a lid for 30 minutes. Strain the stock through a sieve. You should have about 1.25 litres (2 pints); if there is more, just boil rapidly to reduce.

Simple hollandaise sauce

This is an alternative to the French classic. The acidity is provided by lemon juice, replacing the usual vinegar base. This sauce has many variations, some of which I've included in the notes below.

Makes about 200ml (7fl oz)
- 175g (6oz) butter
- 2 egg yolks
- juice of 1 lemon
- salt
- cayenne or ground white pepper

Method Clarify the butter by melting it until its solids have become separated from the rich yellow oil. Remove from the heat and leave to cool until just warm. Most of the solids will now be at the base of the pan. Any other solids on top can be skimmed away.

In a bowl, add the egg yolks to 2 tablespoons of warm water with half of the lemon juice. Whisk over a pan of simmering water to a thick ribbon stage, almost the consistency of softly whipped cream.

Remove from the heat and slowly add the clarified butter, whisking vigorously. This will emulsify the butter into the egg yolk mixture. If the sauce seems too thick and almost sticky while adding the butter, loosen slightly with another squeeze of lemon juice or water. Season with salt and cayenne or white pepper, and add the remaining lemon juice, if needed, to enrich the total flavour. The sauce is now ready to serve. For a guaranteed smooth, silky finish, strain through a sieve.

Keep the sauce in a warm bowl, covered with cling film, for up to 1 hour before use. If allowed to cool, the butter sets and the sauce will separate when reheated.

Hollandaise sauce can take on a lot more flavours, so here are a few suggestions:
Sauce mousseline *Add 1 or 2 tablespoons of whipped cream before serving.*
Sauce moutarde *Add 1 teaspoon of Dijon mustard.*
Nutty hollandaise *(or sauce noisette) Melt the butter to a nut-brown stage, then allow to cool slightly and continue with the recipe method above.*
Sauce maltaise *Replace the lemon juice with the juice of two or three blood oranges reduced to a syrupy consistency, adding the finely grated zest of one blood orange to the juices while boiling to tenderize. The sauce maltaise is perfect for serving with grilled duck, game or fish dishes.*

Mayonnaise

The basic recipe for mayonnaise usually uses only olive oil. However, for many recipes this can be overpowering, with its rich flavour. For a less strong taste, mixing the olive oil half-and-half with vegetable or groundnut oil helps balance this richness.

Makes about 300ml (½ pint)
- 2 large egg yolks (3 yolks for a richer finish)
- 1 tablespoon white wine vinegar
- 1 teaspoon English or Dijon mustard (optional)
- 300ml (½ pint) olive oil (or equal parts olive and vegetable or groundnut oil)
- salt and pepper
- few drops of lemon juice

Method Whisk together the egg yolks, vinegar and mustard. Very slowly add the oil in a steady trickle, whisking continuously. Once all the oil is added, it should have a good, rich, thick consistency. If it becomes too thick, and almost gluey at any time, add a teaspoon or two of water to loosen before continuing. Season with salt and pepper, finishing with the lemon juice. If chilled, the mayonnaise will keep for up to 1 week, providing fresh egg yolks have been used.

Cranberry sauce

This recipe offers a rich sweet-savoury cranberry sauce full of natural fruity flavour.

Serves 8–10
- 450g (1lb) fresh cranberries
- 125–150g (4–5oz) caster or jam sugar
- juice of 2 oranges
- 2 teaspoons very finely chopped shallots
- 5 tablespoons port
- pinch of salt
- 1 tablespoon redcurrant jelly

Method Place all of the ingredients, except the redcurrant jelly, in a saucepan. Bring to a simmer and cook over a moderate heat for 10–15 minutes, stirring from time to time. Once the berries are tender and have begun to break down, add the redcurrant jelly. To help the jelly melt into the sauce, it is best to mix well. Once the jelly has been added, cook for a further minute, then remove from the heat. The sauce can now be served warm or cold.

Extras

Mashed potatoes

These potatoes eat beautifully with almost any dish.

Serves 4–6
- 900g (2lb) large floury potatoes (preferably Maris Piper), peeled and quartered
- salt and pepper
- 75–100g (3–4oz) butter
- 100ml (3½fl oz) milk, or single cream for a richer finish
- freshly grated nutmeg

Method Boil the potatoes in salted water until tender, approximately 20–25 minutes, depending on size. Drain off all the water and replace the lid. Shake the pan vigorously, which will start to break up the boiled potatoes. While mashing the potatoes, add the butter and milk, a little at a time. Season with salt and pepper and some freshly grated nutmeg, according to taste. The mashed potatoes are now ready to serve.

- *For an even softer creamier finish, the milk or cream quantity can be increased to 150ml (¼ pint). Pushing the boiled potatoes through a drum sieve or potato ricer will also create a smooth finish. If using one of these utensils, it is important that the potatoes are sieved while still hot, and mashed while still warm. If left to cool before being mashed, they can become granular in texture.*

Classic roast potatoes

For the very best roasts, using the right potato is crucial. Almost any potato will roast, but if you prefer a crispy edge with a light, fluffy and creamy centre, then floury potatoes are needed. I choose between the following four varieties that will always give you this result – Maris Piper, Cara, King Edward or Desirée. To achieve the right finish, these potatoes will take at least 1 hour to cook; for ultimate crispiness, 1½ hours.

Serves 4–6
- 6–9 medium potatoes
  (allowing 3 halves per portion)
- salt
- cooking oil or lard
- plain flour

Method Preheat the oven to 200°C/400°F/Gas Mark 6. Peel the potatoes and halve them lengthwise. The peeled side of the potatoes can now be scraped with a knife to give a smooth domed shape to all the halves. Place in a saucepan and cover with cold salted water. Bring to the boil and simmer for 5–6 minutes. Drain in a colander, leave to stand for 2–3 minutes, then shake the colander gently. This will begin to break down the edge of the potatoes. These slightly rough edges will become crisp and crunchy during the roasting.

Heat 5mm (¼in) of oil or lard in a frying pan. Roll the potatoes lightly in flour, shaking off any excess. Fry them in the hot oil or lard, turning them occasionally, until golden brown all over.

Now transfer the potatoes to a roasting pan. Pour some of the cooking oil or lard into the pan (approximately 3mm/⅛in deep), sprinkle the potatoes with salt and roast in the oven for 30 minutes before turning in the pan. Roast for another 30 minutes. Remove the crispy roast potatoes and serve.

A knob of butter can be melted over the potatoes to enrich the crispy roast taste.

Noisette potatoes

Noisette potatoes are balls scooped from the potato, using a noisette spoon cutter. These are approximately 2.5cm (1in) in diameter and, once fried and baked, offer a sautéed roast flavour. The potatoes can take on many other flavourings if wished; add fried bacon, onions and herbs, to suggest just a few. For fairly generous servings, I suggest two large potatoes (approximately 225g/8oz) per portion. The potato trimmings need not be wasted – simply boil them and mash on another day.

Serves 8
- 16 large potatoes, peeled
- cooking oil
- knob of butter
- salt and pepper

Method Preheat the oven to 200°C/400°F/Gas 6. Scoop the potatoes into balls as above, rinsing well once all are shaped. Dry the potatoes on a clean tea towel, ready for frying. Heat 2 tablespoons of cooking oil in a large frying pan and fry two or three handfuls of the potato balls on a medium-to-hot heat until golden brown, then transfer them to a roasting tray. Repeat the process until all are coloured. The potatoes can now be finished in the preheated oven for 15–20 minutes, until tender.

Once they are cooked, remove the tray from the oven, then add the butter and season with salt and pepper. The noisette potatoes are now ready to serve.

Buttered Brussels sprouts

This is one of our most classic of winter vegetables. There are a few golden rules to choosing and buying sprouts. To appreciate the great flavour – quite different from cabbage – and their slightly nutty crunch, it's important to buy them as small and tight-leafed as possible. Never buy yellowing sprouts, those whose colour is fading, or those with too many loose leaves. All these signs will tell you they are old and they'll taste pretty old too. Another important point to remember is that, once they are cooked and unless you are refreshing them in iced water, you should always serve them immediately. Holding sprouts at high temperatures for too long – for example, keeping them warm in the oven – leads to a bitter finished flavour.

Serves 8
- 900g (2lb) small Brussels sprouts
- salt and pepper
- 25g (1oz) butter

Method First bring a large pan three-quarters full of salted water to the boil. While waiting for the water to boil, remove any damaged or loose outside leaves from the sprouts to reveal the rich green nugget. When the water is boiling, remove the lid and add the sprouts. It is important not to replace the lid, as this usually leads to the vegetables losing their rich colour. This is a rule that holds true for all green vegetables.

Return to the boil; the sprouts will need just a few minutes for that nutty bite, up to 6 minutes for a softer touch. Larger sprouts may well need up to 10 minutes. If not serving immediately, refresh them in iced water to cool, then drain and chill until needed. These will then take just a minute or two to reheat in boiling water or in the microwave.

To finish, drain the sprouts well, then roll in the butter and season with salt and pepper.

● *It is important, whenever cooking green vegetables, in particular Brussels sprouts, not to overfill the pan with too many at once. This will result in the water taking too long to return to the boil, consequently stewing the vegetable. For large quantities as above, it is best to cook small batches in advance, refreshing in iced water as mentioned in the method, repeating the process until all are cooked.*

Wild mushrooms

Wild mushrooms come in so many shapes, sizes and colours, all offering their own distinctive texture and flavour. Most begin to come into season during the last months of summer, becoming plentiful throughout the autumn. It is best to purchase young mushrooms, which are much firmer to the touch, without bruising or discoloration. It is also important not to store mushrooms of any variety in plastic bags. This will steam and sweat the fungi, causing them to deteriorate quite rapidly.

There is a selection of recipes throughout the book featuring wild mushrooms (all can be replaced with button, cup and chestnut, should wild be unavailable). Some varieties need very little cleaning, just trimming and wiping clean with a damp cloth or brushing to remove any grit. This avoids increasing their natural water content. There's also no need to peel most types: just trim away any stalk or stem bases. Ceps, chanterelles and our everyday

mushrooms all have a stem that is as good to eat as the caps themselves. Here is a list of wild mushrooms featured, and how to clean and trim each.

Cep Known in France as *cèpe* and in Italy as *porcini*, these mushrooms need only trimming at the base of the stem, then wiping well with a damp cloth. They are now ready for slicing. Dried ceps can also be purchased and these need soaking in water to soften them before use. The soaking water makes a good wild mushroom stock. (This also applies to dried morels and mixed dried wild mushrooms.)

Chanterelle and girolle These range in colour from a pale cream to a deep orange-yellow. On the outside of the cap leading into the stalk, the chanterelle has a wrinkly ribbed finish, quite distinctive in its appearance. The girolle is often looked upon as the firmer, smaller variety with a smoother finish. As with the cep, these mushrooms are totally edible, needing just the base of the stalk trimmed. They can now also just be wiped clean and the stalk scraped with the point of a small knife if it is damaged or particularly dirty. They can also be washed in cold water (treat them with care), then lift from the water and dry over an hour or two on a kitchen cloth. Particularly large chanterelles can be cut or torn in half.

Black trumpet mushrooms Known as *trompettes-de-la-mort* (trumpets of death) in France, these are jet-black in colour, and feel quite dry if in good condition. They must, however, be split and washed to ensure all impurities are removed. Cut away the base of the stalk, and split each mushroom into two or three strips. Wash in cold water three times, each time changing the water, then allow to drain on a dry, clean kitchen cloth. Although washed many times, providing the cleaning is done well in advance, the mushrooms will drain and dry well.

Shiitake These come in small, medium and large – the small much more commonly available. They have dark brown caps and a reasonably firm and meaty texture. Not growing wild in Europe (they originated in China and are commercially cultivated by the Japanese), shiitake have become a cultivated 'wild' mushroom. The stalks can be tough to eat, so are best discarded or used to flavour a stock. Wipe the caps clean before use.

Oyster Known as *pleurotte* in France, these are again a mostly cultivated 'wild' mushroom, shaped almost like an ear, varying in colour from an oyster grey to a pale buff grey. The stalk base of individual oysters can just be trimmed away. If you are tackling a group joined by a thicker stalk, this also needs to be well trimmed, being very tough. Small oysters can be left whole, but larger ones are best torn into strips.

Chestnuts

Fresh chestnuts have quite a short season, joining us in the autumn and usually lasting only until December. They are, however, very versatile, and cooked chestnuts are sold throughout the year in many different forms. The French vacuum-packed sweet chestnuts are among the best. Very tender to eat and still maintaining their attractive domed shape, these are available all year round from most delicatessens and supermarkets. Other chestnuts available for savoury dishes or puddings are the tinned unsweetened purée, tinned sweetened purée/*crème de marrons*, sweet rich *marrons glacés*, and tinned chestnuts in syrup (another variety of *marrons glacés*).

The fresh chestnut is low in oil and high in starch, unlike so many other nuts. When purchasing chestnuts to cook, choose rich and shiny ones with a good weight to guarantee a better result. It is also a good idea to buy a few more than needed, as there always seem to be one or two duds, however well selected.

The chestnut can find itself in many a savoury dish, the stuffing for the Christmas turkey and with Brussels sprouts being among the most common and popular. They also work in so many desserts, whether it be in a mousse, ice-cream or filling. Regardless of how you're using the chestnuts, the first stage is to get them peeled and cooked until tender.

Whichever of the following cooking methods you choose, the first stage has to be to pierce the skin. Without this, the chestnut will soufflé and swell on being heated, finally exploding and splitting the shell, leaving you with nothing. Using the point of a sharp knife, make a slit lengthwise on both sides of each nut, not cutting into the flesh. If the incision is not made well enough, a lot of steam will build up inside the shell, overcooking the nut inside and leading to it having a crumbly texture.

Having pierced the chestnuts, here are three blanching/cooking methods you could follow.

To boil, place the pierced chestnuts in a saucepan and cover with cold water. Bring the pan to the boil and cook for 1 minute, then remove the pan from the heat, leaving the nuts immersed in the hot water. The nuts can then be peeled, one at a time, removing the shell and bitter-flavoured skin that surrounds the flesh. It is only while the chestnuts are still hot that they will peel easily and successfully. Should the water begin to cool, simply return to the boil before continuing. At this stage the chestnuts are only blanched, leaving a crunchy bite. To cook them completely, simply boil as above for 5–6 minutes, before peeling.

To bake the chestnuts, preheat the oven to 200°C/400°F/Gas 6. To blanch only, place the pierced nuts on a roasting tray with a sprinkling of water and place them in the oven for 5 minutes. To roast them completely, bake for 15–20 minutes. Whether blanching or baking, it is best to turn off the oven and just remove a few at a time to retain the heat, leaving the nuts easier to peel.

To braise the chestnuts, first blanch them in boiling water and peel as above. Place the chestnuts in a saucepan and cover with approximately 300ml (½ pint) of *Chicken* or *Instant stock* (page 194) or tinned consommé. Add 1 teaspoon of caster sugar and simmer for 15 minutes, until tender. The chestnuts can now be removed and served soft and tender, adding a pinch of salt, or boil the stock and reduce it to a syrupy consistency, before adding the chestnuts and rolling them to give a shiny glazed finish.

● *For an alternative blanching method, the pierced nuts can be deep-fried in hot fat (180°C/350°F) for just 1 minute, then removed and allowed to rest for 2–3 minutes, before peeling.*

Poached eggs

For the 'perfect' poached egg, the secret is to use only the freshest of eggs. These will then need little help, poaching simply in simmering water. Should the eggs need a helping hand, a fairly generous quantity of vinegar, up to one-third of the water content, can be added. This helps set the protein of the whites almost instantly around the yolks, without tainting their fresh flavour. It's very important that the water is always deep. This means that the egg will be poaching before reaching the base of the pan and spreading.

Serves 4
● 4 eggs
● malt or white wine vinegar (optional)

Method Fill a large, deep saucepan with water (replace up to one-third with vinegar should it be required). Bring to a rapid simmer and whisk vigorously in a circular motion. Crack an egg into the centre. As the liquid spins, it pulls and sets the white around the yolk, before the egg reaches the base of the pan. Poach the egg for 3–3½ minutes, before serving.

If wishing to poach the eggs in advance, once cooked plunge them into iced water to stop the cooking process. These can now be trimmed of any excess whites to leave perfectly shaped eggs. To reheat, plunge into rapidly simmering water for 1 minute.

● *All four eggs can be poached together, placing one after the other in the centre of the rotating liquid. However, if cooking beforehand and keeping refrigerated in iced water until needed, poach each separately for perfect results.*

Pastries

Shortcrust and Sweet shortcrust pastry

For plain shortcrust, the fat content can be split between butter and lard; the two work well together, giving a good flavour, and the lard helps shorten the dough texture. Sweet shortcrust, however, is best made purely with butter, its richer flavour complementing the sweet filling. The fats should be cool before use, rather than refrigerated, as this can make crumbing hard work.

Always allow the finished dough to rest for 20–30 minutes. The gluten content in the flour reacts with the liquid (water or milk), giving a better texture to roll and work with. Always roll pastry out on a cool and lightly floured surface. Pastry must remain cold, and the dusting of flour will prevent the pastry from sticking.

Makes about 400g (14oz) shortcrust pastry and about 450g (1lb) sweet shortcrust pastry
- 225g (8oz) plain flour
- pinch of salt
- 50g (2oz) butter (100g/4oz if the lard is omitted), diced
- 50g (2oz) lard, diced (optional)
- 1 small egg (optional) or an extra 2–3 tablespoons water or milk
- 2 tablespoons water or milk
- 50–75g (2–3oz) caster or icing sugar (for sweet shortcrust only)

Method Sift the flour with the salt. Rub the butter and lard, if using, into the flour until a breadcrumb texture is achieved. Beat the egg, if using, with the water or milk and work gently into the crumbs to form a smooth dough (if excess crumbs are left in the bowl, add an extra tablespoon of water or milk). Wrap in cling film and allow to relax in the fridge for 20–30 minutes before using.

When needed, remove from the fridge and allow to return to a cool room temperature before rolling.

For the sweet shortcrust pastry, omit the lard and use all the butter, then simply add the caster or icing sugar once the breadcrumb stage has been reached.

● *The scraped seeds from a vanilla pod added to the sweet pastry mix at its crumb stage will introduce another flavour, which enhances the taste of many fillings.*

● *Another flavour that works very well in the sweet version is the finely grated zest of one lemon.*

● *When lining a flan case or mould, it's best to leave excess pastry hanging over the edge during the cooking time to prevent it from shrinking into the case. Once removed from the oven, gently trim the excess pastry away, leaving a neat finish.*

Quick puff pastry

This recipe offers a slightly quicker method than the traditional way of making puff pastry. The resulting pastry can be used in any recipe requiring the classic puff finish. Any not used will freeze very well. Good puff pastry can also be bought.

Makes about 750g (1¾lb)
- 325g (11oz) butter, chilled
- 450g (1lb) plain flour
- 1 teaspoon salt

Method Cut the chilled butter into small cubes. Sift the flour with the salt. Add the butter, gently rubbing it into the flour but not totally breaking it down. Add 200–225ml (7–8fl oz) cold water and mix to a pliable dough, still with pieces of butter showing. Turn out on to a floured surface and roll into a rectangle approximately 46 × 15cm (18 × 6in). Fold the top one-third over and then fold the bottom edge up over it. Leave to rest for 20 minutes. Turn the pastry by 90° and repeat the rolling, folding, resting and turning sequence three times. Allow to rest for a further hour once complete. The pastry is now ready to use.

Creams and sweet things

Crème Anglaise (custard sauce)

These measurements can be halved for a lesser quantity, if required.

Makes 750ml (1¼ pints)
- 8 egg yolks
- 75g (3oz) caster sugar
- 300ml (½ pint) milk
- 300ml (½ pint) double cream
- 1 vanilla pod, split (optional)

Method Beat the egg yolks and sugar together in a bowl until well blended. Put the milk and cream in a saucepan and scrape in the seeds from inside the vanilla pod, if using, also adding the pod before bringing to the boil. Sit the bowl of egg yolks and sugar over a pan of simmering water and whisk, pouring the hot milk and cream slowly into the mixture. As the egg yolks cook, the custard will thicken. Keep stirring until it begins to coat the back of a spoon, then remove the bowl from the heat, discarding the vanilla pod. The custard can now be served warm or cold.

To prevent a skin forming if cooling, cover the custard with greaseproof paper or cling film.

The custard can be brought back up to heat over a pan of hot water, but it must never boil. If that happens, the sauce will scramble.

Prune and Armagnac custard

This fresh custard provides a wonderfully flavoured finish for many desserts, in particular those featuring apples and pears. Vanilla has also been included; if this is unavailable, a good sprinkling of freshly grated nutmeg makes a good alternative.

Makes approximately 400ml (14fl oz)
- 4 egg yolks
- 50g (2oz) caster sugar
- 150ml (¼ pint) milk
- 150ml (¼ pint) double or whipping cream
- 1 vanilla pod, split, or a few drops of vanilla essence
- 6 ready-to-eat pitted prunes, roughly chopped
- 3–4 tablespoons Armagnac

Method In a bowl, whisk together the egg yolks and sugar until thick, light and creamy. Put the milk and cream in a small saucepan and scrape the vanilla seeds from the split pod, adding them to the pan. The scraped pod can also be added. Bring to the boil and whisk into the egg and cream mix. Return to the stove and cook over a very low heat for just a few minutes, until thick enough to coat the back of a spoon. It's important that the custard barely reaches a gentle simmering point – any hotter than this and the sauce will scramble. Remove from the heat and add the chopped prunes. Leave to cool. Remove the vanilla pod before blitzing the custard in a liquidizer and straining through a sieve for the smoothest of finishes. The preferred quantity of Armagnac can now be added to lift the prune flavour. This custard is wonderful cold or warm.

If reheating, never allow the custard to quite reach a simmer, as this will result in a separated scrambled finish.

- *When making the custard, once the milk is added to the cream mix, it can be cooked in a bowl over a pan of simmering water, ensuring the bowl does not come into contact with the water.*

- *The quantity of milk can be doubled and the cream omitted for a less rich finish, if preferred.*

Chocolate sauce

This recipe provides a chocolate truffle ganache filling, served while still warm, with a sauce-like consistency.

Serves 4–6
- 100g (4oz) bitter dark chocolate, chopped (milk or white chocolate can also be used)
- 150ml (¼ pint) single cream
- 25g (1oz) butter

Method Place all the ingredients together in a bowl set over simmering water, ensuring the bowl does not come into contact with the water, stirring gently from time to time until the chocolate has melted. The sauce is now ready to serve warm.

● *This sauce can be loosened to a thinner consistency with the addition of a little milk.*

● *If refrigerated, the ganache can be shaped into balls and rolled in cocoa powder for home-made truffles.*

● *This recipe can be increased for larger quantities.*

Greengage jam

Greengages contain a medium pectin count, so granulated sugar will work just fine here. Preserving sugar is a larger sugar granule that takes longer to dissolve, hopefully leaving a clearer finished jam, but it does not contain pectin. Jam sugar does and will guarantee you a setting point, so although it's not essential to use it, it does give you a greater sense of security. Explained below is an option to make this into a greengage and lime jam, the citrus touch offering a 'marmalade' bite.

Makes approximately 1kg (2¼lb), easily doubled
● 1kg (2¼lb) greengages
● 675g (1½lb) granulated, preserving or jam sugar

Method Wash and halve the greengages, then remove the stones. These can be discarded or tied in muslin cloth to add to the fruits while simmering for even more flavour. Halve each piece of greengage once more and place them in a large saucepan, preferably a preserving pot. Add 200ml (7fl oz) of water and the muslin bag of kernels, if using.

Bring the water to the simmer over a low heat, continuing to cook gently until the fruits become pulpy. At this point add the sugar, stirring it in well. Once it has completely dissolved, increase the heat to a rapid boil for 15 minutes.

To test for setting point, spoon a little of the jam on to a saucer and chill. As the jam cools, a skin forms; when pushed with a finger, the skin should begin to crinkle if setting point has been reached. If still too wet and loose, continue to boil, checking for setting after every extra 5 minutes.

Once ready, remove from the heat, skim away any impurities and allow to cool for 20 minutes, removing the muslin bag, if using. Transfer to sterilized jars (page 11).

● *A sugar thermometer can also be used, placing it in the pot at the beginning of the cooking process. The setting point will be reached at 104°C/220°F.*

● *For a greengage and lime jam, follow the above recipe, adding the finely grated zest of 3 limes to the greengages. Squeeze the juice from the limes, put in a measuring jug and top up with water to reach the 200ml (7fl oz) of liquid required.*

Home-made quince jam

In the first month of winter there are still some quince to enjoy. With Christmas so close, this fruit provides us all with the opportunity to create a home-made fragrance to offer as the perfect present.

When purchasing quince for jam, a little over the required weight covers the peel and core waste.

Makes approximately 2.25kg (5lb)
● 1.3kg (3lb) quince (net fruit weight)
● juice of 2 lemons
● 1.3kg (3lb) jam sugar

Method Peel and quarter the quince, cutting away the central core. Cut each quarter into rough 2cm (¾in) dice. Place the fruits in a large saucepan, preferably a preserving pot, along with the lemon juice and 1.25 litres (2 pints) of water.

Bring to a gentle simmer and cook until the fruits have become tender, then lightly mash with a fork or potato masher. Add the sugar, stirring until completely dissolved, then bring to the boil, cooking at this temperature for 15–20 minutes. To test for setting point, spoon a little of the jam on to a saucer and chill. As the jam cools, a skin forms; when pushed with a finger, the skin should begin to crinkle if setting point has been reached. If still too wet and loose, continue to boil, checking for setting after every extra 5 minutes.

Once the jam is ready, remove the pan from the heat and skim away any impurities. Leave to stand and cool slightly, then spoon into sterilized jars (page 11).

Tuile biscuits

These biscuits ('tile' is the literal translation of the French word *tuile*) can be used to accompany so many desserts, whether as baskets to hold fruits or ice-creams and sorbets, or simply shaped to offer as an extra crispy bite. The best way to shape the tuile paste is to cut a square, circle, triangle, tear drop, leaf or whichever shape you're looking for from the centre of an ice-cream tub lid. It's the remaining space left in the lid that creates the template once the shape has been cut out and discarded. The excess plastic of the template can be trimmed away leaving a 1–2cm (½–¾in) border. For large biscuits, a 10–13cm (4–5in) diameter lid will be needed. For the smaller, almost *petit four* size, 6–7.5cm (2½–3in) will be plenty. The finished mix will last up to 10 days, if chilled.

Makes 16–18 large or 30–34 small biscuits
- 2 egg whites
- 75g (3oz) icing sugar
- 50g (2oz) plain flour, sifted
- 50g (2oz) butter, melted

Method Preheat the oven to 200°C/400°F/Gas 6 and line a baking sheet with parchment paper. Place the egg whites and icing sugar together in a bowl and whisk for 30 seconds, then add the flour. Once well mixed together, stir in the melted butter to form a paste. Using a palette knife, spread the mix evenly across the shape in the template, on to the parchment paper. Now lift the template, leaving the paste shape in place. Repeat the process until the baking sheet is covered. Bake in the preheated oven for 6–8 minutes (10 minutes maximum) until the tuiles are golden brown. Remove the tuiles from the oven and, while still hot, press them to your desired shape.

To shape a tuile into a cup, place the warm biscuit in, or over the outside of, a cup. For a curved shape, lay the biscuits over a rolling pin, or you can split the cardboard centre of a cling film or kitchen foil roll lengthwise, line it with parchment paper and lay the tuile inside, presentation-side down. Should the tuiles cool and firm too quickly on the tray, you can always return them to the oven for a few seconds to rewarm and resoften, continuing to shape. Tuiles will keep for up to 48 hours in an airtight container.

- *For a nutty finish, nibbed or flaked almonds, or chopped pistachio nuts, can be sprinkled over the tuiles before cooking.*

- *The zest of one lemon or orange can be added to the mix for a citrus touch.*

Stock syrup

This can be used for sorbets, poaching fruits and as a base for sweet-flavoured sauces. The quantities listed here will yield approximately 450ml (¾ pint) of finished syrup. The syrup can be simmered and reduced by a quarter to a third for a sweeter finish when used with highly acidic fruits.

Makes 450ml (¾ pint)
- 300ml (½ pint) water
- 225g (8oz) caster sugar

Method Bring the water and sugar to the boil. Simmer for 10–15 minutes, until the sugar has completely dissolved and the syrup thickened. Allow to cool, and keep chilled in an airtight jar.

index